Gender Circuits

Gender Circuits explores the impact of new technologies on the gendered lives of individuals through substantive sociological analysis and in-depth case studies. Examining the complex intersections between gender ideologies, social scripts, information and biomedical technologies, and embodied identities, this book explores whether and how new technologies are reshaping what it means to be a gendered person in contemporary society.

Dr. Eve Shapiro is Assistant Professor of Sociology at Westfield State College. She received her Ph.D. in Sociology from the University of California, Santa Barbara and has published in a number of journals including *Gender & Society, Sexualities*, and the *Journal of Gay and Lesbian Social Services*. Her current research elaborates the dynamic relationships between identity, embodiment, and community, including how new information and biomedical technologies are changing the gendered sexual and political lives of cisgender and transgender individuals.

Contemporary Sociological Perspectives

Edited by **Valerie Jenness**, University of California, Irvine
and **Jodi O'Brien**, Seattle University

This innovative series is for all readers interested in books that provide frameworks for making sense of the complexities of contemporary social life. Each of the books in this series uses a sociological lens to provide current critical and analytical perspectives on significant social issues, patterns, and trends. The series consists of books that integrate the best ideas in sociological thought with an aim toward public education and engagement. These books are designed for use in the classroom as well as for scholars and socially curious general readers.

Published:
Political Justice and Religious Values by Charles F. Andrain
GIS and Spatial Analysis for the Social Sciences by Robert Nash Parker
and Emily K. Asencio
Hoop Dreams on Wheels: Disability and the Competitive Wheelchair Athlete
by Ronald J. Berger
The Internet and Social Inequalities by James C. Witte and Susan E. Mannon
Media and Middle Class Moms: Images and Realities of Work and Family by Lara
Descartes and Conrad Kottak
Watching T.V. Is Not Required: Thinking about Media and Thinking about Thinking
by Bernard McGrane and John Gunderson
Violence Against Women: Vulnerable Populations by Douglas Brownridge
The State of Sex: Tourism, Sex, and Sin in the New American Heartland by Barbara G.
Brents, Crystal A. Jackson, and Kathryn Hausbeck

Forthcoming:
Transform Yourself, Transform the World: A Practical Guide to Women's and Gender Studies
by Michelle Berger and Cheryl Radeloff
Sociological Storytelling: Reflections on the Research Experience by Sarah Fenstermaker and
Nikki Jones
A Dictatorship: Visual and Social Representations by Jacqueline Adams
Social Statistics: The Basics and Beyond by Thomas J. Linneman

Also of Interest from Routledge:
Sex For Sale: Prostitution, Pornography, and the Sex Industry, Second Edition, by
Ronald Weitzer
The Handbook of Sexuality Related Measures, Third Edition, edited by Terri Fisher, Clive
and Sandra Davis, and William Yarber
The Feminist Theory Reader: Local and Global Perspectives, Second Edition, edited by
Carole McCann and Seung-kyung Kim

Gender Circuits

Bodies and Identities in a
Technological Age

Eve Shapiro

Routledge
Taylor & Francis Group

NEW YORK AND LONDON

First published 2010
by Routledge
270 Madison Avenue, New York, NY 10016

Simultaneously published in the UK
by Routledge
2 Park Square, Milton Park, Abingdon, Oxon OX14 4RN

Routledge is an imprint of the Taylor & Francis Group, an informa business

© 2010 Taylor & Francis

Typeset in Adobe Caslon and Copperplate Gothic by
RefineCatch Limited, Bungay, Suffolk
Printed and bound in the United States of America on acid-free paper by
Sheridan Books, Inc.

Library of Congress Cataloging in Publication Data
Shapiro, Eve.
Gender circuits: bodies and identities in a technological age/Eve Shapiro.
—1st ed.
p. cm.—(Contemporary sociological perspectives)
Includes bibliographical references.
1. Gender identity. 2. Transgenderism. I. Title.
HQ1075.S43 2010
306.4—dc22
2009032557

ISBN10: 0–415–99695–3 (hbk)
ISBN10: 0–415–99696–1 (pbk)
ISBN10: 0–203–85936–7 (ebk)

ISBN13: 978–0–415–99695–2 (hbk)
ISBN13: 978–0–415–99696–9 (pbk)
ISBN13: 978–0–203–85936–0 (ebk)

DEDICATION

For my parents.

TABLE OF CONTENTS

SERIES FOREWORD

This innovative series is for all readers interested in books that provide frameworks for making sense of the complexities of contemporary social life. Each of the books in this series uses a sociological lens to provide current critical and analytical perspectives on significant social issues, patterns, and trends. The series consists of books that integrate the best ideas in sociological thought with an aim toward public education and engagement. These books are designed for use in the classroom as well as for scholars and socially curious general readers.

Gender Circuits explores the complex relationship between technological development, cultural ideologies, social scripts and gendered bodies and identities. Using a vast range of case studies and historical and contemporary examples, Shapiro demonstrates the subtle but persistent ways in which communications technologies, medical technologies, and fashion technologies reflect social conditions and dominant social ideologies and simultaneously shape our ideas about what gender can and should be. This book will be of interest to students of gender, technology, and culture, and also to anyone interested in the reciprocal influences of social context and embodied lives.

Valerie Jenness and Jodi O'Brien
Series Editors

PREFACE

Last year, when I was working on this book, I took myself on a writing retreat to get away from my daily distractions. Since it was off-season, the inn at the retreat was empty and I ate my meals, for the most part, alone. During my first meal at the restaurant I was engaged in friendly conversation by my waiter who asked me what I did for a living. When I shared with him that I was a sociologist, he became quite agitated and launched into a long, rather one-sided conversation. Shifting his weight from one foot to the other repeatedly, Will grilled me about what I thought had caused some of the biggest changes in our society. I was not particularly interested in having a conversation with Will, so I think I just grunted a response and made motions to get back to my meal. Not to be deterred, my chatty waiter shared with me his take on his own question. He informed me that technology was transforming our world, including individuals. At this point my ears perked up; I had not mentioned to Will that I was currently writing a book on technology, and here he was lending credence to my ideas. Will went on to explain that in his view technology was changing how people acted, what people believed, the nature of interpersonal relationships, and indeed who people were. He also shared that as a technophobe he knew that he was missing out on key parts of contemporary life. Without an email account he felt left out with friends, and with no computer skills he felt unable to pursue his true passion, becoming a wine buyer for the inn. What struck me as poignant when talking with Will was that his internal struggle over technology was palpable. He wanted so much to join the fold, so to speak, and simultaneously was afraid of who he might become because of it.

After dinner, when I returned to my hotel room I turned on the Discovery Channel and found myself watching a show about 'human-imals,' people who engage in dramatic body modification in an effort to make visible their sense of kinship with cats, lizards, and other animals.[1] I began to feel as if everywhere I turned I found evidence of how technologies were reshaping people's lives and embodied selves. Perhaps I felt like a magnet for this type of information because I am so attuned to the topic, but I think it is more than that. These conversations have become commonplace in society as a whole. In numerous venues, including in popular media, political debate, and social commentary, attention has been paid to the changing nature of life in North America amid technological innovation. Consider, for example, telephones. While few individuals had cell phones 10 years ago, most teens today cannot imagine a life without them, and pay phones are disappearing from public streets. Similarly, we accept as normal the integration of biomedical technologies like implants, contact lenses, pharmaceuticals, and pacemakers into the human body; many of these technologies were the sole purview of science fiction just a few years ago. All to say, trying to make better sense of how new technologies are reshaping contemporary bodies and identities is an engaging and prescient endeavor at this moment in North America.

Technology and technological innovation has a long history. Technologies have been in a dynamic relationship with gendered bodies and selves throughout history. However, the pervasiveness of technology and the speed of change that we are experiencing in this era are impacting contemporary lives and societies in new and transforma-tive ways. These changes, in conversation with social norms and in line with dominant ideologies are reshaping what it means to be an embod-ied, gendered person. This is true even if we, as individuals, ignore or resist these processes. Dominant power holders construct some beliefs, norms, appearances, and experiences as prized, normal, and valued, while discrediting others. Normative values and expectations shape individuals in myriad ways even when they do not fit into or abide by them. The inspiration for *Gender Circuits* lies at the intersection of these social forces—technology, bodies, identities, dominant ideologies, and social scripts. I begin and end by questioning how technological change is affecting society and individuals. I hope that this book, born out of my own questions, generates new inquiries and offers new analytical tools to help answer your own questions about your life, community, society, and world.

A few notes about language. I have endeavored to write in a jargon free manner. I have, in the process, made a few stylistic choices. First, given my focus on the complexity and historicity of sex and gender categories, I have tried to minimize gendered language. In the absence of common gender neutral pronouns (although I do introduce some in Chapter 1), I use 'they' instead of he/she and 'their' instead of his/her. While grammatically incorrect, this approach has the benefit of avoiding gender-specific language. Second, in an effort to engage in conversation with readers' own lives and experiences, I have at times used inclusive language (for example 'you,' 'we' and 'us'). My intention is not to assume a shared experience or identity with readers or to be condescending. Rather, it is my invitation to you, as readers, to consider whether your own experiences mirror or contradict the examples in this book and how you might make sense of these overlaps and divergences using the analytical tools developed herein.

In addition to text boxes that highlight the definitions of new terms and theories, the notes offer more details about the ideas raised in the book and list many wonderful empirical articles and books on the topics introduced here. They are a wonderful place to learn more about the mechanisms by which particular identities are integrated, technologies are developed, and bodies are shaped. I encourage you, when inspired, to use the notes to find books and articles that elaborate a particular topic and continue your research there.

The analytical approach I use in this book can be used to examine many other areas of embodied identity and social change. I hope that *Gender Circuits* can serve as a launching pad for research on a diverse array of other topics. Because of both space constraints and issues of complexity I have chosen to focus on social changes, gender ideologies, and social contexts within North America. However, there is outstanding work that engages these same issues outside of this region and I encourage you to explore this scholarship.

A project such as this cannot be accomplished by one person alone. I had the great joy and privilege of being trained by an incredible group of scholars including Richard Flacks, Jodi O'Brien, Leila Rupp, Beth Schneider, and Verta Taylor, all of whom have, over the years, shown phenomenal generosity with their time and provided me with invaluable mentorship. Many colleagues were generous enough to read drafts of this manuscript. Patricia Drew and Lisa Leitz read every chapter and cheered me on when I needed it most. Kendal Broad, Leah DeVun, Jessica Fields, Mary Ingram-Waters, Linda Kim, Amanda Moras, and many others read chapters, offered support, and otherwise enriched my life. The members of my writing group, Linda Kim, Amanda Moras, Emily Musil, Jen Sandler, Asali Solomon, and Melissa Stuckey have been the most steadfast of friends, critics, and champions. Many of the strengths and none of the failings in this book are thanks to them. I was lucky to have the research assistance of Jennifer Weekley and to benefit from the wonderful research skills of the University of Connecticut Women's Studies librarian Kathy Labradorf. Sabrina Matthews edited each and every chapter brilliantly and, like always, made me laugh in the process. This book would never have been possible without the guidance and support of series editors Valerie Jenness and Jodi O'Brien and the vision of Routledge editor Steve Rutter. Thank you for believing in the project and for more than a few wonderful conversations. Finally, there are people in my life to whom I owe innumerable thanks and without whom I would never have been able to arrive at this point. Mindy Stevens has brought more joy to my life than I knew it could contain. I cannot imagine a better partner with whom to build a life. My parents and brother made me believe that I could accomplish anything I wanted. All of my accomplishments—indeed, all of the good things in my life—I share with them.

PREVIEW
GENDERED BODIES AND IDENTITIES IN A TECHNOLOGICAL AGE

When I was a child in the early 1980s, my friends and I spent a lot of time thinking about what the world would look like when we had grown up. We imagined that the twenty-first century would be run by robots. We would all live forever as robotic humanoids, with regular tune-ups, replacement parts, and body swaps. Our food would be 'replicated' at our whim as it was on *Star Trek,* and our clothing would be made from plastic. We would all be able to communicate with one another anytime we wanted, from halfway around the globe; our Dick Tracey phone-watches would even send messages to our parents if we made a quick jaunt to Mars for a party. The giant *Transformers* robots would be engaged in an epic battle of good over evil, while Rosie, George Jetson's robotic maid, dusted our homes.

Now that we are at the dawn of the twenty-first century, these predictions sound both hilarious and eerily true. While we do not have regular body swaps we do have face transplants, plastic surgery, stem cell research, cloning, and in-vitro fertilization. Although we do not yet travel on the daily Mars shuttle, we do have an international space station, Mars rover, and space tourism. And lest we get bored, we have cell phones, genetically modified food, and robotic vacuums to keep us occupied.

Technology has infiltrated all parts of modern lives. As predicted by science fiction, technology has changed how people experience the world around them, interact with each other, and go about their daily lives.[1]

> ### TECHNOLOGY
>
> Technology is anything that humans develop to manipulate the natural environment. Its Greek root words mean 'expression of a craft' and signify the breadth of the concept. Technology is the wide variety of objects, knowledge, activities, and processes humans have developed to alter the material (and conceptual) world. I discuss the meaning and scope of technology in more detail in Chapter 1.

Even when economic, racial, sexual, gender, or age status (to mention only a few defining characteristics) puts access to certain types of information or medical technology out of reach, individuals are affected by the social changes that these technologies have brought about. The ability to use technological advancements to access news and information online, communicate through cell phones and text messages, and modify bodies through surgery, medicine, robots, and machines has created new sites of agency and social control, of power and inequality. And, as we will see throughout this book, these changes have gone hand in hand with changes in how people define themselves as individuals, and how much ability they have to make those identities real and embodied. Many contemporary social debates center on questions of technology and its impact on human experience,[2] and scholars have begun to ask questions about how this new technological world is changing who people are.[3] Some social theorists argue that technology will supplement the limitations of nature, and expand possibilities for humanity.[4] Others contend that technology will constrain and imprison civilization.[5] Regardless of whether scholars take a catastrophic or utopian view, most agree that technology raises the question of "whether humanity could become a new order of being."[6] A social scientific approach, which I take up in this book, views individuals as products of both nature and society. From this vantage point we are prompted to ask a range of questions about whether and how the societal changes that are interdependent with technological development are affecting who people are, and can be, in our society.

Understanding the Embodied Self as a Social Product

While the body has long been the domain of medicine and science, scholars of society have much to gain from thinking about how society, the self, and the body interact with one another.

> **EMBODIMENT**
>
> The lived body. A state of being in which the body is the site of meaning, experience, and expression of individuals in the world.[7]

This is particularly true in a technological age where humans have increasing ability to modify the form and function of the body. Historically, prejudice and discrimination have been legitimized through arguments that inequality was the product of natural differences between groups of people. For example, eugenics movements sought a scientific basis for the racial superiority of Whites.[8]

Beginning with late nineteenth-century race and gender rights movements and accelerating in the wake of the Holocaust's reliance on race science, numerous philosophers, scientists, and scholars have argued against the biological basis of social inequalities. For example, feminist scholars over the past 25 years have called into question the 'naturalness' of societal gender inequalities. Through empirical studies and gender theorizing, scholars have demonstrated how embodied

> **SOCIAL INSTITUTION**
>
> An established path for achieving particular social or individual needs or goals. Institutions can be physical structures or societal concepts and are imbued with social power. Social institutions are the means by which social order is established and upheld.

identities (such as race, class, and gender) are not just physical realities but also social institutions that shape individual lives.

This scholarship asserts that the meaning and importance of the body for individuals are as much social products as they are biological; for example, the importance of one's skin color has everything to do with racial inequality and racism. The body, which is the human means of connection to the world, is viewed according to the values, norms, and socially specific meanings dominant in any historical era. But the relationship between society, identity, and the human body is even more complex. Not only does society shape our embodied experiences, but also these socially specific beliefs shape the form and function of the body.

Contrary to the early scientific conception of the embodied self as the untainted reflection of biology, social and biological scientists in the last 25 years have explored how social beliefs shape physiology and biology. What this research has shown is that social beliefs and practices influence the human form alongside genes and hormones. Consider, for example, a prime marker of femininity in North America: the high-heeled shoe. Women wear them as a symbol of femininity, and men do not. Although high heels are not regarded as biologically compelled attire, most members of our society do see wearing them as a trait of being feminine and assume that it is natural for women to be drawn to wearing them, while men are repelled. Connoisseurs of high-heeled shoes often remark on how they show off women's natural curves, accentuating their femininity. This is true—according to our society's definitions of femininity—but it is also the case that wearing these shoes (a culturally and historically specific fashion practice) creates some of the femininity that is assumed to be natural. Over time, wearing high heels will change the shape of a woman's feet and the arch in her back, alter her gait, and strengthen particular muscles in her legs. These changes result in a body comportment that highlights breasts and buttocks, a gait that incorporates swaying hip movements, and legs with long, lean muscles. In other words, following this social norm (there is no gene for wearing high heels, after all) changes women's physiology and produces some of the feminine characteristics we attribute to biology. As this example illustrates, our body both informs and responds to the society we live in. All social dynamics are embodied—experienced by and through the body of individuals—and changes in society inevitably produce changes in the body (and vice versa).

Biology and social practices are not the only forces that shape human bodies; individuals also make sense of bodily experiences socially. The physiological responses, for example, to excitement and fear are remarkably similar; it is our interpretation of the situation that helps us know what we are 'really' feeling. That is, the process of analyzing and assigning meaning to our body and its sensory experiences is a learned one that is shaped by social beliefs, expectations, norms, and values.

NORM

A norm is an informal or formal rule for behavior, belief, appearance, or attitude, within a society or community. Norms can be formalized laws, such as marriage laws that dictate who can form families. Norms can also be mores, societal expectations that are strongly enforced, such as rules about cannibalism. Finally, informal expectations that are not highly punished when violated (such as greeting a neighbor when passing on the street) are a type of norm called folkways.

The social meaning of the body is something that has changed throughout history and these changes affect how individuals make sense of their own physiological experiences. One of the most touching moments in Eve Ensler's popular play, *The Vagina Monologues*, illustrates this beautifully. During the monologue "The Flood," an elderly woman describes becoming shocked and ashamed by her own sexual arousal as a teenager, and developing a life-long sexual shame because of the experience. Socially constructed gender beliefs in the early 1900s painted 'good' women as lacking sexual desire, and forbade public distribution of educational materials about sex and sexuality.

These social conditions meant that discussions of women's sexual needs were absent from most public or private discourse, denying

SOCIAL CONSTRUCTIONISM

A theoretical approach which states that societal structures (on the individual, interactional, and institutional levels) are the product of social processes and are not naturally or biologically inevitable. Social constructionism asserts that the forces that shape the lives of individuals (e.g. gender, race, law, governance structures) are created and recreated over time out of social interaction and guided by reigning worldviews in a society. A social construction is a phenomenon produced through social interaction in conversation with physical reality (e.g. biology). This theoretical paradigm is often contrasted against essentialism, which states that social reality is the product of ahistorical, inevitable forces such as divine will or natural law.

women any positive explanations for their experiences of desire. This social climate had dire consequences, as the woman portrayed in "The Flood" describes. She thinks of her own vagina as a place:

> Like the cellar. There's rumbles down there sometimes. You can hear the pipes and things get caught there, little animals and things, and it gets wet, and sometimes people have to plug up the leaks. Otherwise the door stays closed. You forget about it. I mean, it's part of the house, but you don't see it or think about it.[9]

Every time I hear this monologue I think of my own grandmother who shared with me her story of having her first menstrual period (in the 1930s). Like the character in *The Vagina Monologues*, she had no exposure to reproductive biology or sex education at home, in school, or through popular media. When she began to menstruate, she thought she was dying—she truly believed that something had burst inside of her and she was going to bleed to death. This reaction and explanation may seem ridiculous to modern ears. In contemporary society we have different socially constructed explanations for bodily experiences, and most women have access to more information about their bodies than my grandmother did. In the moment when my grandmother got her first period, however, she made sense of her body using those tools at her disposal and, like the character in Eve Ensler's play, this meaning-making reflected her socio-historical context. In turn, this context and my grandmother's experience shaped her understanding of her body in significant and enduring ways. It is likely that future generations will assign equally different emotions, explanations, and meanings to some bodily experiences than people do today, and this will differentiate their lives from ours in important ways as well.

The body is the intermediary between our internal mind and the external world as well as the visible component of who we are. In contemporary society we assume that identity and personality characteristics reside in the body such that what we look like tells the world something about who we are. Not only do we assume gender, race, and, often, social class based upon what someone looks like, but also we deduce all sorts of other social values.[10] As a society, we evaluate fat people as lazy, blondes as dumb, masculine women and feminine men as gay; such designations go on and on. Each person experiences and internalizes social beliefs and norms through the body and, in turn, the body is assumed to reveal to the world the individual's identities, values, and moral character. In fact, some of the most pressing contemporary social debates—such as concerns over the nature of humanity in an age of information technology, the sacredness of the body in the face of cloning and stem-cell research, and the changing self in an increasingly global society—are about this relationship between embodied individuals and social change. And, indeed, social change does beg the question: How are we changing?

In this book I ask how certain technologies have affected us as modern individuals. One of the ways that I do this is to look at cases where new technologies are changing social beliefs about who we are (or think we can be). These changes can come about as a result of medical technologies that allow us to see, alter, and treat the body in ways that were previously impossible. They can also be the product of those information technologies that allow us to discover, meet, and interact with people and their ideas without ever coming face-to-face.

BIO-MEDICAL TECHNOLOGY

Technology that maintains and/or transforms the human body. Bio-medical technology includes among other practices, genetic testing and manipulation, pharmacology, surgery including micro-surgery, imaging, cloning, synthetic drugs, hormones and vaccines, prosthetics, and implants.

INFORMATION TECHNOLOGY

Technology that facilitates communication between individuals through computer-based hardware and software, Internet access and networking. Information technology includes, among other practices, email, virtual communities, online social networking, and online games.

One of the primary ways that we know ourselves is by identifying with a gender and embodying the behaviors and characteristics associated with that gender. Because gender is one of the main ways that we *all* organize ourselves in society, and experience the world, we will use it as a strategic vantage point from which to examine the changes brought on by technological innovation.

GENDER

A social status and personal identity, defined in the United States as woman or man.[11] As a social status gender is a set of values, beliefs, and norms (rules for behavior) that are created and enforced by society and assigned to individuals on the basis of birth sex.[12] As a personal identity gender refers to an individual's sense of self as a man, woman, or alternative gender.

SEX

Socially interpreted meanings of chromosomes, genitalia, and secondary sex characteristics. In the contemporary United States sex takes the form of male, female, and intersex.[13]

Why Gender is a Good Vantage Point for Inquiry

Gender, like other social categories (race, class, age, etc.), is both a personal identity and a culturally specific set of behaviors, beliefs, and values. Each society has a particular interpretation of what it means to be a 'real' man, a 'real' woman, and in some societies, a 'real' other gender. These particularities are what inspire men and women to dress, talk, act, and look different in different places and during different eras. These gender social scripts include everything from our perception that we have a gender, to those norms that advise whom and how it is appropriate to desire because of this gender.

SOCIAL SCRIPTS

Blueprints for behavior, belief, and identity.

Gender scripts are the resources that individuals use to construct socially legible lives. They structure our everyday interaction and shape each of us regardless of how much or how little heed we pay them. They are far more complex than molds from which each of us is stamped out, however. Scripts offer a range of possibilities for gendered selves from which individuals construct an authentic embodied life. Scripts are not deterministic but they do guide who and what we are. This book will explore the dynamic relationship between dominant beliefs, social scripts and emerging technologies (both information and biomedical) by focusing on gender in order to elucidate the complexities of these dynamics.

I take on these issues by examining the social histories of gender variation and by exploring a number of case studies that elaborate how technology, social beliefs, and gender scripts are in dynamic relationship to individual bodies and identities. Much like a circuit requires connections between each component part to allow the flow of electricity, each of these components is necessary to make sense of contemporary bodies and identities. By taking up unique case studies to observe these phenomena, we can learn a great deal about how we all navigate everyday experiences, social interaction, and technological change. Before we begin, however, we must develop a shared understanding of what phenomena we are focused on, namely embodied identity, gender, and technology. Let us begin by reviewing in more detail the social construction of identity.

Making Sense of Identity

Over the past 500 years scholars of the self and society have tried to make sense of how individuals come to understand who they are.

IDENTITY

An individual's sense of self. The answer to the question, 'who am I?'

For many centuries leading up to the 1600s, Judeo-Christian theology guided Western pre-Enlightenment philosophers to the belief that the self was a reflection or product of a god's will. The belief was that human lives followed a pre-ordained path set out by a god. With the rise of science and a shift of social power from religious institutions to scientific ones, however, Enlightenment philosophers argued that while the 'self' was a pre-formed, fixed mind, unique to individuals, it was not the product of divine will. In 1641 René Descartes argued that we know our 'self'—our stable, internal, answer to the question, 'who am I?'—because we know our thoughts: "cogito ergo sum." In general philosophers during the Enlightenment viewed the definition of who someone was as a static, inborn set of identities and traits. Building on Enlightenment philosophy, but extending a more interpretive perspective, early twentieth-century pragmatic sociologists[14] argued that the self was a social entity, not an independent one. Instead of something pre-formed within a bodily shell, the self was theorized as the product of social interaction. They argued that as individuals we develop who we are by knowing (or imagining) how others see us.[15] George Herbert Mead, among others, suggested that people make sense of who they are through interactions with others,[16] and this has been the dominant approach to identity within the social sciences for the last 50 years.

An interpretive theory of identity highlights the interaction between society and the individual. Consider for a moment how you know who you are. Are you *really* kind or cruel? Gentle or gruff? Forthright or dishonest? Both personal experience and social psychological research suggest that who we are is due, in part, to whom we spend time with, and how they evaluate us. If others see us as kind, for example, we are more likely to feel that we are kind. Unlike eye color, height, or age, our minds and identities are not quantifiably observable; instead, we learn to make sense of who we are (and should be) through our interpretation of our interactions with other people. This is what scholars mean by a social self.

How Do Social Scripts Shape Selves?

Navigating the social world is an endeavor that, on a daily basis, includes multiple interactions with individuals, groups, and institutions; part of how people manage this is by learning and adopting socially accepted patterns for interaction. Instead of going through life having to interpret each experience or interaction anew, members of society develop patterns of behavior that they learn and use as signposts to guide everyday experiences. These recipes for meaning-making[17] help us to define our situation and figure out what to do next. Consider research on sexual social scripts.[18] Shari Dworkin and Lucia O'Sullivan's interviews with men about sexual activity within heterosexual relationships, for example, found that different sexual scripts for men and women shape who initiates sex and how these acts are understood. Their interviews revealed that, "men in relationships feel comfortable if women initiate 'once in a while' or 'more' than currently, but 'not too much.'" [19] That is, dominant social scripts for sex normalize men asking for sex, but make it problematic for women to do so; these scripts shape how men and women interact and make sense of their own sexual selves. Moreover, as men and women engage in sexual activity they learn these rules and experience reward or sanction for rejecting or abiding by them. Dworkin and O'Sullivan conclude that in the process of negotiating sexual relationships, men "wrestle with, critique, adhere to, and remake" gendered sexual scripts.[20] What this research example reveals is how social scripts shape even the most intimate of behaviors, and how they do so in ways that feel like authentic expressions of personal will.

Just as a play has a script for the actors so that they know what to say and do from Act 1 to the final curtain, social scripts guide each of us, and our behavior, through the scenes of everyday life.[21] Once we learn these scripts, however, they become so automatic that we forget that we had to learn them in the first place. In fact, these patterns and interpretations begin to feel so natural that they come to feel like self-initiated responses to events and not socially guided scripts for behavior or packages of meaning. This does not mean that we abide by them all the time, of course. Individuals choose to defy, or inadvertently breach expected patterns for behavior all the time, in the same way that actors add improvisational components to scripted material. That said, social scripts for behavior are transmitted and enforced ubiquitously through social interaction, and contravening them has real-world consequences.

Social scripts become more easily visible when they are performed incorrectly. When I was younger my mother used to amuse me with stories of funny things she said or did when she first emigrated from Romania to the United States. My favorite was her 'how are you' story. When my mother first moved to the U.S. from Eastern Europe she knew limited English; it was enough to communicate her basic needs but not much more. Each morning a neighbor used to greet her in the hall of our apartment building with a friendly 'how are you today?' And my mother would answer ... honestly and at length (despite her limited English skills). She would share with them how she was feeling physically and emotionally, what she was excited to do that day, and what she was missing about home. At this point in the story I would always laugh, as would my mother. She would explain that while her neighbor never said anything, my mother quickly learned that this was not the appropriate response to the question 'how are you?' She had to learn the American script for greeting a casual acquaintance, which differed from anything with which she was familiar. Asking 'how are you' is not a way that friends or strangers greeted one another in

Romania, and so my mother defined the situation based upon her native social scripts, and answered the question literally. We all learn how to define new situations and the scripts for behavior that go with them as we interact with others in society. My mother has adjusted her response to fit the social script of the United States and now answers 'how are you' with a cheery 'fine!'

How Are Social Scripts for Bodies and Identities Changing?

Social scripts guide far more than how to greet friends and acquaintances in the hallway. We also have social scripts for who someone can be—for their identities and body. In North American societies, social scripts for gender teach us that individuals will always be one of two genders—woman or man—as determined by the unchanging physical and physiological features of their female or male body. This gender script leads us to define who someone is based upon the style of their clothing, hair, and body movements, and from this we assume we know many things about them, their body, and their life. Young children still learning the rules, however, often mess this script up. For example, children make firm plans to grow up to be a dog, marry their cat, or become another gender. Firm correction from others starting at a very young age, however, helps children quickly learn the social scripts for the set of identities that they are permitted to grow into. By age three or so, children display a rigid set of rules for gender and go about enforcing them on everyone around them.[22] If you have ever been around small children, you have likely been firmly scolded about your gender presentation or behavior. This process of scripting gender continues throughout life. As teenagers go through puberty, they are taught (through sex-education, media, religion, and family among other forums) the range of sexual selves they can and are expected to be. Adulthood brings gender rules and norms regarding marriage, child rearing, and aging.

Gender

We experience gender in what our bodies look like, how we move them through space, how we interpret our physical and physiological input, and how our bodies interact with other bodies both socially and sexually. Gender is also an experience of the mind—a sense of who we are, and what we are 'like' and 'not like.' But contrary to our societal assumptions, neither our gendered bodies nor our gendered identities are simply inborn. Gender is regarded by most people, institutions, and governments as a fixed descriptive characteristic of individuals based upon one's born sex, and as something that is outside of the realm of social construction. Research on gender, however, shows that it is *not* a direct product of biological forces, but rather a set of values, beliefs, and norms that are created and enforced by society in conversation with biology.[23] Gender scholars have come to understand that there is a difference between the 'sex' of our physical male, female, or intersex bodies and our gender, and that both of these are shaped by the complex interplay between biological and social forces.

INTERSEX

The term used for individuals whose chromosomes, genitalia, secondary sex characteristics, and/or hormones do not correspond to one binary sex category (male/female). For more information see http://www.isna.org, the website of the Intersex Society of North America.[24]

Gender is a Social Endeavor

Gestures and behaviors communicate particular gendered messages that vary by culture and historical moment. Gestures such as batting one's eyelashes or spitting supplement the information already broadcast by bodily appearance, clothing styles, and words regarding one's embodied identity, whether that is race, class, gender, sexuality, nation, age, etc.[25] Consider, for example, how you 'know' what someone's gender is. Can you articulate what it is in how they look or behave that communicates this information? Gendered ways of conducting, dressing, and carrying oneself, like other types of norms, are not adopted by chance; individuals learn, adopt, and are compelled to conform to these scripts through the systems of reward and sanction that underlie social conduct. People quickly learn that failing to adopt the proper gendered body scripts has consequences.

Moreover, embodied gender conveys more than just gender; it also conveys and gives meaning to other socially significant identities such as race, class, and sexuality. We refer to a person's embodiment when we discuss their 'refinement' or 'trashiness,' 'poise' or 'roughness.' Some people are under surveillance by the staff of fancy stores, while others are not, based upon a set of assumptions about class as conveyed through their embodied gender, class, and race. One could, with certain resources, dress up, act differently, or otherwise attempt to shape one's identity to change other people's responses, but this would alter one's own embodiment. Most embodied scripts are difficult to modify, however, and the very act of policing some types of people and not others is one of the many ways that hegemonic norms and social inequalities are reinforced. When working class people or people of color are monitored in stores, it sends a message about who is welcome and who is not—about who the right kind of person is, and who is a problem.

Take a moment to think about how often in the last year you were told that your portrayal of gender was unsuitable. Were you told that something you wanted to do was 'unladylike' or 'girly,' that you were acting 'like a sissy girl' or 'too butch,' that you did not walk, talk, or act like the gender you were supposed to be? Chances are you and most people you know have had this experience. When I ask this question in classes, I have only one or two people out of perhaps 150 who raise their hands and say that they never had an experience in which their gender was policed. If our gender flowed directly from our genes, then we would all produce the correct gender attributes perfectly and consistently. Moreover, gender expectations and behaviors would only change when our biology changed, and, considering that 99.9 percent of the DNA in all humans is identical,[26] humans all over the world would 'do gender' nearly the same way.[27] That is not the case, however; we see vastly different expectations for what qualities men and women should possess across time and place. Around the world men may be expected to be tall, short, thin, stocky, quiet, domineering, gentle, gruff, sexually aggressive, or stoic and subdued. As these examples demonstrate, the qualities defined as masculine (and, of course, feminine) are variable by locale and historical moment.

The idea that sex and gender are the products of natural, biological processes is so ingrained in how we understand the world that it is hard to imagine it being any different. This is what scholars mean when they talk about hegemonic gender.

HEGEMONY

Domination without force.[28] Hegemonic ideas are those beliefs that get us to participate in a system that dominates us, even when we do not benefit from it. In other words, they are beliefs that we take for granted as natural and eternal and that therefore hold incredible power in society to shape individuals' lives, possibilities, and freedoms. For example, the hegemonic belief that gender is a direct product of biology and carries with it natural and eternal differences between men and women, justifies treating men and women differently and unequally. Because hegemonic beliefs are understood as natural and timeless, imagining change is difficult.

There are numerous examples, however, that contradict this assumption that gender is a fixed, natural reality; in fact, gender is far more variable than most people take into consideration. A straightforward example of the diversity of gender arises when we contemplate our own lives and how often our own desires, behaviors, and presentations go against the idealized gender norms. The fact that the 'ideal' body changes over time also refutes the concept of gender as fixed, defined simply by biological reality.

Fashion is a great example of the continuously changing concept of an ideal body. Styles for men and women come in and out of fashion, all the while shaping what we consider as traits of femininity and masculinity. Through the late nineteenth century young boys in Europe and North America were dressed in skirts and dresses until early childhood, but dressing boys like this would be perceived as gender-bending today. In the 1920s the perfect woman's body was petite, small breasted, and boyish, and women wearing pants was unthinkable—at least for feminine, 'good' women. In the 1980s both men's and women's fashion rebelled against the long hair, platform shoes, and bell-bottom pants of the 1960s and 1970s. Business suits, men's leisure suits, and acid-washed jeans refocused men's fashion on the qualities that then defined masculinity, while women's clothing became more tight fitting, following what was then established as feminine. More recently, the rise of the 'metrosexual' man who pays attention to his hair, clothing, and style is reshaping what it means to be masculine, as opposed to earlier decades where North American men were not expected to pay attention to their looks. With an understanding of how social trends and norms shape embodied gender, it is possible to make sense of these changes over time and place.

It is hard to think about gender, which our whole society treats as natural, as shaped and defined by each society. In fact, even though scholars have studied and theorized how gender is a socially constructed category shaped by social norms, hierarchies, and power relationships, most of us continue to treat it as something that is a natural and fixed part of who we are (and always have been). In part we do it because gender shapes our lives, our experiences, and even our bodies consistently and dramatically. Gender helps to determine what clothes we wear, what toys we play with as children,[29] our school experiences, what we think we can be when we grow up, how we fall in love (and with whom) and whom we should desire sexually. In many times and places gender determines what political rights we have,[30] the jobs we can obtain, and what roles we are expected to take on in our own families.[31] How, then, can gender be part of all these decisions and processes if it is created by society and therefore not a tangible thing?

Gender as Socially Constructed but Meaningful in Our Lives

The contradiction posed by the reality that gender is socially constructed while also significant in shaping our lives is one of the most challenging aspects of understanding gender and its importance. The first way to approach this contradiction is to understand gender as something that "does not exist (in nature)" but is "real (in terms of life consequences, including various structural inequalities, physical violence, etc.)."[32] In other words, even though gender rules and norms are things that are created by society, and therefore not facts of nature, their consequences are tangible and meaningful, and are experienced mentally, emotionally, and physically by individuals.[33] For example, contemporary North American gender norms suggest that 'real' men are naturally well muscled and athletic. These socially constructed beliefs about what it means to be a man affect how boys and men prioritize working out, learning sports, and building muscle. The investment of time and energy into strength building and participating in athletic activities leads to boys and men who are more muscular and interested in sports, which completes the circle and reinforces the idea that men are naturally big and strong. Meanwhile, this focus on muscularity and athleticism—adherence to a set of socially informed gender beliefs—shapes men's bodies, making them larger and stronger. These foci also shape how men function within and interact with the world, what they spend their time on, and what their own beliefs about gender are. In fact, the demand for muscles is high enough that increasing numbers of men (not to mention professional athletes, as evidenced by the 2007–2009 baseball scandal) use steroids to accomplish the task.[34] What is particularly ironic about steroid use is that it can lead to a number of bodily characteristics that undermine normative masculinity, including breast growth, shrinking of the penis, and increased emotionality.

This is a clear example not only of how social beliefs about bodies prioritize some characteristics over others at different times, but how these social beliefs shape both our bodies and our identities. Because we believe that gender naturally exists, and because we believe that there are natural differences between men and women, societal forces create, uphold, and reproduce gender. To put it another way, the *"cultural messages* that form our expectations and 'rules' about gender determine the gendered experiences of our bodies—our *embodied knowledge,* and these messages and our resulting gendered practices help to shape our physical bodies as well."[35] Throughout the rest of this book I will examine how new technologies are changing the social scripts, or what

Crawley, Foley, and Shehan call 'cultural messages,' for who individuals can be in the world. Moreover, I explore who this is allowing people to shape their gendered bodies in new ways.

Accounting for Gender Variation in Society

There is more variation in gender than we acknowledge as a society, and in recent years there has been increased public attention paid to gender change. From talk shows to TV documentaries to movies to newspaper articles, there has been an explosion of coverage about transgender and transsexual individuals and lives.

TRANSGENDER

Transgender can be used as an umbrella term that refers to individuals who change their sex or gender after birth through social or medical means. It can also be used to refer more specifically to individuals whose gender differs from their birth sex but who do not take medical steps to alter their body accordingly.

TRANSSEXUAL

Transsexual is a term that refers to individuals who take medical steps (e.g. hormones and surgery) to bring their body into alignment with their gender. Transsexualism is currently pathologized through the psychological diagnosis of Gender Identity Disorder.

A quick LexisNexis newspaper search pulls up more than 1,400 U.S. newspaper articles in the last year on transgender individuals, rights, and communities. We can compare this to only 1,000 articles between March 2002 and March 2003, and only 320 ten years ago.[36] Not long ago, transgender individuals were relegated to appearances on Jerry Springer-like talk shows,[37] or portrayals only as the brunt of jokes in movies like *Sorority Boys*. Now, however, their lives and experiences garner increasing attention and more favorable coverage by mainstream media. In the past few years there have been a number of television shows about transgender youth and adults including Sundance

Channel's *TransGeneration*, an eight-part documentary about transgender college students, and *Changing Sexes: Female to Male 2003*, a documentary shown on the Discovery Channel. Transgender characters have been included on TV shows like *Ally McBeal*, *Nip/Tuck*, *SouthPark*, *Ugly Betty*, and *All My Children*, while talk shows and news programs alike have done stories/episodes on transpeople's lives, experiences, and challenges. In addition, a number of books have been published about gender change, including the best sellers *She's Not There: A Life in Two Genders*, by Jennifer Boylan, and Renee Richards' *No Way Renee: The Second Half of My Notorious Life*.

Increased attention to transgender and transsexual individuals both reflects and spurs change in society. School, work, and government policies about gender change have become increasingly common, and a number of states have enacted non-discrimination policies regarding gender presentation. Across the board we have seen more attention paid to transgender lives, and both media attention and public discussion about how people can be gendered have increased awareness and affected how most people in North America think about gender. If who we are is shaped by our society, then wider social understanding of transgenderism challenges our social and personal beliefs that there are only two genders that flow directly and innately from two types of sexed bodies. One way that we see the effects of this social broadening is in responses to transgenderism. As opposed to my own experience as a young person in the 1980s, I now see that most students in my courses have some understanding of gender non-conformity. Moreover, there are clear generational changes in how people make sense of transgender lives.

Consider, for example, a recent case in Florida. Largo, Florida's city manager, Susan Stanton, was fired in 2007 after coming out as transsexual.[38] After 14 years of highly praised service, city commissioners voted five to two that Stanton should be fired because of her decision to come out and change her public identity and body—what is often referred to as 'transitioning'—from male to female. This showed that she lacked "honesty, integrity and trust" according to Commissioner Andy Guyette.[39] Stanton was taken aback by this response; she shared in a newspaper article a year later that, "I was totally unprepared for the reaction and rejection of [sic] almost everyone who'd been close to me."[40] Susan was called sick, deviant, and a 'weirdo' by city leaders, abandoned by friends, and ridiculed on national television. These responses are, unfortunately, what we might expect given dominant social scripts for gender and the attendant marginalization of transgender and transsexual individuals in society. But, if you look at the response of Stanton's 14 year old son, Travis, you see a very different understanding of gender in general, and of transgender individuals more specifically. In a school essay Travis wrote the following about Susan:

> Throughout my whole life, I thought my dad was a really tough guy. He went out with the cops and busted bad guys. He shot guns, fought fires. He was an aggressive driver. He liked football and lots of sports.
>
> Then one day my thoughts changed about him when we had a family meeting and he told me how he felt about himself. He said he felt like a woman on the inside and was going to change into one. He said he tried his best to be a manly guy, but he couldn't stop his feelings to become a girl.
>
> At first, I thought I was in a dream. I thought he was 100 percent manly man, more manly than most guys.
>
> After a few days, I thought about it. I knew he was making the right choice to become a girl. Although I cannot relate to his feelings, it must be really hard to hide something like that . . . I think that everyone should be who they are and not try to be the same as other people. If you ask me, this has got to be the most manliest thing he has done in his whole life. It takes a real man to come out of his shell and say, 'Hey, I am who I am.'[41]

This has surely been a difficult time for Travis, but his essay is not only deeply moving, but it reflects a flexible understanding of gender and identity. He takes for granted, almost, that one's sex and/or gender can change. And he is not alone; many people rallied around Susan. In fact,

230 supporters, most of whom were young, transgender activists and allies, showed up to her hearing with city commissioners, and have supported her new identity.

Travis recognizes that the way he is making sense of gender is different from how other people have viewed it. In an interview, Travis Stanton reflected that, "everyone thinks my dad has hurt me and my life is ruined. But that's not how it is at all. I just think I get things more now . . . We do stuff together all the time. It is like being with my aunt or something, only he's still my dad."[42] What this example suggests is that exposure to new gender norms and social scripts has transformed the ways that some young individuals make sense of gender and gender non-conformity; the possible ways of being gendered in the world are changing, and these changes are affecting younger generations in transformational ways.

Gender non-conformity is not a new thing. It has existed throughout recorded history, and across all cultures and ages. In Chapter 1 I explore how gender has been understood over time. Before the rise of science when medicine became the authority on bodies, most individuals were treated as their desired gender if they took on the corresponding social roles and responsibilities.[43] In more recent times, psychology has offered the diagnosis of Gender Identity Disorder (GID) for individuals who express dissatisfaction with their assigned gender or sex.[44] Some contemporary psychological theories treat the desire to change sex or gender as a product of a disordered sense of self. Most recently, in the last 15 years, transgender activists have pushed for new understandings of gender non-conformity, unfettered by medical definition, and have challenged the pathological categorization of GID. These challenges are forcing scientific and medical practitioners to rethink the treatment of gender non-conformity.

The Impact of Challenging Gender Norms

Even though our society views gender as if it is an unwavering reflection of biology, contemporary engagement with transgender lives and issues, along with other examples of gender variation and flexibility, have challenged these assumptions. Just as Susan Stanton's son (and the other individuals who rallied around Susan) reflected a new, broader set of beliefs about gender, other groups are also challenging the idea of a fixed, biologically driven gender. These challenges have happened more in some groups and communities than others. The question then becomes, what would cause a group of people to think of gender as something that can be changed; moreover, as something that they could think about changing within themselves?

What does it mean when whole *groups* of people assert that questioning gender and changing how they understand their gender identity is a legitimate endeavor? I encountered a community doing just that when I began studying a drag performance troupe several years ago.[45] Drag performances are lip-synched performances that play with gender. Drag has often been understood as the theatrical performance of an 'opposite' gender for entertainment, but in the group I studied, drag meant any gender performance. In this performance group there were female-bodied people performing as men (drag kings), transgender kings and queens (transgender performers, performing masculinity or femininity, both in accordance with and differing from their chosen, self-defined gender), and bio-queens (women performing femininity). Members of this group—the Disposable Boy Toys (DBT)—were short and tall, fat and thin, masculine and feminine, man and woman identified. What is noteworthy about the group for the purpose of this discussion is that while society might consider all of the members to be female (born into female bodies, raised as girls and women), the members themselves would not all define themselves as such. What, then, would lead many of these performers to make sense of their own bodies and identities in new and different ways?

No member's sex, gender, and sexual identity in this group align the way that our societal assumptions—assumptions so taken-for-granted that they are usually unexamined, even unnoticed—say they should. These variations from common identity pairings were not the case, however, before they became drag performers in DBT. Almost everyone in the group defined their own gender differently after performing together for a few years than they did before they joined. What I found in my research was that the ability for members to embody gender differently had everything to do with the way the group as a whole made sense of gender as a chosen and evolving identity. The group, which spent rehearsal, performance, and social time together, created a social space where participants were able to and even encouraged to try on, practice, and embody different genders. Because drag in DBT was inherently about gender play—whether any given performance crossed gender lines, claimed new gender definitions, or portrayed transgender lives—it enabled members to play with a variety of masculine and feminine genders. And this play changed how people were gendered in their everyday lives.

Many women performers went from naming themselves simply "female" to claiming a radical femininity, described as "chosen," "proud," and "transgressive." Similarly, a number of participants came to resist singular gender classification and prefaced naming with "if I have to choose," or "I guess I am." Some female-bodied performers came to take on male or masculine gender identities including butch, ambiguously masculine, masculine female, Female-to-Male transsexual, and transgender male. Even when their bodies remained female, members felt able and empowered to define their gendered self in a new way. Regardless of identity, members described gender as a conscious act and explained these gender shifts as outcomes of their participation in DBT.

One performer, Summer's Eve, who was a feminine woman who performed an exaggerated femininity on stage, noted,

> We joke in DBT about drag being the gateway drug for gender regardless of what that gender is. Some members came into a masculine butch, some members came into a female-identified butch, and some members came into fiercely femme.

This example reveals what other research on identity also suggests; that how we make sense of our self is shaped by the world around us, who we spend time with, and what we do.[46] The possible ways of being gendered (for example, having a female body but dressing, behaving, and identifying as a man) expanded for members of DBT. The group encouraged its performers to play with gender and supported them through identity change, and this expansion of social scripts for how you could be defined changed members' gendered identities. We will return to this example in later chapters, to examine in more detail when and how these social scripts change.

In a technologically saturated age where individuals have access to more information, more real and virtual communities, and more medical intervention, the implications of this are significant. The world around us, both in general and in terms of the specific people and communities we interact with, shapes who we are and who we think we can be. At the beginning of this preview, I suggested that how people come to know and understand their self has changed throughout history. Even though we go about our lives as if what we are is some intrinsic, stable part of ourselves, the social scripts that dictate who we can be in terms of our gender and other characteristics, shape these identities. By examining how technology has created new physical and social possibilities for gender we can learn a lot about *how* our modern technological world is changing who we are in fundamental ways. Scholars have traditionally examined the development and acquisition of gendered social scripts through face-to-face interaction within social institutions such as school, family, and religion. In our contemporary, fragmented world, however, it is becoming increasingly routine to come to know others and ourselves through technology.

Technological, social, and physical conditions all interact with one another within a specific social context and through a variety of institutions. Many factors including race, class, gender, and age shape each person's access to and use of medical and information technologies, as well as their relationship to dominant social scripts and ideologies. As technology advances, each new set of body and identity possibilities is interpreted through dominant social scripts and beliefs, and these things work together to shape our identities and bodies.

A New World Order: Life in a Technological Age

According to my Palm Pilot (where I took the initial notes for this text), on July 30, 2007 I listened to the car radio while I drove to work. I am sure my Bluetooth cell phone earpiece was in my ear, but I was able to hear a program on my car radio in which Dr. Danna Walker, a Journalism professor at American University, described her students' reactions to an enforced media blackout.[47] Walker asked students to refrain from all electronic media for 24 hours. Students in her "Understanding Mass Media" course reacted with a range of emotions, from frustration to anger to claims that it was "one of the toughest days I have had to endure."[48] The comment that most struck me from this broadcast was from one of Walker's students, who declared that spending the day without technology made her feel homeless. "I was walking down the street literally with nowhere to go, and I just did not know what I was going to do." I found this a phenomenal statement about the centrality of technology in our twenty-first century lives; then again, should I have been shocked, given how encumbered by technology I was at that very moment?

In North America at the turn of the millennium, individuals privileged enough to have ready access to technology use cell phones, computers, televisions and, if pushed, antiquated radios to gain information, achieve tasks, and communicate with a multitude of real-life or virtual acquaintances. We have become a society that must trust science to keep us healthy and use technology to overcome nature. It is easy to see how these rapid technological advances have shaped how we communicate with each other, how we spend our free and working time, how we learn about the world around us, and about how our bodies change over time. But the technological tendrils that permeate our lives have not stopped with communication or medicine. New technology is changing everything about our lives and world, including our bodies and identities.

That technology is ubiquitous in the everyday life of most North Americans is incontrovertible.[49] From our daily use of cell phones, computers, IPods and Blackberries to the genetic engineering of our food, bodies, and medicine,[50] to the World Wide Web and electronic media, technology mediates most of our daily experiences in the twenty-first century. Even for those of us who lack economic privilege, technology has come to play a prominent role; food stamps are electronic and computers are required for many social and economic tasks, which exacerbates existing social inequalities through unequal access to technology. Technology is the middleman, as it were, between our social world and us.

Think about the speed with which we go about our days, days filled with the multi-tasking, double booking, and phone calls while traveling to the next place our physical presence is required. A leading scholar of identity and society, Jodi O'Brien, writes about how in our modern world we come to 'lean forward' in time, always paying attention to the next thing we have to do, spurred on by our increasing ability—and increasing expectations—to speed up our lives using modern technology. Regardless of all of the time saving devices introduced to our life in the last 20 years, or maybe because of their introduction, people feel more short on time than ever before.[51] The many news articles on the increasing speed of life—more than 50 in major U.S. newspapers alone in 2007—are testament to the feelings of being overwhelmed by technology and our ambivalence to this phenomenon.

One familiar example of the impact of technology (and our mixed feelings about it) is the effect cell phones have had on our everyday behavior. Cell phones give us a way to contact others at any time we choose, but the other edge of the sword is that we are expected to be reachable at every moment of the day. I know in my own life I am engaged in an ongoing tug-of-war with my father. If I do not return his phone calls within an hour, he will call again . . . and again . . . and again. I believe this is more than just a 'father thing.' When I was in college I could go for days ignoring his phone calls, but now, although I am older and more independent, along with my cell phone comes his expectation, and even demand, that I be reachable at all times. My father very likely feels that he is equally on-call. In these and many other ways, technology is not just the means through which we increasingly interact with the world around us, but it also acts as an instrument to shape *how* we interact, and these changes further shape who we are as embodied individuals.

Information Technology as Mediator between Physical and Mental Life

Technology increasingly plays the role of middleman between our physical and mental selves. Not only do we communicate with friends and strangers over email and through online social networking sites like *Friendster*, *MySpace*, and *Facebook*, online social spaces have become places to 'be yourself.' This is particularly true in the increasingly popular virtual worlds such as *Second Life*, which had 16 million registered users as of July 2009.[52] These users spent a total of one billion hours in the *Second Life* world 'Lindenland.' Much more than a game, *Second Life* is literally a copycat world where individuals can create schools, businesses, and governments and interact in virtual copies of real-world places. Comedians and musicians have gone on tour in *Second Life*. *Maxim*, a men's magazine, voted 'Second Life Girls' number 95 in their list of "100 Hottest Females of 2007."[53] Lindenland 'residents' go to school in virtual classrooms (while earning real-life college credits), go out to dance clubs, participate in charity races, and even date. Realtors facilitate the buying and selling of virtual land (for real money), and contractors offer their services to help people build their avatars (a two- or three-dimensional image representing you or your character), virtual houses, and businesses. Real-world businesses have virtual stores where individuals can (and do) try on, buy, and sell real-world goods, conveying those transactions between virtual world and real-life. Virtual bars and restaurants offer places for individuals and groups to eat virtual food, drink virtual drinks, and interact with one another through virtual representations (accurate or not) of their physical bodies. In other words, you can 'do' all the things you usually do with your body in real life, virtually in *Second Life*, plus a lot more: for instance, you can fly.

These online interactions have meaning for people in the real world. In September 2007, 2,000 real Italian union workers spent 12 hours in virtual protest over stalled contract negotiations, outside of IBM's virtual headquarters in *Second Life*. Their avatars gathered outside of IBM's virtual island and voiced their grievances, and these virtual protesters took advantage of the real-world possibilities offered in *Second Life* as well as more fanciful ones; alongside the anticipated union activists in union shirts and employees carrying protest signs, a large yellow banana held a sign that read, "Fair work, fair pay, please don't take our money away," while a green triangle stood by stoically.

Most important, perhaps, is that this virtual protest mattered. The Italian CEO of IBM resigned soon after the protest and union contract negotiations were reopened. Within days 9,000 real life union workers had a new real-world contract.

As *Second Life* demonstrates, people are using online spaces in a myriad of ways to mimic and even carry out social, political, and community activities alongside, or instead of, activities in the real world. And just as real-world interactions shape what we think about who we can be as individuals, these technologically mediated spaces offer new experiences and definitions of who we are. Since its inception in 2006, *Second Life* has attracted more than 16 million users who have created virtual depictions of who they are and what they look like, or want to look like. With the ability to customize your avatar-self and use it to interact with others, *Second Life* offers a whole new set of social spaces to develop and assert one's personal identity. Not only do individuals create visual representations of self, they use these virtual bodies and identities to have real-time experiences with other people, all mediated by the technological interface of computer networks. As I explore further throughout this book, online forums are sites for community development, romantic relationships, and sexual experimentation. Moreover, in the process these forums are facilitating identity changes for many people.

Biomedical Technology as Mediator between Physical and Mental Life

It is not only information technology that is shaping our experiences of bodies and identities. In our modern medical age we learn and experience our own physical bodies through technology as well. We may have some intuitive sense, fever, or stomachache, but know we are 'really' sick only because a medical test tells us so. When we miss class or work we must legitimate illness through a note from the doctor, rather than through some personal accounting of how we felt or how our body manifested an illness. In our new biotech world, we can get full-body medical scans that will tell us everything that is—or will be—wrong with us. Armed with this knowledge, and some disposable income, we can treat ourselves with new pills and lotions for ailments we never knew we had. Are we sick, then, because of how we feel or because of what technology tells us? Do we trust our bodies as sources of knowledge less as we trust technological intervention more? How do we come to know ourselves in situations where real-world experiences exist alongside virtual ones?

In 1985 Donna Haraway, a feminist philosopher, wrote an article foretelling the encroachment of technology into human bodies and identities. In it Haraway argues that we have all become cyborgs—a combination of machine and organism—in this modern technological world.[54] Our bodies are no longer left in their natural state to grow, age, and die, but instead are modified with and through machines. We modify and reconstruct our bodies using lifestyle and daily maintenance drugs, contact lenses, tattoos, tanning salons, hair dyes, prosthetic limbs, and plastic surgery. Haraway argues, "communication technologies and biotechnologies are the crucial tools recrafting our bodies."[55] In this techno-world, the body comes to be an ongoing production of society, constantly changing through technological intervention. These are significant changes. Media Studies scholar Anne Balsamo, in her research on gender and technology, argues that these changes are shaped by and, in turn, shape the individual attributes that society inscribes onto the body—elements like gender and race.[56]

Take the double eyelid surgery called blepharoplasty, popular among Asian women, as an example of society's production of the body in this techno-world.[57] In an effort to create 'White looking' eyes that are wide with a creased eyelid, many Asian women in North America go under the knife. While men can and do get the surgery, it is overwhelmingly pursued by women.[58] It is no surprise, given the beauty demands we put on women, that women make up the overwhelming majority of plastic surgery patients. The surgery, which uses sutures to create a crease in the eyelid (something typical of White eyes but atypical of Asian ones), is a clear example of using technology to change the body in both a gendered (given its overwhelming use by women in North America) and racialized way. The use of this surgical intervention is tied to social norms and expectations within North America and plays out differently in other nations. For example, in many Asian countries men utilize the surgical intervention at much higher rates than they do in North America, and the cultural meaning of the surgery is different given the minority status of White individuals.

Blepharoplasty is the most popular cosmetic surgery for Asian-American women, and is a hotly debated issue within Asian-American communities. While the surgery itself is more than 100 years old, its popularity has exploded in recent years as medical advances have made it less invasive, safer, and more affordable. In her critique of plastic surgery as the erasure of race and disability, feminist philosopher Sara Goering notes that, "the fact that most of the practices aim at one specific kind of body [creating White features] suggests that much more than personal preference is at issue."[59] In our world, globalization has included the increasing homogeneity of beauty norms (indeed we see an increasing preference around the world for Western/White features, styles of dress, and beauty trends). We can make sense of unnecessary surgery designed to create 'Western looking' eyes as a product, at least in part, of specific *cultural beliefs about beauty*[60] and the gifts of ease and access offered by advancing medical technology. These interventions change the perception of what Asian women should look like by changing what some actually do look like, and in the process they are both reinforcing and challenging social scripts about what it means to be a woman or man in the twenty-first century.

Investigating the Impact of New Technologies

In the following chapters we will investigate how gendered bodies and identities are changing in a society that is being reshaped by technology. In between these substantive chapters I offer several short case studies that explore how societal gender ideologies, new technologies, and social scripts are in dynamic relationship to individual bodies and identities. The first one, which follows this preview, examines how the technological innovation of tattooing has been used historically to 'do' masculinity in North America. Chapter 1 follows by developing a more nuanced understanding of technology and examining how the social histories of gender and technology have been intertwined. After exploring how gender has been understood and shaped by the technologies developed in different historical eras, I elaborate how a sociological approach best recognizes the connections between gendered bodies, identities, social scripts, ideologies, and technologies. It is this type of approach that is most useful for understanding nineteenth-century battles over dress reform highlighted in the second case study.

In Chapter 2 I use this approach to make sense of how new information technologies are reshaping gendered bodies and identities. I take up examples such as virtual interactive worlds, online support groups, and transgender discussion boards. I introduce research on these new technologies and ask whether and how information technologies are offering people new social scripts for gendered bodies and identities and changing the real-life experiences and identities of individuals. The significance of these dynamics is profiled in the third case study on transgender social movement organizing and the Internet.

In Chapter 3 I examine how technological advances in plastic surgery, body modification, and medicine help individuals to shape their physical bodies in new ways. I focus on the dynamics at play in surgical and hormonal interventions, steroid use and plastic surgery, and examine whether and how social scripts and individual identities are changing as part of these bio-medical technological innovations. The last case study examines the treatment of intersex individuals in North America and charts the normative and counter-hegemonic outcomes of this approach. Finally, I return in the Review to the questions we began with—how are new technologies changing who we are and how we can be defined as gendered beings? And where are these changes leading us as individuals and as a society?

CASE STUDY: FOCUS ON TATTOOING AND MASCULINITY

Tattooing is an increasingly prevalent form of intervention into the body in North America. As a technology—it is after all a clear intervention into the natural body—tattooing has changed very little over the past several thousand years. Save for one significant innovation in the late 1890s when the tattoo machine was created, the principles and basic methods have remained the same. Tattoos are created by inserting ink (natural or synthetic) under the dermis layer of skin using needles (which historically could be made of a variety of materials such as shells, bone, quills, and metal). Because tattoos are pictorial and/or word images literally written on the body, they alter the embodied landscape of individuals. In addition, because of the body-identity connection assumed in contemporary body ideologies, these inscriptions are assumed to have significance for the individual.[1] Yet, the social meaning of tattoos has changed drastically over the past 150 years, and these changes have concurrently shaped the meaning and import of tattoos for individuals. Tattoos are part of a historical process of continual redefinition and negotiation of gendered terms, especially within the context of masculine identities.

In contemporary North American society tattoos are viewed as meaningful acts of identity building or personal expression. For example, television shows such as *Miami Ink* on The Learning Channel document acts of narrative identity formation, often profiling the personal stories behind a client's tattoo. Because of these expectations individuals are called on to narrate the meaning of a tattoo for themselves and others (I discuss this process of narrative identity in the next chapter) and they do so using the social scripts available.[2] Sociologist Mary Kosut elaborates on this relationship and explains that,

> Although tattooing is a way to construct one's body and self in one's own desired image, it is also a phenomenon that reflects cultural influences. An important characteristic of the tattoo as a

form of communication is that it largely "speaks" through non-verbal transmission.[3]

The stories individuals tell about their tattoos are the product of both the internal self and embodied experience and are shaped by the dominant beliefs and scripts of the day. Personal and societal meaning-making about tattoos comes from the interaction of a number of social forces: dominant ideologies for bodies and gender, social scripts for acceptable bodies and identities, technologies of tattooing, and the bodies and identities of individuals within a group or society.

An example of this complex play of forces is tattoos within gangs (a particular social context with its own social scripts for behavior). Gang tattoos take highly regimented forms as a way of communicating to others an individual's personal experiences within the group, such as their history of violence, loss of loved ones, and sense of loyalty. Each element of the tattoo holds a range of meanings, depending on its location on the body and the symbols contained therein.

In different eras social scripts for tattooing in North America have labeled bodies as beautiful or deviant, military or criminal, aristocratic or working-class. Tattoos have been used by individuals as accessories, badges, and to symbolize among many other things social status, rites of passage, community affiliations, personal triumphs and tragedies, racial, ethnic, political, sexual, and gender identities. Tattoos have also been deeply gendered; scripts for men's and women's tattoos have distinct forms and conventions in North America as well as in many other cultures that practice tattooing. Examining tattooing as a gendered technology reveals a lot about how gendered bodies and identities are in dynamic relationship to new technologies and social scripts.

Tattooing dates back to 6000 B.C.E. and has been present in many cultures around the world. Early European explorers came into contact with tattooing practices among the Moors (North African peoples) as well as within indigenous communities in Central and South America and on the Pacific Islands. Tattooing was not adopted by European explorers until the mid-eighteenth century, however, when sailors and merchants began acquiring tattoos during their travels. The practice became more widespread in the West after Captain James Cook named the practice and brought several natives from the South Pacific back to Europe with him. As trade and colonization accelerated, tattooing was increasingly practiced in Europe and the North American colonies. Simultaneously increased contact with Japan in the late nineteenth and early twentieth centuries introduced Westerners to classic Japanese tattoo art, a much more artistic and graphic style than that which dominated in Europe and North America. During this time tattooing was almost exclusively practiced on men. Even though women in other societies such as the Ainu of Japan practiced tattooing, in the West, tattooed women were extremely marginalized.

Tattoos themselves carried with them information about man's trade—adventurer, merchant, rebel, or sailor—and in the process reinforced the meaning tattoos had within the society. Because the men who donned tattoos in the 1800s were from a social stratum associated with radical politics and social non-conformity, these characteristics came to be associated with tattoos as well. In other words, tattoos conveyed ideas not only of the specific gendered and classed identity of the subject but also his social and political affiliations. For these very reasons men who were free thinkers, radicals and outlaws embraced the tattoo and its associations; it is this mutually constitutive process that is at the heart of how new technologies reshape bodies and identities in conversation with other social forces.

For a brief period of time (from the late 1800s to early 1900s) the European gentry was enamored with tattoos. While it had been the purview of sailors (by choice) and criminals (by force), tattoos became all the rage among upper classes in these few decades. A number of European royalty were tattooed including Prince Waldomar of Denmark, Grand Duke Alexis of Russia, Queen Olga of Greece, and King Oscar of Sweden.[4] This trend was part of a larger fascination with all things 'native' and 'primitive' sparked by the expanding European colonization of Pacific and American lands. It was in the midst of this tattooing fad that the practice came to North American White communities (it was prevalent among some indigenous groups long before then). Both wealthy men and some women were tattooed but these tattooing practices and motifs differed from one another, just as they differed from the prevailing lower-class styles and customs. These differences were the product of differences in social scripts and embodied identities available to men and women of different social classes.

Tattoos were employed by elite individuals to inscribe markers of aristocratic status on the body. An article that appeared in the *Boston Morning Journal* in 1897 emphasizes the very classed nature of the tattoo fad of the late 1800s:

> Have you had your monogram inscribed on your arm? Is your shoulder blade embellished with your crest? Do you wear your coat-of-arms graven in India Ink on the cuticle of your elbow? No! Then, gracious madame and gentle sir, you cannot be *au courant* with society's very latest fad—the tattooing fad. It has just reached New York from London and Paris. It may develop into a mania.[5]

By emphasizing its European roots and suggesting that individuals inscribe their crest or monogram, the article makes clear that this type of tattoo was associated with both cosmopolitan fashions and aristocratic genealogies in the late 1800s.

By the early 1900s tattooing had once again become highly contested and over the next several decades lost social status and became associated with marginal subcultures. This shift was due in part to the increased access working-class individuals had to tattooing with the advent of the electric tattoo machine; the more accessible tattoos were, the less elite they became.[6] In 1891 the tattoo machine was patented by Samuel O'Reilly and this made the tattooing process more efficient while less costly and painful. In addition, at the turn of the century, a number of criminologists began to hypothesize that tattoos were proof of criminal intent or propensity. While forced tattooing of prisoners in Europe had fallen out of fashion, criminal connotations persisted and voluntary tattooing was seen as proof of deviance. At the same time public health campaigns linked tattooing to sexually transmitted diseases; some doctors went as far as to claim that tattoos were external representations of pathology and deviant proclivities. According to criminologists the tattoo was a stigmata of as-yet uncommitted crimes, and according to medical experts the tattoo was a symptom of as-yet undiagnosed disease.

This connection between tattoos and both mental and physical pathology has carried over into some current social science and medical research and into popular culture.[7] These enduring legacies continue to shape the meaning of tattoos and the social scripts that govern their gendered embodied significance. For example, tattoos are often used in literature and film as shorthand for a man's shady past, questionable character, or ill intent and a woman's lack of femininity or morality. In the 1951 Tennessee Williams' play *The Rose Tattoo* (made into an eponymous film in 1955), the main character's husband, a truck-driver who smuggles contraband, has a rose tattooed on his chest. When he is shot and killed by the police, his wife discovers not only his illegal activities but also his adultery. By the play's end, the tattoo in the play's title symbolizes the husband's double deceptions.

By the mid twentieth century, tattooing was most common among young military and working-class men in North America, and primarily featured military, death, and pinup imagery. Small tattoos were often used like badges to mark significant events, and the tattooing session itself was one such event. Surviving the pain of tattooing is viewed as evidence of machismo or manliness, and it is this willingness to accept the pain that has historically situated tattooing as a rite of passage for men (often at puberty or adulthood) within a variety of cultures world-wide.[8] Many of the qualities defined as central to masculinity within dominant social scripts, including bravery, endurance, and immunity to pain, are qualities tested in the act of acquiring a tattoo. These qualities are available to men regardless of social class and historically tattoos were a way for lower class men to compensate for their compromised masculinity. Because many of the socially sanctioned markers of masculinity (e.g. a high paying job, material wealth, and social power) were out of reach for poor men, they drew on tattooing and its related masculine social scripts to bolster their sense of manhood.[9]

In the West this has been particularly true within military groups. Tattooing in the military is a longstanding practice. The first professional tattooist in the United States was Martin Hildebrand who traveled around during the American Civil War tattooing both Union and Confederate soldiers in what was likely the first widespread use of tattoos by soldiers. Hildebrand's tattoos were primarily political and patriotic images that made explicit for which side, North or South, the soldier fought.[10] The practice of tattooing in the armed forces continued to be widespread into the twentieth century, according to tattooist Charlie Wagner, profiled in the *New York Times* in 1943: "Fighting men want to be marked in some way or another. High-class fellas, too—men from West Point and Annapolis. Sailors used to be my big customers, but now it's soldiers."[11]

Today, different branches of the military claim particular symbols, tattoo locations, and rituals so that the whole experience, from the act of getting the tattoo (which symbolizes bravery) to the images inscribed (symbolizing dedication to the group) connect an individual to his military 'brothers.' For example, the U.S. Marines often have a blade and skull tattooed onto their left shoulder while Navy sailors use an anchor. Sociologists Coe, Harmon, Verner, and Tonn interviewed military college cadets and found that for these men getting a tattoo was a social bonding act done in groups and used to mark their membership in the community.[12] Both the cost and the pain of the tattoo were sources of pride and the men's sense of masculinity.

Similarly, research suggests that tattooing is a significant social practice within other men's groups and communities in North America.[13] Tattoo scholar Janine Janssen argues that, for many men:

> A tattoo is not only a form of establishing an identity (e.g. as a sailor or biker), there is also a relationship between tattoos and male bonding. By wearing a specific tattoo they can show each other and the rest of the world what kind of men they are (e.g. gang members or soldiers). Not only the final result—the tattoo—but also the process of 'inscribing' the body can be a manner for expressing one's masculinity.[14]

Not only do they select a single design in common, these men will have their tattoos done as a group, suggesting a ritualistic quality to the tattoo process. Examples like this illustrate how the technology of tattooing, informed by the social norms and scripts of an era, has been used in the service of gendered body and identity work.[15] In North America masculinity has intertwined with tattooing in a variety of ways including in its historical legacy and enduring social meanings, in the process of acquiring a tattoo, its location, and the imagery it contains.

In the post-World War II political and social climate that stressed conformity to White middle-class values, tattoos were increasingly disparaged. By mid-century tattooing had been taken up by prison and motorcycle gangs and came to symbolize violent, rebellious masculinities. The historical legacy of tattooing links the act to archetypical masculinities, however (e.g. sailors, soldiers, Popeye, and the Marlboro man). Even though tattoos were held in distaste in the 1950s, their connection to idealized masculine figures in these advertisements created a tattoo craze. For example, in the 1950s and 1960s Marlboro cigarette ads featured cowboys, musclemen, and suave debonair men with Marlboro eagle tattoos on their hands.[16] Concurrently, the conventionalized form of these tattoos, drawn from media or trademark imagery, tended to reinforce dominant paradigms of masculinity, such as rugged independence and physical strength. It was only in the midst of the 1970s' social change movements that tattooing began to be revived as an acceptable form of bodily manipulation. In this era of anti-establishment attitudes and rejection of authority, the tattoo was reclaimed, and many counter-culture musicians and celebrities sported highly visible tattoos. The tattoo was burnished with rock-and-roll glamor.

Since then both the number of individuals soliciting tattoos and the stigma associated with the practice have shifted considerably. A recent national survey conducted by the Pew Research Center estimated that 36 percent of the U.S. population between the ages of 18 and 25 and 40 percent between 26 and 40 had at least one tattoo. Estimates for Canada are similar.[17] Not only is this figure a large proportion of the North American population, but it points to a dramatic increase in the use of this particular body technology; in the same survey only 10 percent of individuals between 41 and 64 years old reported ever getting a tattoo.[18] Charting the same generational shift, survey data from the early to mid-1990s estimated that fewer than 3 percent to 10 percent of the U.S. population had a tattoo, while a 2006 survey found that 24 percent of individuals under 50 had one.[19]

A more detailed analysis highlights how these changes are also deeply gendered. Historical data points to a dramatic disparity in rates of tattooing between men and women. The stigma attached to tattooed women has been much stronger than that attached to men. In one 1950s account of tattoo culture, for example, tattooist Samuel Steward recounted that he personally refused to tattoo women unless they were 21, married, and had permission from their husbands![20] Certainly not all tattooists were this blatantly sexist, but statistics do suggest that women accounted for a small minority of tattoo clients up until the 1970s. Even by the late 1990s Copes and Forsyth estimated that while between 10 percent and 20 percent of men in the United States were tattooed, only 7 percent of women were.[21] In contrast several surveys conducted in the early 2000s found no significant differences in rates of men and women clientele; women were requesting tattoos at rates even with those of men.[22]

The increasing parity between men and women tattoo-ees does not erase, however, the gendered aspects of tattooing or the particular function tattoos continue to play in relation to masculinity. A number of scholars have documented how tattoos on men and women are interpreted in vastly different ways boosting masculinity while threatening femininity.[23] There are also significant differences in the placement and imagery of tattoos between men and women. For example, while women are more likely to situate a tattoo on a part of the body that is easily covered, men often select a highly visible area that is associated with male secondary sexual characteristics, such as biceps and forearms.[24] The imagery in men's tattoos is also often chosen to represent masculine traits including toughness, individuality, and braveness. The scale of men's tattoo designs is usually large too. In their study of young British men Rosalind Gill, Karen Henwood, and Carl McLean found that men turned to tattooing in part as an effort to publicly stake claim to particular identities.[25] In a historical moment when men's bodies are under increasing scrutiny but, simultaneously, men are not supposed to care about their looks, body work is fraught with tension for men. Young men "must simultaneously work on and discipline their bodies while disavowing any (inappropriate) interest in their own appearance."[26] As a result of these constrained social scripts for acceptable masculinity, Gill, Henwood, and McLean argue that young men make sense of tattoos as identity and community-focused endeavors. Moreover, they found that the available social scripts for young men's masculinity were so limited that although all the young men interviewed espoused personal reasons for getting a tattoo, their narratives were surprisingly uniform.

Drawing together this range of scholarship makes evident how the technology of tattooing has been both shaped by and influential in social scripts for masculinity and individuals' embodied experiences. Sociologist Paul Sweetman summarized that:

> As corporeal expression of *the self*, tattoos and piercings might thus be seen as instances of contemporary *body projects* (Shilling 1993): as attempts to construct and maintain a coherent and viable sense of self-identity through attention to the body and, more particularly, the body's surface (Featherstone 1991).[27]

As body projects, tattoos carry with them legacies of social signification about men, masculinity, and social class. Whether upper-class men in the 1900s tattooing their elite lineage, or 1850s sailors charting their travels, tattoos have been purposefully used by men to establish and reinforce their manhood. These legacies, built out of dominant ideologies about the gendered body and self, have in turn shaped the use of this technology by different groups of men over time.

1

A SOCIAL HISTORY OF TECHNOLOGY AND GENDER

Just a few minutes into the movie *Kinky Boots*, the based-on-real-life story of a rural British shoe factory struggling to survive in a global market, Lola curses her biggest obstacle as a drag queen. Holding up her boot to display its freshly broken heel, she laments, "Like most things in life, it cannot stand the weight of a man."[1] With this remark, Lola pinpoints a key barrier in her ability to successfully dress as a woman. Lola's problem (and that of her real-life compatriots) is the construction of women's shoes: they are not built to support male bodies. High-heeled shoes are not typically constructed to accommodate the average size male's heft, foot size, or gait. All high-heeled shoes, particularly 'stilettos,' characterized by particularly thin heels, require technical acumen in their design because the structure of the shoe focuses immense pressure on a very small area (a petite woman in stilettos can exert 20 times the pressure of a 6,000 pound elephant under her heel!).[2] In fact, it was only in the 1930s that the manufacture of stiletto heels became possible at all, when the specialized design of inserting thin metal tubes into the heel structure of shoes was developed. The standard construction of heels, however, can only withstand a certain amount of pressure, and more often than not male bodies exceed these limits. This structural problem, combined with norms for high-heel shoe size and width, makes finding and wearing high-heeled shoes, by males, virtually impossible.

In the film, after being literally hit over the head with the problem, and as a last ditch effort to save his failing factory, owner Charlie Price recognizes his niche market—shoes for 'drag queens' (aka males who perform dressed as women). He works with Lola to design shoes that will allow male bodies to successfully function in women's high-heeled shoes. As fanciful as the film is, the story and the problem it centers around are genuine. A 2006 *New York Times* article inspired by the film interviewed a number of drag queens and shoe designers about the real-life challenges posed by lack of footwear for drag queens.[3] What the interviewees make clear is that without footwear that fits their feet, male-bodied individuals struggle to perform femininity (whether as drag queens or as transgender and transsexual women). High-heeled shoes are one of the few items of clothing that remain strictly gendered in this age of increasingly androgynous clothing (particularly when compared to bygone eras of corsets, full-length dresses, and top hats); if one is to portray normative femininity—regardless of biological sex—one must be able to wear the appropriate footwear. The solution to this shoe problem is the creation of new approaches to, methods for, and products targeted at male bodies doing femininity. In other words, successfully dressing the part—a key component of embodying gender—requires the development of new technologies.

What is true for shoes is true more broadly with respect to gender; what defines it, how gender is manifested in the body, and what social scripts are available to individuals are to a large extent shaped by technology. This chapter is focused on the dynamic relationships between technology, gendered bodies and identities, dominant ideologies, and social scripts.

In the Preview I defined social scripts as culturally specific blueprints for behavior that shape social and individual expectations and productions of gender. Building on this foundation, this chapter examines how technologies prevalent at different historical moments have been used to make sense of gendered bodies, to police gender ideologies and scripts, and to create or inhibit space for gender non-conformity (defying gender norms and expectations). In other words, I investigate how the histories of gender and technological innovation fit together. These histories suggest that how people understand, conform to, or contest embodied gender changes as technologies change from era to era. People use the technologies available to them at any given time to produce gender (either normative or non-conforming) and in turn, the resulting gender scripts, bodies and identities shape technological development. For example, women in the twenty-first century can wear pants and still conform to gender scripts, while women in the nineteenth century could not (see the second case study); twenty-first century women can employ plastic surgery to create more curvaceous bodies while nineteenth-century women used corsets and girdles. Over time, as technological innovation transforms ways of knowing and shaping bodies and identities, social knowledge of and scripts for gender change as well.[4]

Why Focus on Technology?

Feminist scholar Bernice Hausman suggests that technologies of the time shape what people think they can be, both physically and ideologically. In her research, Hausman traces how the development of medical technologies in plastic surgery and endocrinology (the science and medicine of hormones) led to the development of contemporary transsexual identities.[5] The social changes brought about by technological innovation expanded existing scripts and created new ones for embodied genders. It is not that gender non-conforming individuals did not exist, but rather that how people understood possible gender change was different.

These and other similar changes are the product of ideological and theoretical innovation (for instance the idea that sex is different from gender) as well as tangible technologies (such as the example of shoes for drag queens), all of which allow individuals and society as a whole to imagine and manifest new ways of existing in the world. The case studies that appear throughout this book suggest that technology is an integral part of social changes around gender. Technology interacts with dominant ideologies, scripts, and embodied identities to produce an array of socially recognizable gendered selves. These social forces influence and build on each other to produce a range of socially legible gendered identities and bodies from which individuals construct their lives. As Hausman summarizes: "The development of new technologies (especially those where contact with the body is most intimate, such as medical technologies) also effects the production of new subjectivities [aka identities]."[6]

Neither technological innovation nor changes in gender identity are modern phenomena, even though people often talk about both as if they are products of contemporary social, political, economic, and scientific changes. In fact, both have very long histories. Examining technology and gender through a mutually constitutive lens can help make sense of how the changes in gender and technology that are at the core of this book are historically situated. Throughout history, gender scripts, ideologies, bodies, and identities have been shaped by the technologies of the time. To better understand these concomitant histories, this chapter begins by exploring how scholars have defined and studied technology. I continue by reviewing theories of technological innovation in society and use these theories to explore technologies of gender and gender nonconformity throughout history. Finally, I demonstrate how a sociological approach that takes into account ideology, scripts, technologies, and embodied identities is the best approach to studying and understanding the dynamic relationship between gender and technology.

Making Sense of Technology

The word technology comes from the Greek *tekhnologia*, which is derived from the words 'techne' meaning craft, and 'logia' meaning 'discourse' or 'expression.' While technology is often defined in terms of machines, its linguistic origins, meaning 'the expression of a craft,' suggest its scholarly use to refer to anything people develop to manipulate the natural environment.

Technology is a complex amalgam of objects, knowledge, activities, and processes, all of which affect our material environment. Anthropologists trace technology back a million years, to the point when early humans harnessed the power of fire,[7] certainly a significant manipulation of the environment. From this distant innovation, to the development of the most recent supercomputer, technological development has been an integral part of the lives of human beings.

Technology does more than alter our material world, however, as

TECHNOLOGICAL INNOVATION

The leading transnational institution in charge of encouraging and monitoring technological innovation is the United Nations Educational, Scientific, and Cultural Organization; UNESCO defines technological innovation as the development of "know-how and creative process that may utilize tools, resources, and systems to solve problems, to enhance control over the natural and man-made environment to alter the human condition."[8]

these changes give rise to changes in the behavior of individuals and even entire cultures.[9] Our very bodies and identities have been shaped by technology in profound and dramatic ways. The advent of clothing, for example, which included the development of know-how about sewing, the harvesting of plants or animal skins for cloth, the creation of methods and processes for production, as well as an evolution of the clothes themselves, allowed migration out of Africa around 200000 B.C.E. Clothing provided warmth and protection from the environment such that individuals could migrate into colder climates.[10] These technological developments changed where and how people lived on Earth from that point forward, allowing geographical expansion, cultural differentiation, and social change. The relationship between technology and society is a reciprocal one; as people create technology, technology shapes people and the societies they live in.

A Brief History of Technology

While the first technological leaps occurred when humans began to use or control natural resources as tools to shape their environment (fire, spears, and wheels, for example), technological advancement gained momentum with the rise of scientific inquiry in the 1400s. Prior to the fifteenth century, when scientists or laypeople approached the natural world as an area of inquiry, they did so in ways informed by religious paradigms.

For example, Katharine Park, a history of science scholar, has documented that early dissection was deeply informed by both religious

PARADIGM

A system of thought or theoretical framework that structures how a group or community makes sense of the world around them. Paradigms are comprised of ideas, beliefs, assumptions, and ways of knowing and provide a particular perspective on the world.

and gender beliefs (and scripts), even though it was a scientific attempt to learn about the human body.[11] Park maintains that in the fourteenth and fifteenth centuries, individuals made sense of human bodies (both anatomically and physiologically) through religion. Family and scientific practices such as dissection were engaged in service to those doctrinal views. For example, many of the early dissections performed on women were done in an effort to find religious relics embedded in the bodies of 'holy women' so as to prove their divinity. What Park argues is that the development and use of early medical and scientific technology were always influenced by social paradigms and scripts, including those about gender.

With the popularization and professionalization of science, individuals began to privilege knowledge of the natural world that was developed through empirical research and the application of the scientific method. The rise of science afforded people the idea that we can—even should—understand the natural world through the use of observation and analytical reasoning. This encouraged and facilitated the development of new technologies to shape and manipulate the natural environment. As society fell more under the jurisdiction of science, there followed a shift in social, political, and economic power. Whereas theocratic ontologies—world views guided by religious doctrine—pointed toward church leaders and divinely chosen royalty as the legitimate authorities in society,[12] science naturally pointed to scientists and logicians.

More than a simple shift toward empirical study of the natural world, this transfer of influence from theology to science altered the whole structure of society and granted social and political power to a variety of scientific institutions. Medicine came to be the authority over

> ### ONTOLOGY
>
> A worldview; a grand theory about the nature of the world and existence. An ontology is a group or community's answer to the question, 'what exists in this world?'

ill and healthy bodies, logic-based legal institutions over crime and punishment, and biology, chemistry, and physics over the natural world. And in all aspects, a focus on new technologies was part of this change. Since its acceleration in the fifteenth century, technological innovation has been a key component of scientific and social change.

Challenging Technological Progressivism

As tech-savvy modern individuals in North America we have a tendency to think of technology as always moving society forward—what Daniel Kleinman calls *technological progressivism*.[13]

> ### TECHNOLOGICAL PROGRESSIVISM
>
> A paradigm that suggests all technological innovation produces beneficial social changes. A sociological analysis of technology that takes into consideration other social forces contradicts this paradigm and suggests, instead, that technological innovation is shaped by myriad social institutions.

It is important to remember, however, that technology is not always progressive. While technology often creates new possibility, new tools and methods are sometimes developed with the intent of maintaining the status quo. For example, medical techniques have historically been employed to maintain 'racial purity' and existing racial inequalities, which are decidedly non-progressive. As new biological technologies were developed in the nineteenth and twentieth centuries they were first deployed to find 'true' differences between Whites and people of color. These studies were often referred to as 'race science,' and the subsequent findings were used to justify slavery, colonialism, and genocide. Many technological advances, such as race science and embryonic sex selection,[14] reflect social debates and tensions over power, morality, and social structure. It is important to remember that technology is always driven by, shaped, and understood through individual and societal values. The topics innovators choose to focus on (or choose to ignore), the methods they employ (or dismiss), and the items they produce (or choose not to produce), are decisions shaped by personal and social paradigms and values.

An example of how technology follows a path dictated by social climate is the birth control pill. Since the advent of the birth control pill in the 1960s feminist scholars and activists have criticized pharmaceutical companies for not creating oral contraceptives for men. The view that reproductive management (along with reproduction itself and childrearing in general) is a 'women's issue' is a product of our society's values concerning women and men, reproduction, and sexual activity. Scholars and feminists alike have suggested that the placement of contraceptive and reproductive responsibility almost exclusively on women is a product of a larger set of social beliefs that men's bodies (like men more generally) are the normal, default, unmarked category while women's bodies are other, different, and at times even in need of treatment.[15] For example, while changes in male's testosterone levels are seen as a natural part of aging, menopause (female changes) is defined medically as an "estrogen-deficiency disease."[16]

Nelly Oudshoorn, a scholar who has researched the development of a male pill, asserts that the lack of contraceptives for men reflects the scientific and medical bias that allows women's bodies to be designated as legitimate sites of medical intervention, particularly in terms of reproduction. This focus on women was matched, until very recently, by an equally prevalent, opposing absence of men's bodies in reproductive medicine.[17] Because male bodies were viewed as the baseline for normalcy they were not seen as warranting investigation, let alone intervention, as we usually study the exception to the norm instead of the norm itself.

This societal designation of women's bodies as anomalous helps to explain why 13 new contraceptives have been developed for women since World War II, while there has not been a single new contraceptive developed for men in the last 100 years.[18] For this to change, the very infrastructure of reproductive medicine—and the gendered social scripts for who a patient can be, that undergird it—needs to be expanded. As Oudshoorn documents, when the World Health Organization encouraged research on male contraceptives in the 1970s, the scientific community was unequipped to heed the call. Scientists had to substantially reorganize family planning institutions, create new drug testing standards, clinics, and research specialties, and even develop new definitions of who could be categorized as a reproductive patient, before the research could move forward.[19] For researchers to develop the new technologies necessary to create male contraceptives, a sufficient shift in societal gender paradigms and scripts was required.

This is only one example of how technological development is neither predestined nor separate from social values, norms, or beliefs. While often construed as always progressive, technology is instead intimately shaped by dominant beliefs and other social forces. The development of new technologies is tied to social paradigms in a myriad of ways; technology is always already a social endeavor.[20] To understand the relationship between technology and gender, then, is to make sense of the interactions between gender paradigms, scripts, bodies, identities, and technology.

Theorizing Technology

The meaning and significance of technological development has been a central theme for social theorists of the past 200 years. Some scholars view technology as dehumanizing; Max Weber, for instance, argued that technological innovation would only exacerbate the increasing rationalization and bureaucratization of society that were already stripping people of their creative life force.[21] Other similar dystopian perspectives represent technology as making people less unique, less free, and less happy.[22] Other theorists, such as Karl Marx,[23] saw technology as the path toward an egalitarian society. Although the technological innovations of the Industrial Revolution had led to short term inequalities, Marx argued that science and technology would ultimately offer liberation by moving society beyond capitalism.[24] Other technological utopianists also argue that new technologies will transform institutions, values, and culture, to create a more perfect society.[25]

One of the most comprehensive social theories of technology was formulated by philosopher and historian Michel Foucault. Foucault was interested in how systems of knowledge shaped society and individuals, and he developed a complex definition of technology in an effort to grasp how and to what ends technologies shape everyday life and individuals.[26] Foucault argued that technological innovation takes many forms including the creation of new products, new words and meanings, new means of shaping one's body, and new ways of controlling members of society.[27] He advanced the idea that these technologies are both shaped by and shaping individuals and society as each new innovation goes through the inevitable processes of upholding and challenging social paradigms and structures.

Consider, for example, body modification. Modern medicine allows people to alter the appearance, shape, and function of their body, and whether these alterations take the form of the currently popular gastric bypass surgery, breast augmentation, or blepharoplasty (eyelid surgery), the technologies that enable body modifications reflect deeply entrenched gendered body scripts in North American societies.[28] Some individuals fit 'naturally' within these hegemonic norms of beauty and attraction, but the majority of people seek an approximation of these body expectations through one or more forms of technological intervention. From clothing choices to tanning, from treatments for baldness to major plastic surgery, individuals change the form and function of their body in efforts to achieve socially valued body shapes, facial features, and standards of beauty. People create new measures for altering their physical appearance, and as more people make use of these measures, society at large begins to more often approximate—and subsequently more often expect approximation of—an accepted ideal. As Foucault theorized, technology (as guided by social paradigms and scripts) created by people, changes people and society.

Technology as Social

Foucault's theory of technology captures the ways in which technology is intertwined with social ideologies, scripts, bodies, and identities. For example, as feminist activism challenged the dominant ideologies about gender in the middle of the twentieth century, new technologies were developed that called into question the naturalization of male and female social scripts. One consequence of this trend was the differentiation of *sex* from *gender*. This differentiation allowed feminist scholars to distinguish bodily traits (sex) from the social status (gender) attributed to individuals because of their sex. The language of sex and gender was an intervention into the natural world—a technology—since it changed how individual behaviors and social practices were interpreted and rendered significant.

Technologies can also be used to reinforce social inequalities and hegemonic norms.[29] In *The History of Sexuality*, Michel Foucault examined how individuals' sexual expression and identity were shaped and policed throughout history by use of what he calls 'technologies of power.' Foucault employs this phrase to refer to the means used by those in positions of influence to control the behavior and beliefs of individuals. He asserted that regulatory systems, such as obscenity laws about sexual conduct, were developed and used in concert with the field of psychology to define and enforce normal versus deviant sexual behaviors, desires, and identities.[30] Similarly, technologies have been used to police gendered bodies and identities in line with prevailing gender ideologies and social scripts.[31] Gender theorists Epstein and Straub explain that, "the 'normative' and the 'transgressive' in our sense of our bodies, our sexual practices, our erotic desires, and our gender identities exist in and through the cultural discourses that construct and enforce them."[32] What people think of as appropriate or transgressive gender, and how each individual presents gender, is therefore a product of the technologies of power wielded during any historical era. The case study on the innovation of women's pants, which follows this chapter, offers an example of how technological innovation and fights over societal gender ideologies are connected.

Technology and the Individual

Direct interventions into the body are theorized by Foucault as technologies of the self.

> **TECHNOLOGIES OF THE SELF**
>
> The way individuals shape their self (body and identity) to their own (and society's) liking.[33]

In addition to working in dynamic relationship with other societal forces such as dominant ideologies, technologies are used by individuals to shape and reshape their bodies and identities.[34] Technologies of the self are ways of shaping and reshaping who and what we are; for example, bodybuilding can be viewed as a technology of self that allows individuals to change their physical body to achieve a particular shape, identity, or aesthetic.

Consider the numerous ways men are encouraged to develop and exhibit highly developed muscles. Considering the historic Muscle Beach in Venice, California and numerous men's fitness magazines, the increasing attention to film actors' muscle definition in mainstream media and the presence of weight-rooms at most schools, gyms, and recreation centers, immense pressure is exerted on boys and men to develop highly muscled bodies. North American cultural expectations very clearly tie muscular definition to masculinity and research over the past 25 years suggests that men's attention to muscle mass has steadily increased. In national U.S. surveys only 18 percent of men expressed dissatisfaction with muscle definition in their upper bodies in 1972, while 38 percent did in 1996. Similarly, 91 percent of college men surveyed in 1994 reported a desire to be more muscular.[35] These are dramatic numbers. In an effort to embody socially valued masculinities, then, many men engage in time consuming and often painful workout regimens to achieve the type of musculature associated with hegemonic masculinity. The technologies of the self that are utilized toward this end include nutritional supplements, exercise regimens, and weight-lifting machines. The extensive work many men do on their bodies can be interpreted as a response to gender paradigms that define men as naturally strong and dominant scripts for masculinity that connect strength to manhood.

At the same time that individuals use technologies to achieve particular aesthetics, social scripts for bodies shape the use and development of new technologies. Embedded in social gender scripts are assumptions about technologies of the self. For example, the belief that men are naturally stronger is built on the fact that boys and men are encouraged to be more physical from birth, which increases their muscle mass and strength. Similarly, the contemporary gender norm of women's bodies as hairless is reliant on the fact that women will use razors, waxes, and lasers to achieve this aspect of gender.

Technologies of the self are used to construct both normative and non-normative gendered selves.

NORMATIVE GENDER

Individual gender expression that is in line with dominant social scripts for masculine men or feminine women. Another way to refer to this is gender conformity.

NON-NORMATIVE GENDER

Individual gender expression that conflicts with dominant social scripts for masculine men or feminine women. Another way to refer to this is gender non-conformity.

Consider, for example, men dancers. In contemporary North American culture dance, particularly classical forms such as ballet, are considered feminine endeavors. Men who dance are often assumed to be effeminate gay men who failed at normative masculinity (when used in this manner homosexuality is intended as a slur to signify de-masculinization). This is such a common trope that the story of a boy dancer, Billy Elliot, was turned into a blockbuster movie and Broadway show. In the movie and play *Billy Elliot*, a young boy struggles to take ballet lessons in the face of significant and violent resistance from friends and family.[36] While the moral of the story is that Billy should and did eventually do what he loved—dance—the film gets its humor from the incongruity of a young working-class boy in England becoming a professional ballet dancer. Billy's interest in dance is blamed on the death of his mother, on the failing of his father, but never on an innate talent or love of dance; these things are seen as incompatible with 'normal' (aka normative) masculinity. Technology plays a part in both enforcing normative gender (e.g. dance as feminine) through technologies of power, and in non-normative gender. Men who pursue dance use new technologies to help train for and choreograph performances, strengthen and treat injuries, and maintain particular body size and shape norms particular to dance subcultures. In the process, men dancers use technology to produce masculine bodies and identities that are non-normative.

As with any aspect of technology, whether and how individuals participate in technologies of the self depends on a multitude of personal, social, and embodied factors. Some people pursue counter-hegemonic technologies, others normative ones, and others engage in a combination of both. The technologies of the self that are demanded of people in order to conform in one situation may be unacceptable when attempting to conform to norms in another. The ways in which individuals navigate this complex terrain are determined by the social scripts at their disposal. The rest of this chapter explores how standards for gender normativity have changed over time, shaped by technologies of the day, and how these changes have affected what was expected of individuals in order to be appropriately—or inappropriately—gendered in society.

Theorizing Gender and Technology Together

Technology plays a central role in producing gendered selves and bodies. Gender paradigms in a society set out the core beliefs about gender, and shape how individuals and institutions structure gendered lives. Social scripts establish what is appropriate for men and women in our society, and shape how each of us 'does' gender on a daily basis. Social theorists Candace West, Don Zimmerman, and Sarah

Fenstermaker discuss this production of gender as 'doing gender.'[37] Their theory explains why the accomplishment of gender feels effortless and inevitable until and unless we go against the grain, do it wrong, do not conform.

DOING GENDER

A theoretical approach that makes sense of gender as an accomplishment and not as a set of individual characteristics. Gender is something that is 'done' in interaction and is imbedded in all parts of social life.

What they argue is that gender is something produced in interaction and not a trait possessed by individuals. Doing gender in the process of social interaction is inevitable; because it is a primary organizer of everyday life it is inescapable and produced in all interaction. We learn these rules about how to behave in both formal and informal ways, in institutions and through every day trial and error.[38] As discussed in the Preview, we can see evidence of how, beginning in infancy, these processes of self-regulation are learned through social interaction. Children learn, through family, media, and other institutions what it means to be a boy or girl, and then practice these distinctions with themselves and others. These rules and expectations and the gender scripts that they are a part of are not deterministic, however. While the technologies of any age shape how individuals can make sense of and intervene in the gendered body, and the available gender scripts constrain the choices they have about gendered identities, individuals are still agents of their own lives. We engage in behaviors or not, whether normative or non-conforming.

Gender non-conformity has been documented throughout history, from Greek mythology to contemporary studies of young transgender children.[39] Throughout history, attention has been paid to individuals we would now call transgender, as technologies of power were used to police what constitutes normalcy.[40] Philosophers, historians, and more contemporarily, anthropologists and psychologists have all documented gender non-conformity, often because these individuals fell outside of the normative gender scripts of the day. Standards were defined through technologies of power, and designated cisgender and heterosexual as normal and transgender and homosexual as abnormal.

CISGENDER

A word used to describe individuals whose gender identity matches the expected norms for their sex (for example, a masculine gender identity and male sex). The prefix 'cis' means aligned with or on the same side of. Cisgender, then, means a gender identity aligned with one's ascribed sex (i.e. non-transgender individuals). The term has been taken up by many in the transgender activist and scholarly community in an effort to resist the normalization of non-transgender individuals and the simultaneous pathologization of transgender people. Instead of defining sex/gender alignment as 'normal' and other sex/gender pairings as abnormal, a cisgender/transgender framework establishes both as legitimate ways of being in the world.

Examples of gender non-conformity were used as foils (i.e. comparisons) against which 'normal' gender identity could be elaborated. Indeed, in his *History of Sexuality* Foucault argues that, "the biological and the historical are not consecutive to one another . . . but are bound together in an increasingly complex fashion in accordance with the development of the modern technologies of power that take life as their objective."[41] The process of setting up normal and deviant sex and gender categories was aided by social, political, and scientific technologies of the self that attempted to define, treat, and cure deviant behaviors and individuals. Historical studies of gender non-conformity in anthropology, psychology, medicine, and science were part of this social negotiation of sex, gender, and sexuality. Reflection on these historic cases also offers what Susan Stryker calls "transgender effects," or moments where "the spectacle of an unexpected gender phenomena illuminates the production of gender normativity in a startling new way."[42]

We cannot necessarily predict how an individual will respond to their particular combination of life experience, socialization, scripts, and technologies, but this does not mean that we cannot or should not examine and theorize how these dynamics function in general, what their consequences are, or how they have played out in people's lives. Even if an individual chooses to defy guidelines set out by existing gender norms and scripts, they still use the technologies available at any given time to do so. One way to trace a history of gender body and identity norms through time is to look at how new technologies have helped individuals make sense of and transform gender according to their own needs and circumstances.

How Technology Has Shaped Gender and Gender Non-Conformity

It may seem absurd to ask what makes a man a man and a woman a woman; we often assume the answer is obvious. But when we look at definitions of sex and gender both historically and in this contemporary moment, a clear-cut distinction is elusive. Although we think of modern biological science as providing definitive answers, numerous scholars have explored the ambiguity of sex and gender dimorphism. While the technologies of our age have provided more insight into the body than ever before, including about the specifics of sex and gender, social beliefs about gender continue to shape how scientists, doctors, and scholars see and interpret the 'facts.' Judith Lorber, one of the foremost contemporary gender theorists, puts it this way:

> When we rely only on the conventional categories of sex and gender, we end up finding what we looked for—we see what we believe, whether it is that 'females' and 'males' are essentially different or that 'women' and 'men' are essentially the same.[43]

Whatever criteria we use—chromosomes, genitalia, secondary sex characteristics, or hormone levels—the lines between male and female bodies are blurred (see the final case study for a longer examination of this). Sex categories may appear stable but the fact is that there is more variation than we are aware of. Those biological 'facts' we use to distinguish and divide bodies into two sexes are based on entrenched social beliefs depicting gender as binary and do not necessarily reflect an underlying natural or scientific sex binary. The use of binary categories to 'prove' that two sexes equals two genders is both a cultural construct and also a circular argument.[44]

Technologies of Sex and Gender Formation

Competing debates and ideas about sexual differentiation emerge in the earliest biomedical texts, persist through the Middle Ages, and continue up to contemporary times. From their earliest iterations, philosophical and medical texts in the West offered explanations for a diversity of sexes/genders. The two dominant philosophical traditions, Galenic/Hippocratic and Aristotelian, produced conflicting ideas about the body and these manifested in fundamentally different ideas about male and female bodies and selves. For example, Hippocrates' *On Regimen*, one of the earliest medical texts (dating back to the fifth century B.C.E.), explained six sex/gender possibilities based on outward bearing: manly men, manly women, feminine men, feminine women, hermaphrodite men and hermaphrodite women.[45] In the fourth century B.C.E., however, Aristotle contravened Hippocrates' definition by asserting that women were differentiated from men (in status and physiology) because of the coolness of their humors.[46] These different sex and gender paradigms demonstrate how the ontology within which sex and gender were understood shaped how people made sense of sex and gender diversity. In the Roman period (129–200 C.E.) Galen argued that women's and men's bodies were the same, save for women's genitals, which were "turned inside out." Scholars built on Galen's theories through the fifteenth century. In contrast, Pattrick Geddes, an eighteenth-century professor of biology, asserted that the very cells in women's and men's bodies were different, claiming that men's cells gave off energy while women's cells stored it.[47] These different paradigms for sex led to radically different 'truths' and technologies of gendered bodies.[48]

Different historical eras have had different dominant ontologies and attendant gender paradigms that responded to and in turn affected the social structures and hierarchies of the day, and technologies were key participants in this process. In 1796 Samuel Thomas von Soemmerring claimed to be the first anatomist to document a female skeleton (see Figure 1.1). While Soemmerring likely exaggerated his case, it is true that drawings of female bodies were not included in anatomy texts until

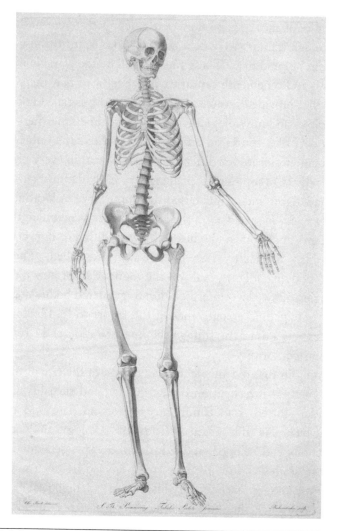

Figure 1.1 Drawing of a female skeleton from *Tabula Sceleti Feminine* by Samuel Thomas von Soemmerring.[49] Reproduction made from an original at the Boston Medical Library in the Francis A. Countway Library of Medicine.

the 1730s.[50] This suggests either that differences between male and female bodies were seen as insignificant, or that women's bodies were not considered an intellectually important subject, while men's bodies were.

There was a variety of competing theories of sex difference prior to this scientific focus, for instance the idea that women were physically and morally distinct because they were ruled by different humors than men; women's humors were cold and wet compared to those of men, which were hot and dry.[51] These theories fell by the wayside in the late eighteenth and nineteenth centuries, in the light of new medical technologies that provided greater access to and more detailed information about biology and physiology than ever before. Soemmerring's illustration was part of a concerted effort within eighteenth-century science and medicine to locate sex differences literally within every part of the human body.[52] On top of this, challenges by early feminists to reigning gender paradigms and scripts raised the importance of locating gender difference—and inequality—in the body in order to maintain the status quo. If men's and women's bodies really were different in every aspect, then gender inequality was biologically proscribed. These new gendered body paradigms, built on the foundation of new biomedical technologies, allowed a reinterpretation of gendered bodies and identities, and one of the key outcomes of this effort to find biological sex differences was a dramatic shift in the interpretation and treatment of gender non-conformity.

Beginning in the mid-nineteenth century with the rise of the scientific and medical investigation of sex, gender, and sexuality, authority over gender shifted from community agreement, law, and the state to medicine.[53] As the medical fields of sexology, endocrinology, and psychology developed, individuals who expressed gender nonconformist desires and/or identities were labeled by doctors with the revival of pre-modern terminology like real or psychological 'hermaphrodite,' and through the minting of new terms, such as 'gender invert' and 'eonist.'[54] These new technologies did more than name people; they defined appropriate ways to manifest, identify, and treat gender nonconformity. Gender non-conforming individuals whom medical practitioners had previously left to their own devices were suddenly subject to medical diagnosis and treatment.

Technologies of Gender Conformity

The late nineteenth century marked the inception of medical authority over sex, gender, and sexuality, and these medical technologies shaped more than just gender non-conformity. Technologies shape gender paradigms, scripts, identities, and bodies more broadly. Normative body scripts, however, are often invisible or naturalized. Take for example the ubiquity of the corset: throughout the nineteenth century corsets were worn by women in Western Europe and North America. Corsetry was more than fashionable dress, however; prevailing gender ideology of the day demanded corsetry because corsets were understood to construct and enforce appropriate, hegemonic, womanhood.[55]

While corsets have a long history (corset-like garments have been documented in ancient Egypt and were commonly worn in Europe since the Middle Ages), they were most important (socially and in terms of shaping gender scripts) between the nineteenth and early twentieth century. Almost all women, of all races and class divisions, wore corsets through the 1800s due, in part, to the belief that as the weaker sex their body (and mind) needed to be supported. Consider, for example, the Chicago Corset Company's advertisements for the "Ball's Health Preserving Corset" and the "H. P. Misses' Corset" (see Figure 1.2).

Two corsets are featured in this 1881 advertisement. One, "Ball's Health Preserving Corset," asserts that its newly patented technological innovation—the coiled wires—made corsets more comfortable and healthier than 'traditional' boned corsets (which used rigid stays made of bone to keep their shape). Also implied in the advertisement is the necessity of corsets for women. The solution to the 'unhealthy' consequences of traditional corsetry was not to stop their use, but rather to develop new technologies to make corsets healthier. Creating the hourglass, 'feminine shape'—what we can think of as the normatively gendered body of that era—was considered more important than the medical problems corsets often caused. That is, gender ideologies that

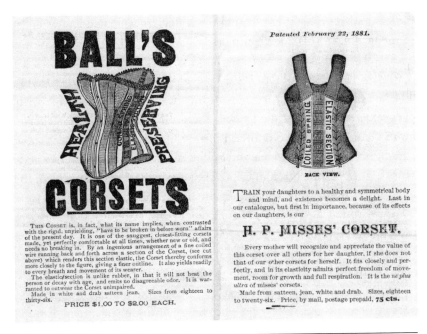

Figure 1.2 Advertisement booklet for Ball's Health Preserving Corsets and the H. P. Misses' Corset. Chicago Corset Company, 1881.

defined ideal women's bodies produced technologies that reshaped how individual women looked and identified. This dominant ideology and the associated scripts for normative womanhood are even more explicit in the second advertisement for a corset intended for girls. The "H. P. Misses' Corset" advertises that wearing the corset will shape young girls' bodies and *minds* appropriately. In fact, the corset's description begins by admonishing women: "Train your daughters to a healthy and symmetrical body and mind, and existence becomes a delight."[56] The implication here is that girls' and women's bodies need corseting to develop both physically and morally!

The corset was seen as a medical and moral necessity for women in the nineteenth century, and came to signify normative femininity.[57] Simultaneously, and perhaps more significantly, the ways that it shaped women's bodies and affected their movement through the world reinforced social beliefs about womanhood. For example, tight lacing damaged women's organs and led to fainting and restricted movement, something seen as clear evidence of women's fragile natures. Corsets dominated women's fashion through the early 1900s until social and technological changes led to new gender norms that, among many other social alterations, displaced corsetry. Advances in the mass production of clothing and elastic as well as women's increased participation in the paid labor force and attendant need for less restrictive clothing meant that fabric bras and girdles became less expensive and more practical than corsets. Simultaneously, gendered clothing norms and scripts changed when flappers hit the scene after World War I.

The rise of the flapper aesthetic in the 1920s was more than a fashion trend. It was an intentional, pointed, and dramatic rejection of Victorian femininity and female domesticity. As young women cast off their corsets and long skirts, they turned toward a new modern womanhood characterized by independence, urbanism, and youthfulness. These new gender scripts were shockingly masculine compared to the accentuated curves and delicacy cultivated by corsets and late nineteenth-century feminine gender norms. As part of these new gender scripts women cut their hair into short bobs, and bound their breasts with cloth to create more youthful, boyish appearances.

All of this gender bending caused a social uproar and gender crisis. Gender scripts for women changed swiftly and dramatically and this shift was tied up with women's newly acquired right to vote (1918 in Canada and 1920 in the United States), and increasing presence in the public sphere.[58] New technologies including jazz music, mass produced cigarettes, suffrage, and short skirts radically transformed the available gender scripts for women. The body practices associated with flapper femininity—dancing to jazz music, drinking alcohol, smoking, voting, working, and embracing single womanhood—went against the Victorian gender scripts that had dominated society before World War I, and transformed who young women could be. Technological innovation in the early twentieth century, in concert with shifting gender paradigms, revolutionized normatively gendered bodies and identities. The meaning of gender non-conformity was also being renegotiated as part of and resultant to these paradigmatic shifts.

Technologies of Gender Non-Conformity

In every historical era, the technologies of the day have been used to delineate the boundaries between male and female, between men and women, and these technologies have shaped how individuals and societies at large make sense of sex, gender, and their diversity. Neither the complexities of people's lived experiences nor the ideologically driven theories of sex and gender are modern phenomena. Evidence that individuals have lived cross-gender or gender non-conforming lives can be found in almost all cultures, and there have been gender non-conforming pharaohs, kings, queens, Catholic Popes, soldiers, musicians, governors, criminals, and everyday people. It is difficult to talk about transgender individuals before the development of modern sexual and gender identities, in part because sexuality and gender have often been conflated.[59] We can, however, look to historical and cross-cultural examples of gender non-conformity as evidence that these practices, and their contemporary corollaries, are not new or unique. In addition to individuals who have lived cross-gender lives, in many times and places other possibilities were available. While Western societies have not often offered third (let alone fourth or fifth) gender options, many other societies have, and some still do. Some cultures not only accommodate these alternate genders but also see them as legitimate ways of being, powerful and important to the society at large.[60] We find these third genders embraced and even named in many cultures including in some Native American and Canadian tribes (Berdache), in Indian society (Hijras), in Albania (Sworn Virgins), and in Maori communities (Takatapui).

In the process of recording gender non-conformity, historical research has also documented the ways that the rigid binary categories of male/female and man/woman have been constructed, reinforced, and defied across time and place.[61] How gender non-conformity has been defined and understood reflects the prevailing ontology, social scripts, and technologies of the time, making it difficult for contemporary scholars to know how to talk about and make sense of gender non-conformity from the past. In an effort to reveal histories of gender non-conformity, should we transcribe current identities onto historical gender diversity?[62] Or would that obscure the complexity and historical specificity of those experiences by ascribing ahistorical identities onto experiences from the past?[63] As historian Elizabeth Reis asks, "can we really compare Joan of Arc's cross-dressing and militarism in fifteenth-century France with Sarah Emma Edmonds, who lived as a man and fought in the American Civil War" without eliding the specificity of their historically situated experiences?[64] This dilemma is not unique; gay and lesbian scholars have struggled with the same issues when deciding how to make sense of historical sexual diversity in the absence of contemporary sexual identities.[65]

Comprehension of past gender non-conformity is also complicated by the histories of colonialism. One of the reasons that gender non-conformity was documented in cultures around the world was because White Western explorers sought evidence to prove that their own cultures were more advanced than 'primitive' ones (recall the history of 'race science' discussed in the Preview). Almost everything that we know about gender non-conformity within Native American and Canadian tribes, for example, comes from the notes of White explorers as viewed through a lens that justified colonial racism. In fact the word used to describe individuals living cross-gender lives, 'Berdache,' is not a Native word, but one adopted by Europeans from a pejorative[66] applied by French missionaries and explorers. The naming of alternative gender schema in Native tribes, then, reflects the ideology and gender norms of the White men who 'discovered' them, rather than indigenous meaning-making. Documentation of non-Western histories of gender non-conformity reveals as much about Western norms and beliefs as it does about indigenous gender diversity; unfortunately, this can make it difficult to comprehend precisely the attitudes of those cultures toward gender non-conformity, or to compare them to contemporary views. As gender scholar Vic Muñoz argues, the pathology of Western gender and transgender paradigms have been mapped onto diverse indigenous gender and sexual identities.[67]

While gender non-conformity throughout time cannot always be called transgenderism, individuals have used the technologies available in any given era to construct gendered bodies and identities in both normative and non-normative ways. Contemporary gender status for both non-transgender and transgender individuals is judged primarily through visibility—whether one's body (inside and out) reflects one's chosen gender according to biomedical criteria and as judged by medical authorities. In contrast, before the rise of medical intervention into gender, the ability for an individual to choose how to do gender was more often rooted in social or legal agreement. This often meant that power-holders, legal authorities such as kings, governors, Congress, or judges, claimed a need to confirm an individual's chosen gender.

The colonial Virginia case of Thomasine/Thomas Hall illustrates the different body scripts and technologies at play in the 1600s; in 1629 Hall was called before the General Court in Virginia because his/her gender was unclear—s/he wore both women's and men's clothing. It was the *clothing* that was key here; as the primary gender code of the day, clothing inscribed gender. Ultimately the courts ruled that Hall's refusal to 'choose' a single gender had to be reflected in his/her clothing. It was not the truth of biology or even body that mattered, but rather social presentation vis-à-vis clothing. In other places and eras as well, taking on a gendered social role and appearance was sufficient to claim one's desired gender.[68] These cases demonstrate how the act of substantiating sex and gender has changed over time in concert with technological innovation and dominant gender paradigms.

In the early 1900s the dominant paradigms for sex and gender shifted away from the 1800s model of male and female bodies as dramatically different. Instead, male and female bodies were viewed as having the same core biology and physiology but shaped by different 'sex hormones' both in-utero and throughout one's lifespan. This led to psycho-medical redefinition of sexuality and gender. Early efforts conflated sexuality and gender, mixing all gender or sexual non-conformities under the umbrella term 'inverts,' and attributing the roots of sexual and gender variation to physiological and hormonal differences. Over time, sexologists and scientists came to differentiate between sex and gender, shifting toward an identity/mental model instead of a physiologically centered one, and these new technologies opened up new scripts for gender non-conformity. This paradigm shift entitled people to treat gender non-conformity with hormonal and surgical intervention; if the structure of male and female bodies was essentially the same, then biomedical technologies could allow individuals to move from male to female or vice versa. The shifts in scientific gender paradigms opened up the possibility for gender change in the early 1900s, and it is then that we see the emergence of transsexuality, defined as the desire to transform one's body *through hormones and surgery.*[69]

Along with these new biomedical technologies occurred an increase in the quantity and selection of information technologies, such as newspapers, magazines, radio, and eventually television, which disseminated information about sex-change research, transsexual individuals, and other forms of gender non-conformity. The new information about and language for gender non-conformity were in themselves new technologies of meaning-making, and exposure to them opened up new identity and body possibilities for individuals. As historian Joanne Meyerowitz suggests, "stories in the press allowed a few American readers to imagine surgical sex change and seek it for themselves."[70] Meyerowitz describes what was perhaps the most significant media coverage of transsexuality in North America, when in 1952 the *New York Daily News* broke the story that an 'Ex-GI' had just undergone a 'sex-change' to become the blonde, beautiful, Christine Jorgensen. Jorgensen's return to the United States in 1953 was covered in every major domestic news outlet, propelling her successful nightclub act for several years. "Jorgensen was more than a media sensation, a stage act, or a cult figure," Meyerowitz concludes. "Her story opened debate on the visibility and mutability of sex."[71] In that historic moment, one person telling her story in the public realm catapulted transgender issues into everyday society. Jorgensen's story, and the repercussions of it being publicized, reinforce how new technologies, in this case information and biomedical technologies, participate in significant social and individual change. They are responsible for instigating paradigmatic changes as well as new social scripts, all of which allowed new body and identity possibilities for individuals.

The trend toward classification and treatment of gender non-conformity in North America continued through the 1950s, 1960s, 1970s, and 1980s. Medical and psychological diagnoses were introduced and used to classify, pathologize, and treat gender non-conformity. Harry Benjamin, building on the theories of Magnus Hirschfeld and other early sexologists, worked with transgender individuals in North America in the 1950s. Regarded as the father of modern trans-sexual 'treatment,' Benjamin wrote the groundbreaking book *The Transsexual Phenomenon* in 1965, thus opening the formal genre of transsexual medical literature. While there were a handful of articles that dealt with what would later be termed 'gender dysphoria'[72] before his book was published, Benjamin's was the first comprehensive analysis and medical treatment guide for transsexual individuals.[73] The guidelines that Benjamin laid out in this and subsequent texts are still in use today through the World Professional Association for Transgender Health; formerly known as the Harry Benjamin International Gender Dysphoria Association, this international organization sets transgender treatment protocols.

As part of the medicalization of transsexuality, Gender Identity Disorder (GID) was introduced as a mental disorder and defined in the American Psychiatric Association's *Diagnostic and Statistical Manual* in 1980. Gender Identity Disorder is defined in the most recent edition of this set of guidelines for psychological diagnosis and treatment, (*DSM-IV*), in the following manner:

> There are two components of Gender Identity Disorder, both of which must be present to make the diagnosis. There must be evidence of a strong and persistent cross-gender identification, which is the desire to be, or the insistence that one is of the other sex (Criterion A). This cross-gender identification must not merely be a desire for any perceived cultural advantages of being the other sex. There must also be evidence of persistent discomfort about one's assigned sex or a sense of inappropriateness in the gender role of that sex (Criterion B). The diagnosis is not made if the individual has a concurrent physical intersex condition (e.g. androgen

insensitivity syndrome, or congenital adrenal hyperplasia) (Criterion C). To make the diagnosis, there must be evidence of clinically significant distress or impairment in social, occupational, or other important areas of functioning (Criterion D).[74]

One of the consequences of this process of medicalization has been the construction of a specific gender script to which transgender individuals need to adhere in order to access sex reassignment surgery (SRS). This new script reinforced existing hegemonic gender paradigms and scripts. As gender non-conformity became pathologized, and the science of sex came to rule the 'Truth' about gender, access to SRS was restricted and required a significant series of diagnoses, tests, and commitments from the individual. Under the rules set out in the DSM, for example, to be cleared for surgery an individual had to state that s/he had always felt trapped in the wrong body, wanted to be normatively gendered after going through sex reassignment surgery, and aspired to a 'stealth' (i.e. keeping secret one's transgender status) heterosexual life. The required statements also implied that individuals would leave behind any transgender identity, community, or activism. While many people genuinely held the obligatory feelings, beliefs, and outlook, and still others may have come to experience them as genuine, the prerequisite adherence to these dictums is tied up with hegemonic gender paradigms. By requiring a very specific transgender script, psycho-medical gatekeepers were able to reinforce hegemonic gender scripts and beliefs in the process. The advent of modern medical technologies not only changed how science and medicine made sense of gender and gender non-conformity, it created new technologies of power which influenced how individuals experienced and made sense of their own gender non-conforming bodies and identities.

We also see the symbiotic relationship between hegemonic gender paradigms and transgender treatment in the public response to gender non-conformity. Hand in hand with the demand for a particular and restrictive narrative for 'treatable' gender non-conformity has come criticism of transgender individuals as dupes of the gender system.[75] Scientists, scholars, and people at large have held transgender individuals to more stringent standards of gender-norm resistance than cisgendered people. Transgender people have been accused of somehow maintaining hegemonic gender norms and inequalities, of destroying gender diversity, of failing to be gender non-conforming at all times and of simultaneously being too flamboyant, radical, or militant. Essentially transgender people have been held responsible for maintaining the entire gender system through their own 'normative' masculinities or femininities while simultaneously being required to produce hegemonic gender to access medical services.[76] Applying these disproportionately rigorous standards to those who practice gender non-conformity is a technology of power still being used to downgrade the social status of transgender people. While all members of a society conform to, uphold, resist, and rewrite normative gender scripts through day-to-day interactions, holding transgender people accountable for both the conservation of hegemonic gender norms and preservation of gender diversity has let non-transgender individuals off the hook. In reality, the process of 'doing gender' is one in which we all participate and therefore all have the ability to use technologies of the day to challenge, rewrite, and expand socially available gender scripts.

New Technologies, New Genders

The rise of medical science to the peak of social influence is the technological development that has offered the greatest possibility for the creation of new and more diversely gendered bodies. Individuals are now able to choose a variety of medical interventions to produce new and varied gendered identities and bodies. These interventions include hormone therapies to produce masculine or feminine secondary sex characteristics and various plastic surgeries ranging from procedures to remove or implant breasts in order to mimic established gender characteristics, to sex reassignment surgeries that create differently gendered genitals. Medical science has simultaneously taken on the job of policing gender and sexuality through the pursuit of pathological diagnostic and curative models and treatments. While pathologization of gender non-conformity has been contested over the past 25 years, reducing its dominance, these scientific standards continue to hold sway over and have very real impact on the lived experiences of transgender individuals.

Neither technologies nor scripts are deterministic; they do not lead to one outcome, one set of gender scripts adopted by everyone, or one product, sign-system, power, or self. Their resonance and impact is mediated by particular social contexts and personal histories. To fully consider how technologies have shaped gender historically and in our current society, one must keep in mind the complexity of these relationships. As I examined earlier in this chapter, the use of medicine as a technology of power is not unique to gender; medical science has been used to enforce the racial and class-based status quo throughout history.[77] Science is, of course, the most legitimized knowledge source within a scientific paradigm, and the attendant scientific and medical technologies are used to uphold and defend established social inequalities and prejudices. With regard to the application of gender curative therapies, for example, these therapies are disproportionately directed at young boys; we have much more tolerance for gender non-conformity in girls. This asymmetry is predictable given our societal privileging of masculinity and its attendant traits; to value the desire to be a boy is much more understandable than the reverse.

Even when new gender scripts are put forward, as in cases of transgender social movements (see the case study on transgender organizing and the Internet for a more detailed discussion), their legibility to others remains constrained by hegemonic paradigms. Leslie Feinberg has been a transgender author, activist, and transgender pioneer for the last 40 years. Ze has written numerous fictional and nonfiction books

GENDER NEUTRAL PRONOUNS

Ze is an alternative pronoun used by some transgender individuals to express the fact that they identify neither as a man nor a woman. Similarly, hir is used instead of his or her. These pronouns have been suggested by some activists like Leslie Feinberg as new ways to refer to individuals that transgress the gender binary.

about transgender lives and has toured the country speaking at activist, educational, and political events.

In hir transgender history, *Transgender Warriors*,[78] ze shared a story common to hir experience.

> "You were born female, right?" The reporter asked me for the third time. I nodded patiently. "So do you identify as female now or male?"
>
> She rolled her eyes as I repeated my answer. "I am transgendered. I was born female, but my masculine gender expression is seen as male. It's not my sex that defines me, and it's not my gender expression. It's the fact that my gender expression appears to be at odds with my sex. Do you understand? It's the social contradiction between the two that defines me."
>
> The reporter's eyes glazed over as I spoke. When I finished she said, "So you're a third sex?" Clearly, I realized, we had very little language with which to understand each other.
>
> When I try to discuss sex and gender people can only imagine woman or man, feminine or masculine. We've been taught that nothing else exists in nature.[79]

Leslie Feinberg's poignant reflection about hir own illegibility points to how our ability to make sense of an individual's sex and gender rests in part on the gender scripts available to us. Try as she might, the reporter could not understand what Feinberg meant by transgendered, in part because she had no corresponding gender script on which to draw.

As Feinberg's experience of invisibility renders visible, the stakes are obviously high for transgender people. But these controversies also affect cisgender individuals; we are all influenced by and involved in the creation of gender(s). The creation of new gender scripts benefits all people, not just transgender individuals. One set of new scripts might validate a wider range of emotions for men, allowing them to express themselves more freely; other new scripts could change expectations for women's body size, moving us from a society where most women dislike their bodies to one where most women held positive body images. As Cressida Heyes concludes, "a wide range of gendered subjects stand to gain from challenges to enforced binaries within the nexus of sex, gender, and sexuality."[80] And yet, our ability to recognize and legitimate new gender scripts remains limited by the dominant ideologies and technologies of the day. As new technologies emerge, however, the ability for individuals to transform their own bodies and identities, and to share new gender scripts and ideologies expands.

People continue to refuse to conform to gender norms, of course, just as some have throughout history. Alongside these changes in technologies and normative definitions, gender non-conformity has manifested differently as well. It is continually shaped by the technologies available for the production of gender as well as by the social gender scripts of the era. Trying to make sense of gender non-conformity by isolating it, either by viewing it as solely a biological hiccup, or entirely a product of social experiences and choices, elides the complexity of transgender experience. Only when we examine gender as a product of the varied, complex interplay of biology, social scripts, dominant ideologies, personal histories, and technology can we develop an understanding of gender and sexuality that reflects the diversity found in society. Approaching the analysis of gendered lives and technological innovation together reveals how they are mutually constituted alongside dominant ideologies and scripts.

A Sociological Approach to Analyzing Gender and Technology

The first two chapters of this book have focused on the complex relationships between gendered bodies and identities, dominant ideologies, social scripts and technological innovation. The many examples and case studies reviewed thus far point to technology as a dramatic axis of social change that has historically shaped, and continues to reshape, who we are as people. The cases also reveal that technological innovation is always tied up with dominant paradigms, social scripts, and embodied lives. Sociological theories of identity reveal that identity formation is a social, interactive process that responds to and participates in social change. Moreover, social scripts—the stories for who we can be—work alongside dominant paradigms to shape who we are and think we can be as individuals.

Throughout this chapter these components have been examined in relationship to one another, and the theories and case studies have demonstrated how gender identities and bodies are transformed within the context of changes in dominant paradigms, social scripts and through technological intervention. Consider, for example, how gender ideology in the nineteenth century shaped women's bodies through the use of corsetry. Or how new scientific methods and technologies reshaped the nature (and nurture) of gender throughout the 1500s. Instead of existing in one-directional relationship to each other (for example technologies changing social scripts but not social scripts affecting technological innovation) dominant ideologies, scripts, technologies and gendered bodies and identities appear to be mutually constitutive, each component interacting dynamically with the others. That is, all of these components are engaged in a complex interplay with one another, each shaping and being shaped by the other constituent parts. Examining all of these social forces in interaction is what I mean by a sociological analysis.

SOCIOLOGICAL ANALYSIS

An analytical approach that takes into account individual, interactional and structural/institutional dynamics within a particular social context.

Because social forces are not directly observable (but are rather something individuals experience in the process of interacting in society) it is difficult to see how gender ideologies and social scripts have shaped each of us as individuals; our own embodied gender feels and *is* very real; the impact of new technologies on our bodies and identities is rendered invisible by the mundane nature of social life. Simultaneously, dominant paradigms and social scripts, transmitted through interaction with socializing agents like parents, teachers, peers, and media, disappear under the guise of everyday interaction.

Analyzing gender in a way that accounts for each of these aspects allows us to see how paradigms, scripts, technologies, bodies and identities all contribute to everyday gendered life. This sociologically based gender framework allows us to examine how individuals make sense of their gendered bodies and identities, how gendered forces are transmitted, learned, adopted, and contested through interaction, and how societal institutions produce and challenge gender scripts and gendered technologies. Such an analysis sheds light on the myriad configurations produced by ever-changing relationships between body, identity, social script, technology, and dominant paradigms, and renders visible the social forces that produce the complex reality individuals experience in society.

How Does a Sociological Approach Illuminate Gender Identity Change?

Analyzing the impact of technology on gender in this way is a layered and complex process. A short example from my research on drag performance helps to illustrate this dynamic process. Recall from the Preview that the Disposable Boy Toys (DBT) was a drag performance troupe that fostered significant gender change for most participants. In my research I found that the ability of individuals to present and experience gender differently, and ultimately identify in new ways, was intricately connected to the gender paradigms, scripts, and technologies within this specific group context.

In interviews DBT members understood that performing in this particular drag troupe was critical to changes in their personal gender identity and embodiment; they recognized the ways in which new paradigms, scripts, and technologies reshaped their gendered lives. The mechanisms by which this happened include exposure to new theories for gender (i.e. gender paradigms) and new examples of how individuals could be gendered (i.e. social scripts), as well as access to new tools for doing gender and information about gender non-conformity (i.e. new technologies). The ability of individuals to develop new social scripts within this context, embody them through the use of new technologies, and then—as drag necessarily includes performance—enact them on stage, was transformational.

On the individual level exposure to new gender scripts and paradigms helped members of the Disposable Boy Toys rethink what gender meant and what their own gender could be. In addition, access to new technologies allowed many participants to reshape their gendered bodies. For example, the dominant gender paradigm in DBT was that gender was a performative act, something that individuals learned to do on stage in the case of drag, as well as in everyday life. This new gender paradigm, which defined gender as a set of social beliefs rather than as a biological truth, allowed each individual to reframe what their own gender meant. An overwhelming majority of DBT members suggested that participation in The Disposable Boy Toys provided new gender paradigms and scripts and that these altered their own embodied genders. In fact, the majority of members had different gender identities and bodies after participating in the group. Some were more feminine women, some came to identify as transsexual (and change their body accordingly), and some developed new female masculinities.

One of the central ways that DBT affected its members was by providing access to new technologies. In rehearsals and during shows members learned how to create a particularly masculine or feminine bodily presentation by creating or enhancing those characteristics attributed to the gender they intended to portray. Each of these experiences drew on gendered technologies for reshaping the body, whether it was learning to bind their breasts or choose lingerie, walk in high heels or strut 'like a man,' put on makeup, or glue on facial hair. Simultaneously, members learned new gender paradigms and social scripts, refining their understanding of gender, transgenderism, and gender non-conformity. Trevor Bennett, a young and newly out lesbian member, learned about gender non-conformity for the first time within the group. Trevor shared that:

> Before I joined I thought that women wanted to become men so they could be with a female partner and have some societies [not] reject them. As my knowledge [grew about] things like gender, and I met people that were transgendered, I realized that it's not

about conforming to society's expectations; it has nothing to do with that.

Trevor learned a language for and approach to transgenderism by participating in the group. Within the context of DBT individuals were exposed to new paradigms and scripts for gender as well as new technologies for body and identity work. These new paradigms and scripts changed the range of possible gendered identities and bodies individuals could construct for themselves.

From another perspective, focusing on the effects of socializing agents reveals how rehearsal and performance practices in the group along with chances to perform new genders on stage all facilitated new gender identities and bodies. For many participants DBT was the first place they came into contact with social constructionist and performative theories of gender, theories that the group discussed at length and integrated into educational workshops. In the process new scripts and paradigms were transmitted to participants through interaction. Damien Danger joined DBT as an androgynous looking woman but came to identify as transgender within a year of involvement with the troupe. Damien reflected that:

> A lot of people don't have access to questioning gender because it is such an ingrained institution and [they] don't even realize there is another option. I feel like conversations [in the group about gender] helped its members learn more about themselves and the world at large.

As Damien Danger describes, participation in DBT gave participants a new paradigm for gender. In addition, working within a social context that espoused a wide array of gender scripts allowed individual participants to experience a broad range of possible gender identities and bodies.

Sometimes members even made these new gender scripts the focus of their performance. Nate Prince, a butch identified member (i.e. masculine) who was sometimes assumed to be transgender, talked about this when recalling a solo performance created to female vocals:

> I did the India Arie song [Video] to say I don't wear pantyhose, and I don't shave my legs all of the time, and I don't look like a supermodel but I'm still a woman. I wore my boxers and [men's undershirt] and I showed here are the ways to be a woman.

By acting out new gender scripts, in this case new ways of being a woman, individuals learned, practiced, and shared new gender possibilities with each other.

Finally, attending to the institutional level, a sociological analysis reveals how the gender practices within DBT altered the gendered institutions individuals engaged with. For example, many members felt that DBT's public performances and workshops, and the new gender scripts and paradigms that were part of those, affected the gender dynamics in the local gay and lesbian community, at the university (where DBT often performed), and in local government. Many participants expressed gratitude for the visible presence of DBT and thought that it made Santa Barbara, both within and outside of the Gay, Lesbian, Bisexual, and Transgender (GLBT) community, a safer place to transgress gender norms. Bill Dagger, who identified as 'genderqueer' (a transgender identity that transcends man or woman) felt that:

> DBT made it possible for me to wear the outfit that I'm wearing now, the shirt and tie, on campus without getting harassed. The presence of people who were openly discussing trans and queer issues in a performance way that was specifically about gender made it easier to walk around and not get harassed.

What Bill Dagger suggests is that the gender possibilities created by DBT changed the university atmosphere. DBT also helped participants navigate the gendered aspects of other social institutions. For example, members often engaged in lengthy discussions about how to navigate changing one's gender, including how to approach legal issues such as name change protocols, which doctors in town treated female-to-male identified individuals, and what organizations and groups were available for support.

Over its life-course the array of genders in DBT changed because the component paradigms, scripts, technologies, bodies, and identities present in the group changed. A robust analysis that accounts for both gender and technology can pull apart how social forces came together within the Disposable Boy Toy drag community to facilitate individual gender identity change. Individuals, exposed to new gender paradigms, scripts, and technologies within this unique social context, used these resources to alter their gendered identities and bodies in a variety of ways. The dynamic relationships between technology and embodied gender that are revealed through a sociological analysis of this drag performance troupe highlight the strengths of this approach.

Research on technology and gender in the social sciences suggests that bodies and identities change as new technological processes emerge, informed by the realm of possibilities offered in dominant paradigms and social scripts. New technologies interact with social scripts and gender paradigms to produce particularly gendered identities within different contexts. Moreover, research shows that dominant beliefs and paradigms combine with the diverse array of bodies and identities within a particular context to shape our vision of who we can be as embodied individuals. A sociological approach offers an analysis of gender and technology that recognizes the interplay between these individual, interactional, and structural forces.

CASE STUDY: FOCUS ON BLOOMERS AND NINETEENTH-CENTURY WOMANHOOD

In North America in the mid-nineteenth century a social battle raged over women's dress, and primarily White women's attire. The fashions of the day kept White women covered from head to toe in long sleeves, corsets, and multiple layers of skirts. While these styles reflected race and class status and ideals of women's domesticity, they severely hampered those women's ability to move freely; corsets restricted breathing and layers of skirts made running and jumping impossible. While sports (in particular bicycling) were becoming popular, women were unable to participate fully because of their clothing. Amelia Bloomer and others advocated for the rights of women to wear a female version of pants—what became known as 'bloomers'—but experienced stiff opposition from individuals who viewed this dress reform as equivalent to cross-dressing. Simultaneously, most women of color and poor women were exempt from these dress norms, not because they were free of hegemonic pressures, but because they were viewed as different kinds of women (if they were viewed as women at all). The fragility, domesticity, and purity said to characterize White upper-class women's femininity was not thought of as part of these lower-class women's character. How could it be when it was poor women who were responsible for doing the household labor from which White upper-class women were being protected? Even when poor women and women of color took on styles of dress and body codes in line with hegemonic norms of White femininity, their gender performances were viewed as inadequate; their very race and class identities made hegemonic gender unattainable. Convergently, part of the panic about 'dress reform' was driven by the decreasing distinction between the clothing of different racial groups and social classes.

During the Victorian era (i.e. mid to late nineteenth century) clothing for both men and women was shifting dramatically. Highly specialized class- and profession-based clothing was moving toward less formal and less regimented styles. This was due in part to the Industrial Revolution and attendant social changes. One of the technological innovations of the Industrial Revolution was the sewing machine, which was developed in the late eighteenth century and was in widespread use by the mid-1800s. This technology made more clothing accessible to more people across social class lines. Whereas most working class and poor individuals owned only one or two sets of clothing before this, the sewing machine (and quick-to-follow technologies of mass produced clothing) allowed most individuals to afford a larger wardrobe. While fashion had safely been the purview of only the upper classes because of its expense, it was now within reach of a much broader range of individuals. Most significantly, however, the sweeping social changes (in paradigms and social scripts) provoked by the rapid technological innovation of the era were reflected in and played out around men's and women's clothing. For men this meant that from the mid 1800s onward, their clothing grew less ostentatious and increasingly homogenous across social class lines. For upper class White women it was a fight over pants.[1]

The movements for and against 'dress reform' took shape in the late 1800s. It was sparked by a number of social changes including women's increased participation in public life (as teachers, college students, writers, and abolitionists), feminist movements advocating for the right to vote, work, and lead alongside men, and post-American Civil War politics. All of these social changes were producing new social scripts for womanhood and challenging dominant gender paradigms that made sense of women as weak in mind and body, innately maternal, and in need of men's moral and intellectual guidance. Instead of confronting these issues head on, both advocates and critics focused the debate of women's role in North American society on pants (or in this case, the women's version: bloomers). As sociologist and fashion scholar Diana Crane summarized:

> Trousers were particularly controversial in the nineteenth century because nineteenth century ideology prescribed fixed gender

identities, enormous differences—physical, psychological, and intellectual—between men and women. The dominant point of view allowed for no ambiguity about sexual identity and no possibility for evolution or change in the prescribed behaviors and attitudes of members of each gender . . . Dress reforms proposed by women's movements were inconsistent with this point of view.[2]

New forms of dress for White upper class women were a technological innovation, but one fraught with social tension over gender, race, and class.[3] In an effort to control White women's clothing, power holders—including doctors, politicians, and religious leaders—weighed in on the importance of women's 'traditional' dress. Many suggested that bloomers (and the bicycle riding that they were affiliated with) "destroys the health of women, and unfits them for the important and sacred duties of motherhood." Kansas District Representative Lambert made this statement in January 1897 when he introduced legislation to the Kansas State Legislature that would outlaw bloomers and public bicycle riding for women.[4] A similar sentiment was expressed in a *New York Times* editorial about dress reform, alongside a telling assertion that dress reform compromises the gender of White women: "This generation has long been aware of the existence of *alleged* women who insist that it is the right and duty of the sex to wear trousers."[5] What these statements point to is how intertwined technological innovation (bloomers) was with changes in gender ideologies, social scripts, and embodied womanhood.

This mid-1800s battle over women's dress had far more to do with the social tensions over first wave feminist activism and the shifts with men's and women's social roles that were taking place, than with any innate need for women to wear skirts. Its manifestation with concern to clothing, however, was sparked by new clothing technologies like bloomers and factory-made clothes. Take, for example, the cartoon (Figure 1.3), titled "Woman's Emancipation," which was published in *Harper's New Monthly Magazine* in 1851.[6] The tension over women's place in society vis-à-vis men is made clear, and bloomers were seen as a catalyst for gender upheaval in society. The fear was that if women were able to wear pants, they would also want to take on all of the other gendered behaviors associated with men, such as smoking or cavorting in public, or even those activities previously assumed to require men: escorting women, for instance. We, as viewers, are clearly supposed to be as aghast as the woman in the background is.

The development of new technologies—bloomers—as part of feminist advocacy and dress reform, provoked new technologies of power in an effort to maintain the existing gendered power structure of the day. Technologies of power such as laws against bloomers and bike riding were deployed to maintain the status quo. As part of the early nineteenth century advent of mass-produced clothing, Elizabeth Smith Miller designed the first women's pants in 1851.[7] These innovations, alongside the new language and aesthetics that were part of feminist

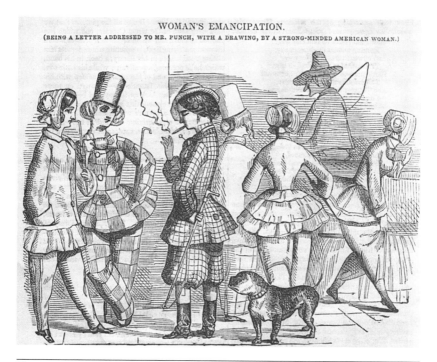

Figure 1.3 A cartoon drawing from *Harper's New Monthly Magazine* in August, 1851, depicting the social consequences of allowing women to wear Bloomers.

activism for women's participation in the public sphere, were met with new rules about women's dress that were, in fact, attempts to restrict women's increasing public social power. Many of these dress rules, incidentally, such as the requirement that women wear skirts or dresses to class at the college/university level, remained in effect through the 1960s, at which time a new wave of feminist activism again challenged them. While few people today would suggest that a woman wearing pants was a blatant example of gender non-conformity, 150 years ago doing just that called into question a woman's very gender identity. This is just one of many examples of how technologies have been used to construct new gender possibilities, delimit normative gender and sanction gender non-conformity throughout history.

2

INFORMATION TECHNOLOGIES AND GENDERED IDENTITY WORK

There is no doubt that the Internet is a 'socially transformative' force; what seems to be at issue here is rather the specific nature of that ongoing transformation as well as its particular object. Rather than adopting a utopian or pessimistic view in which the Internet is viewed as either a vector for progressive change in the classical liberal tradition or as the purveyor of crude and simplistic 'stereotypical cultural narratives,' it seems crucial to first narrow the focus a bit and examine the specific means by which identities are deployed in cyberspace.[1]

For people under the age of 25 with adequate resources to expect reliable access to the Internet, it is increasingly common to participate in virtual worlds like *Second Life* (recall the brief discussion of *Second Life* in the Preview). In recent years there have been academic and popular press articles about the world of *Second Life* that cover nearly as much subject matter as the press deals with in the 'real' world. Topics have included *Second Life* in relation to addiction, sex, teaching, business, team development, streaming sports events, law and copyright/intellectual property, lifelike clothing, harassment, ethical responsibility, *Second Life* libraries and librarians, cultural affinities (or lack thereof) for *Second Life*, medical and health education, and virtual consumption. There is a book about the *Second Life* newspaper, the *Second Life Herald,* another on non-profit organizing in *Second Life,* and many, many more articles have appeared in sources as diverse as *The*

Wall Street Journal, The Chronicle for Higher Education, Time magazine, and *Phi Delta Kappans*, the magazine of the premier professional association for educators.

For people in their late 20s or older, entrance into so-called 'massive multi-user virtual environments' (MMUVE) is slower and often relatively recent. New research suggests that more than 93 percent of teenagers are online (compared to 79 percent of adults) on a regular basis.[2] Among all of those who spend time online, there has been a rush to experience *Second Life* or another MMUVE. An average of one million new members enter 'Lindenland' each year, and more than 1.4 million dollars of goods were sold between January and March 2009.[3] There have been write-ups in all the national papers and articles in many magazines, not to mention plugs by National Public Radio, Microsoft, Apple, and many other corporations, encouraging you to visit them on their island in Lindenland. Although MMUVEs have users of all ages, as of 2007, over 18 percent of individuals aged 18–30 had created an avatar online, compared to 5 percent of older Internet users.[4] This data, combined with the rapid increase in membership of MMUVEs, suggests that a sizable and rapidly increasing number of young adults have participated in virtual, interactive communities.

What Is Going on in the Virtual World, Second Life?

Entrance into *Second Life* can be illuminating, exhilarating, and troubling all at the same time; my own experience offers an example of this. Upon arrival in *Second Life*, an individual is placed on 'Orientation Island' where they are given an avatar whose body looks much like a Barbie doll. The first order of business for new Lindenland residents is to construct a virtual self, or avatar. Using a number of controls it is possible to select from different 'skins,' adjust numerous bodily features, and construct a body to represent an individual's character in *Second Life*. Considering the overwhelming variety and complexity of choices available, it is no surprise that I, as a new resident, immediately hunkered down for several hours to create an avatar. Individuals can play with height, weight, skin color, gender, facial features, hairstyle, and clothing while seeking the perfect combination of who they *are*, who they *want* to be, and how they *want* others to see them. Personally, I wanted to create an avatar that reflected 'who I was,' if not physically, then metaphorically. What I came up with was myself—only better: a little more conventionally attractive, smoother skin, a little less chubby, and definitely dressed in nicer clothing. It is not really surprising that someone might choose to make themselves a 'little better' given the option. It is easy, painless, and reversible.

When an avatar leaves 'Orientation Island' to begin exploring Lindenland's many public and private spaces, they will encounter a world that ranges from hyper-realistic to fantastical. Standard modes of locomotion around the islands include walking and flying. At first I navigated around in a rudimentary way without particular direction, wandering around looking for other people. I explored several public parks, and then dropped by the Transgender Resource Center to get a sense of what was going on. While people's avatars did reflect a certain fanciful diversity—I saw faeries, animals, hybrids, and inanimate objects personified alongside men, women, and visibly gender non-conforming avatars—this world was simultaneously homogenous. Almost everyone was thin, beautiful, well dressed, and had chosen features typical of North American societies' Anglo-European ideals including skin tone, facial and body structure. Why was gender, racial and body size homo-geneity the outcome of allowing people to construct their own avatars? Is this homogeneity intentional, purposefully or unconsciously produced by this virtual world's designers or participants? Or is it a product of those who participate in *Second Life*? If it is intentional, what does that suggest about how broad, all encompassing, and deeply rooted discrim-ination is in our social world? And, if it is unintentional, what indication is this of how narrowly 'outside the box' we are actually able to think? At first glance, it seemed that most people did what I did by creating their ideal self. In the process, however, we created a world that reflected social body norms and hegemonically valued existing gender, race, and class scripts. Given the chance to truly choose to be anything, people usually bowed to the established social scripts and produced socially desirable bodies and identities—and in the process collectively created a world that reproduced the inequalities present in real-life society.

Making Sense of Second Life

From a sociological perspective dominant paradigms, social scripts, technologies, bodies and identities are analyzed in dynamic relationship to one another such that all aspects are mutually constitutive and interconnected. It is possible to make sense of how and to what effect gender paradigms and social scripts shape the identities produced through online technologies, by examining virtual worlds like *Second Life* from this perspective. Moreover, it is possible to hypothesize how these virtual identities might matter on 'real world' individual and structural levels. This chapter uses this analytical approach to make sense of whether and how online activities both reflect and shape individual gender identities and societal gender scripts. Why, when individuals can potentially do or be anything in these virtual worlds, do they reproduce hegemonic embodied cultural norms? Extending this, I examine whether these online worlds, including the construction of avatars, online interaction, virtual communities, and our participation in them, are of any true significance. As Lisa Nakamura cautioned in the quote that opened this chapter, what is at issue is the nature of individual and social transformation online.

The Internet as New Technology

When the first easy-to-use web browsers, *Netscape Navigator* and *Internet Explorer*, were introduced to the public in 1996, Internet participation skyrocketed. Until then only a handful of nerds, computer scientists, and government workers used the Internet in any meaningful way.[5] Indeed, in June of 1995 less than 15 percent of U.S. adults "ever used a home, work or school computer and modem to connect to computer bulletin boards or information services."[6] By November 1997, two years later, almost 40 percent of U.S. adults were online, and now, 10 years later, Internet use has reached 79 percent of all adults in the U.S.[7] Statistics for Canada have been comparable.[8]

As a technological innovation hailed as both liberating and destructive, both lay and academic interest in cyberspace has flourished over the past 15 years.[9] Whether centered on the comments of Al Gore or an article in the *New York Times*, the Internet's social impact has secured

CYBERSPACE

Originally used by science fiction writer William Gibson,[10] cyberspace refers to the intangible, metaphorical 'space' that networked computers construct through and for electronic communication.

a place at the center of public discourse. Scholars from many fields, such as media studies, communication, feminist studies, sociology, anthropology, and history have all examined the relationship between cyberspace, society, and individuals. Many researchers have explored the Internet as a significant technological tool for social change.[11] Sociologist Dana Fisher asserts that the Internet makes the work of social change organizations and activists more efficient and cost-effective, just as older media did in the past, drawing parallels that liken email to the phone, websites to newspapers and magazines, and list-serves and email lists to broadcast media.[12] Other scholars suggest that technology has transformed how individuals live their lives, make change in their communities, and relate to society at large. But, like other technological advances in the past, the Internet does not reach all members of any society equally. In fact, sociologist Daniel Myers explains that not only is access to technology a product of social inequality, but it widens the socioeconomic gap between those with access to information technologies and those without.[13]

Evaluating Information Technologies

While scholars and social critics have argued both utopian and dystopian visions of the Internet, most agree that it has saturated the lives of individuals in the industrialized Global North and some Global South countries with information and means of communication. This has created a 'worldliness of selves,' as Ben Agger termed it, "their [selves] ability to go anywhere/anytime, their saturation with popular culture, their penchant for travel, their tendency to change jobs, spouses, their bodies," in a postmodern world.[14] Early research on cyberspace examined the social construction of online reality and argued that individuals engaged in online forums in ways that either revealed or betrayed their true, essential, embodied self.[15] Other scholars have focused on how and why behavioral norms and scripts are sometimes different online, while other times they are not, suggesting that while online environments allow some escape from existing gender/race/class norms, individuals may continue to rely on existing social scripts to ground online interaction in familiar dynamics.[16] More recently, scholars have rejected the online 'ruse' vs. real-life 'self' dichotomy, suggesting that individuals both reinforce and contest existing social scripts and identities online. The Internet can be understood as a place where real selves as well as false ones can be constructed and produced.

Philosophers like Jean Baudrillard have posited that in techno-saturated post-modernity, image has become more significant, more real, than reality.

POST-MODERNISM

A period in history (usually defined as late twentieth century onward) characterized by the fragmentation of time, place, and identity due to social, cultural, and technological changes. Post-modernism is often summarized as a rejection of the modern focus on reality, unity, and universal truths.

Whether we, as individuals in North America, are talking about art, media, or bodies we have come to trust what we see from media like television or the Internet as much or more than what we personally experience. Some scholars argue that new embodied identities are possible because we are no longer bound by the linear, singular rules of face-to-face interaction.[17] Feminist theorist Donna Haraway, whose article foretelling the encroachment of technology into human bodies and identities was discussed briefly in the Preview, argues that this techno-saturated reality has created cyborg humans.[18]

A cyborg world is one where technologies have become so intertwined with modern life that humans have become a hybrid of machine

> **CYBORG**
>
> The combination of machine and organism characterized by the breakdown of a nature/culture dichotomy.

and organism. As such, we are fragmented individuals composed and recomposed of multiple, contradictory, fluid, and fractured selves. This cyborg theory is not only an effort to understand the influence of technology on individuals, but is also an effort to empower individuals who fall outside of hegemonic norms. Haraway offers up the idea of a cyborg identity in an effort to talk about the power of selves on the border of multiple identity configurations comprised of attributes such as race, gender, class, and ability. She argues that oppositional identities such as those held by women of color, which contradict naturalized hegemonic norms, are locations of resistance and social change. One point of continuity between Haraway and these other theories of technology is the idea that technology can produce new and reconstructed bodies and identities.

What Is Identity Work, and Is it Happening Online?

The construction and reconstruction of identity have been conceptualized as identity work.

> **IDENTITY WORK**
>
> The "range of activities individuals engage in to create, present, and sustain personal identities."[19]

Individuals shape and reshape who they are through language, behavior, appearance, and affiliation, within particular contexts. Individuals do identity work in the process of everyday life and interaction and, in the process, reinforce and contest established personal and social identity scripts.

Identity work is also done in a multitude of more purposeful ways, such as through self-help or therapeutic efforts, group-focused collective identity construction, or as part of significant life changes. For example, Donileen Loseke studied how shared narratives (what Loseke calls "formula stories") for domestic violence have shaped the personal identities of battered women. She found that because our societal understanding has shifted from viewing domestic violence as a private problem to a public one, a paradigm shift that has taken place over the last 25 years, formulaic stories have emerged that define and explain violence and appropriate personal and social responses to it. As women in violent situations seek social support they encounter these narratives and are asked to produce their own story of abuse in a way that aligns with these social scripts. In the process of creating their personal narrative that may be shared, for example, in a support group meeting, individuals work to fit their own complex array of experiences into the established patterns, sometimes conforming and sometimes rewriting them.[20] In the process of fitting one's story into the expected form individual identity is shaped by the paradigms and social scripts dominant in this social context, and shaped too by the personal experiences of the individuals.

Much of the early research on identity work online was utopian in that it ignored the ways in which one's ability to take on new identities online is mediated by real-life structural constraints. For example, this early research ignored the real-world limitations created by gender, race, and class inequalities. This early research does, however, highlight how cyberspace and cyber-technologies are important sites of identity work for individuals. Social scientists like Daryl Hill, David Gergen, and Simon Gottschalk have taken these theoretical tenets and used them to make sense of whether and how people are constructing new identities and subjectivities through computer-mediated communication.[21] What they have found is that the ability to create and deploy new and different identities online can inform or change individuals' understandings of their real-life selves.[22] Once thought of as a deeply embodied process of real-life interaction and self-development, new media scholars have suggested that identity work is also done fruitfully online. In part, they argue, it is the Internet's text-based nature that is key because it allows people to construct identities without having to situate them within differently gendered, raced, or classed bodies. Additionally, the very nature of the Internet as a place where you can interact with a multitude of anonymous others offers a "public arena where people feel they can 'privately' engage in identity work."[23] The Internet can function in part as a collection of 'virtual communities' where individuals interact in collective publics but do so without necessarily revealing their real-life identities, thereby lowering risk of stigma, sanction, and violence.[24] This, combined with its availability at all times and relative affordability, makes the Internet an institutional context primed for identity exploration. As Daryl Hill summarizes, "we come to know ourselves by seeing ourselves reflected back to us through information and communication technology in a way never available before."[25] Similarly, Amy Bruckman suggests that the Internet allows people to try out, emphasize, and experience new or different aspects of their self, and that the very structure and features of the Internet, as text based and anonymous, make it an "identity workshop."[26]

IDENTITY WORKSHOP

A virtual or real space that encourages identity development by encouraging identity exploration, play, and adoption.

We must be very careful of idealizing online interaction, however, by viewing all identity play as significant and radical. Sometimes play is just play, and the creation of new and different identities online is insignificant. This is akin to how not all drag performance is an assertion of transgender identity; for instance, the common practice of dressing in drag for Halloween is usually unrelated to a person's believed or embodied gender. In the same way, not all gendered behavior online is reflective of a 'real' or even desired offline gendered self. Reality is much more complex, wherein the diverse array of online identity assertions have a variety of relationships to offline embodied selves. Rather than some imagined inevitability, it is the real possibilities offered by computer-mediated communication that are so significant. Rules of authenticity are as different online as they are across different real-life spaces, and the Internet can be a context that offers new opportunities to play with and sometimes adopt new identities. And research shows that these online identity constructions matter for real-life selves.[27]

All of this research suggests that new computer-mediated technologies can be important sites of identity play and construction. Philosophers and empirical researchers have theorized why this might be true and suggest that some features of computer-mediated communication make identity work possible. They also suggest that the context-specific norms and social scripts within online communities matter in much the same way they do in real-life groups. What then might be the significance of social norms and scripts in *Second Life* and other online worlds? While there is a gap between virtual and real-life selves, a variety of research has suggested that the two exist in a dialectical relationship, each shaping the other. Not only does our real life shape how we construct online selves, but these online selves in turn shape who we are in real life.

Bridging Online and Offline Identities

Nobody lives entirely in cyberspace—it is, after all, just a shorthand way of describing computer-mediated communication between individuals who may or may not share a temporal or geographical location. People are always navigating between two worlds, bringing real-life identities, experiences, and bodies to bear on online interactions, and vice versa.[28] Sandy Stone reflects that, "it is important to remember that virtual community originates in and must return to the physical."[29] Those of us who interact in both real life and cyberspace, then, have contemporary lives characterized by multiple individual selves that emerge and play out in different social spaces.[30] These multiple personas are not new to the Internet; individuals have always cultivated and experienced a variety of identities shaped by the social and interpersonal demands of a variety of situations.[31] The Internet is just a new space, among many already established ones, where individuals construct through narrative, or 'story,' their lives in multiple ways.[32]

Narrative Identity, Discourses-in-Practice and Discursive Practices

In my own life, I have been and become many things including a designer, a lesbian, a researcher, an actor, a drag king, and a feminist. For each of these new identities, I learned how to narrate, to tell the story to myself and to others of how I was born and became this self. I did this, as we all do, in order to be viewed as authentic in each of these identities. I mined the stories of my own life for those that would bring context to and substantiate each of these identities, choosing to tell of my artist-mother, my first childhood crush on a girl, my scholar-father, my involvement in theater, my lifelong gender non-conformity, and my activist spirit. I learned how to talk about myself as these different selves in ways that resonated with other similarly identified individuals, and through the process solidified the pieces that make up this identity of 'who I am.' This is what social psychologists Holstein and Gubrium call narrative identity.

NARRATIVE IDENTITY

A theory that individuals create an ever-changing sense of self-identity in the process of telling stories about their lives. As new experiences shape the stories people tell about who they are, they come to think of themselves in new ways, engaging in an ongoing cycle of self-identification.

In their prolific work Holstein and Gubrium investigate how individuals develop and make sense of identities throughout their lives. They argue that people create the story of who they are by using the narratives valued in a particular community or context, what Holstein and Gubrium call "discourses-in-practice," narratives which are accepted through modes of storytelling, or "discursive practices."

Consider the domestic violence study by Loseke profiled earlier. What Loseke argues is that the discourses-in-practice of how an individual should make sense of and respond to domestic violence include a narrative that moves from serious violence to taking responsibility and control to holding strong even though "it won't be easy." In her study, if

DISCOURSES-IN-PRACTICE

The social scripts from which individuals construct a legible identity.

DISCURSIVE PRACTICES

How the self is constructed through storytelling processes and procedures.

individual stories did not fit into this pattern, into accepted discourses-in-practice, they lacked resonance with the group. In these cases facilitators and other participants were not as supportive or sympathetic, or expressed doubt about the abuse or the organization's ability to help. Alongside these discourses-in-practice, domestic violence support groups provided particular discursive practices that helped individuals learn and adopt the context-specific discourses. The experience of sharing one's story in a group, for example, affords practice at appropriate presentation in the context of that group, and at constructing a formula story that satisfies both the individual's need to substantiate their own experience and the group's need to relate to the narrative. As Loseke summarized,

> The institutional technologies of narrative work in these places are subtle techniques such as asking questions, rephrasing stories, ignoring some aspects of women's stories and dramatizing other aspects. Women's stories in these groups are interactionally shaped in ways compatible with the discursive environment informed by the formula story of wife abuse.[33]

The support groups are focused on identity change among participants so that an individual's 'battered woman' identity is in line with the social scripts privileged within the groups. The resulting self-stories, built out of group social scripts, are not untrue. However, they are reshaped to resonate with both the individual and the group. This process occurs in most, if not all, groups.

In a similar example, Holstein and Gubrium describe how individuals construct their identity as a 'recovering alcoholic' within Alcoholics

Anonymous groups by incorporating elements of the A-A script into their story. Members build their narratives within the accepted formats for personal story-telling (discursive practices), namely through introductions and shorter 'shares,' sometimes after a longer account by one member.[34] Longer accounts are often by an established member who relates their story in terms of the shared experiences of being an alcoholic, hitting rock bottom, searching for a way out, finding A-A, acknowledging powerlessness, and finding support and recovery through A-A. While everyone has their own personal history, people use discourses-in-practice (social scripts) in order to produce authentic, legible stories. This process of narrative identity formation demonstrates that identity is produced in groups through "the constellation of procedures, conditions, and resources through which reality ... is apprehended, understood, organized, and represented in the course of everyday life."[35]

Discourses-in-practice and discursive practices are the mechanisms by which identity work is done, and Holstein and Gubrium use these concepts to theorize how dominant paradigms and social scripts affect individual identity. [36] In the A-A example Holstein and Gubrium identify that the dominant paradigm within the group for understanding alcohol abuse is that alcoholism is a disease that can be treated with a 12-step A-A program. Within the group, scripts for who you can be and how you can move from alcoholic to recovering alcoholic (the discourses-in-practice) follow a particular pattern and are actively transmitted from older to newer members. In this way Alcoholics Anonymous offers a strong example of how the paradigms and scripts dominant within a given context work in interaction, generating particular types of identity work that manifest a specific set of individual identities.

Storying Ourselves into Being

As I have in this book, Holstein and Gubrium begin with the idea that identities are not something people are born with, but rather are created through the process of narrating one's life within a social context. We tell stories about who we are, and in the process figure out how to understand our experiences and develop a sense of self-continuity, even as new experiences and events change our identities and selves. Life, then, is an ongoing process of creating and recreating stories of who we are. These stories are not dreamt up out of nothing; instead, as Holstein and Gubrium explain, individuals "artfully pick and choose from what is experientially available to articulate their lives and experiences."[37] These available *scripts* are the resources from which individuals construct identities and selves in culturally legible ways. For example, a person is more likely to describe a life-long interest in helping people in order to 'story' why they became a doctor, because as a society we hold that story in higher esteem than one of profiteering or of divine calling. And yet these stories, or scripts, are not stamps that mold uniform identities and selves out of once differing people. In fact, these scripts are rewritten, modified, defied, and reconstructed by individuals, communities, and whole societies in the process of self-identification, social change, and technological innovation.

If we, as individuals, story our identities into being, we do so using the resources at our disposal and within the particular social and institutional contexts we have discussed, including school, family, and virtual communities, that provide a set of legitimized scripts. When starting college, for example, entrance into this new institutional setting is often marked by a shift in young adults' self-identity. College can be viewed as an identity workshop where increased anonymity, distance from parents, exposure to new experiences and communities, as well as participation in structures that specifically encourage new identity formation such as picking a major or joining a fraternity or sorority, all encourage young people to redefine themselves. And as part of redefining ourselves, we draw on the multitude of experiences we have had in our life, what Holstein and Gubrium would call resources, to pick and choose particular incidents to highlight. Consider your own experience. While you likely participated in hundreds of different activities in high school, you talk about some more than others, assigning them differing levels of importance in shaping who you are. And, what is important now is likely to have evolved from what was important to you during high school. Part of why you highlight some activities and interests and not others is because they help you define and validate who you are. As your identity changes, those stories you choose to highlight also change tailored to the social contexts in which you present them.

Looking at my own life so far, all of my high school experiences as part of the 'theater crowd' played a big part in my narrative of who I was when I got to college. When telling people who I was I shared stories about the plays I acted in and the technical backstage work I did and about my professed aspirations, which displayed my knowledge of the theater world; I used the language of the theater, and was sure to correct others who used it wrong. While I had plenty of other stories I could have shared from high school—maybe my involvement in Key club, soccer, or the science fair—these theater stories were the ones I shared because I wanted to be a 'theater person' at college. I majored in Theater, and made sure to learn the local norms and scripts that were associated with that path including who taught what classes, what the different paths toward a degree were, and what the slang was within the theater department. In the process, I came to see myself as a 'theater person,' and so did the people around me.

Re-storying Ourselves into New Ways of Being

When I changed majors to Sociology during my last year of college, I drew on a new set of stories to legitimize this change. I told different stories about my life than I had as a 'theater person.' This time I chose ones that focused on my academic achievement, interest in social movements, and feminist beliefs. I narrated new stories about why I left theater, and why sociology was the place I landed. Just as I had learned which stories resonated with a theater self-identity, and how to tell those stories, I learned new discourses-in-practice and developed new discursive practices to support my new sociologist self.

This process of re-storying one's life necessarily produces new identities that reflect the available social identity scripts of a particular time and place. But, it is not a rote stamping process, as social psychologist Douglas Mason-Schrock notes:

> In this process of sense-making through story, the master patterns are adapted, modified, and later passed on in slightly altered form.

Variations multiply, and so does the number of possible selves. And as lives are fitted to stories, lives may be led differently and new stories thereby created.[38]

What Mason-Schrock is suggesting is that as we tell stories of who we are, we adapt them to our needs. This process transforms the discourses-in-practice that we draw on to construct our storied selves.

Mason-Schrock studied a support group for gender-non-conforming individuals to understand how people storied their transsexual identities. He found that individuals learn and practice how to fit their own biographies into established narratives of authentic transsexual selves within support groups. Holstein and Gubrium's theory of narrative identity argues that we use the storytelling norms and patterns (discursive practices) to fit our own biographical details into existing narratives (discourses-in-practice), and this is exactly what Mason-Schrock found during his research on transsexual self-narratives. He summarized this process in the following way:

> Narratives were maintained and transferred to new members largely through *modeling*. In this process, first of all, those transsexuals who were adept at telling self-narratives did so voluntarily. In telling their stories, they gave the new members clues about the types of significant events to look for in their own biographies. If the newcomers listened closely, they could find the rhetorical tools that could be used, with some slight alterations, to signify their own differently gendered "true self."[39]

According to Mason-Schrock group members shared tools for identity work, which helped new members create authentic and acceptable transsexual selves. As I noted above, though, this process does not simply stamp discourses-in-practice onto individual lives; people take cues for producing authentic identities from the available discourses, and mold them to their own lives and stories. Moreover, this storying does not make these identities artificial; this is the same process that we all go through in developing and refining our identities. While this collective identity construction process might seem inauthentic or suspect in a gender non-conforming group, one must remember that we assign a benign naturalness to these very processes when they conform to hegemonic norms. I find it useful to think back on my own changes between high school and college when considering the realness of identity change. When collective identity work creates normative identities we accept that process as a normal and expected part of life, and transgender identities are no different.

The available scripts from which individuals construct a transsexual self come from a variety of sources. In addition to group members' and community storytelling, other invested parties construct scripts. As I explored in the last chapter, one consequence of treating transsexualism as a pathologized identity is that it has allowed the medical community to appoint itself gatekeeper for transsexual treatment. In order for individuals to gain access to medical treatment they have *had* to tell a very particular narrative about their life history and future desires as a gender non-conforming individual; not surprisingly, this acceptable script reinforces hegemonic gender norms. Given scholarship on an individual's need for storytelling using appropriate discursive practices and content that fall within the boundaries of the proper discourse-in-practice, it is no surprise that the process of learning and telling this particular transsexual narrative has reinforced its validity as a social script for transsexual identity. Many scholars have suggested, therefore, that the dominance of this identity script is the product of processes of medicalization that have reinforced and privileged one particular story. As shifting social paradigms and technological developments change the relationship between medicine and the transgender community, then, the available and legitimate identities that transgender people story into being will likely transform as well. The last case study in this book highlights some of these changes.

This expected expansion of identities and narratives is not unique to transgender identities. Research and theories related to computer-mediated communication suggest that these technologies are central participants in the expansion of social scripts and lived identities of all individuals. Coming full circle to look back at *Second Life* and the meaning of constructing new identities in virtual worlds, questions of online and offline identities become more compelling. If we narrate our identities into being within particular communities and contexts, does this happen within new online technologies? And if so, how?

Narrative Identity Online

In a recently published book titled *Alter Ego: Avatars and Their Creators*, author Robbie Cooper juxtaposes pictures of avatars and photographs of the individuals who created them.[40] The avatars Cooper documents range from almost perfect digital representations of their creators to fanciful avatars that bear little or no resemblance to their real-life corollaries. The images in the book beg questions about the relationship between identity and avatar, between virtual presentation and lived reality. Existing work on behavior and identity suggests that individuals strive for consistency between who they are and how they behave, and that behavioral changes affect individuals' sense of self and identity.[41] Scholars have found that individuals develop identities and a sense of self through interaction with others and through the support or sanction of associated behaviors.[42] It is no surprise, therefore, that recent studies have found that changes in online self-representations (aka avatars) affect the behavior and self-perception of individuals. A number of scholars have argued that elements of online interaction exacerbate these effects; for example, when individuals lack other social and visual cues for comprehending another person's identity—over the telephone, or online, for example—they tend to rely more heavily on identity cues and group norms (what some have called deindividuation effects) to make sense of the situation, and of who they are interacting with.[43] A recent study highlights this relationship between online avatars, behavior, and identity.

Does Online Activity Really Shape Who We Are?

Two researchers at Stanford, Nick Yee and Jeremy Bailenson, have recently examined the impact of avatars on individual behavior. In experiments that altered how an individual's avatar appeared to that individual but without affecting its appearance to others, Yee and

Bailenson were able to isolate the impact of self-perception on behavior. Their experiments show that when individuals have more attractive avatars, they behave in ways that suggest an increased personal sense of attractiveness and confidence.[44] This remarkable dynamic—what they term the "Proteus effect," named after the shape shifting Greek god— suggests that computer-mediated communication can directly impact how people behave, and potentially identify, in online interaction. Yee and Bailenson conclude that, given these results and research on the dialectical relationship between real-life and online interaction, these behavioral changes have significance. Every day, millions of users interact with each other via graphical avatars in real-time online games and communities. In these interactions avatars are our only self-representations, and are usually constructed as something of our own choosing. But, it is not a one-way process; our avatars change how we behave.[45] The implications of this are significant; in the real world, embodying a certain identity means adherence to physiological scripts that may require particular skills, tools, or even medical intervention. As suggested in the Preview, however, computer-mediated communication has made intentional self-presentation and transformation accessible, quick, and impermanent, and this mutability is one of the key features of virtual interaction.[46] If what we do online truly affects who we are in real life, then this set of technologies is radically transforming individuals' embodied identities.

Consider, for example, the impact of online support groups. Research has shown that both in real life and online, men and women behave very differently in support groups. Women tend to seek and demonstrate friendship, emotionality, and support. Men share information, organize meetings with experts, and develop plans of action. These behaviors are in line with dominant gender norms for men and women. Sociologist Clive Seale researched behavior in online support group communities to find out whether the anonymity of the Internet changed these dynamics. What he found was that the use of computer-mediated communication was indeed significant in this way, particularly for men. Seale examined the stories of men and women who participated in online cancer support groups dominated by another

gender (i.e. women in prostate support groups and men in breast cancer
ones). What he found was that men who sought support online after
the loss (or impending loss) of a woman partner, began to behave in
ways that run counter to hegemonic masculinity's focus on emotional
control and distance. Men in these groups describe increased emotionality and tenderness and many embraced these new behaviors as valuable deviations from traditional masculinity. These new behaviors were
clearly meaningful for these men beyond fitting in online; men describe
how their 'selves' have changed in response to both their experiences of
cancer and their participation in the online support group. For example,
Seale quotes one participant who wrote,

> I suppose it is a fact that some men find it hard to get [emotion]
> across as well as they should! Me, after all we went through, it has
> left me with some sort of feeling of opening up more and just
> saying whatever I feel. This thing has some strange side effects on
> emotions that I don't think you can read or learn about other than
> experience them personally.[47]

What is most interesting about this finding is that these same changes
were not reported in studies of real-life support groups for men part-
ners of women with breast cancer. This identity shift toward a non-
normative masculinity does not appear to happen in real-life forums.
Seale concludes, "individuals may be using the relative freedom of the
Internet to enact forms of masculinity and femininity deviating from
the stereotyped gendered norms."[48] What this example suggests is that
the Internet can, and often does, function as a place to develop non-
hegemonic gender identities. For the men in Clive Seale's study the
Internet facilitated the creation and adoption of new gender identity
scripts.

Gender Identity Change and the Internet

Both Holstein and Gubrium's model of narrative identity and the type
of sociological analysis I have engaged, suggest that the significance of
the Internet goes far beyond putting people into contact with one

another; they indicate that it is transformative for both individuals and society. Making sense of how this happens will help us elaborate how new technologies are reshaping embodied identities. In their research into both real-life local support groups and online support forums, Douglas Schrock, Daphne Holden, and Lori Reid[49] found that the Internet mattered in dramatic ways to transgender individuals. People attributed important changes in their lives to these support and social groups. Additionally, individuals saw real-life and online groups as critical to the changes in identity they experienced. More specifically, these groups helped transgender people shape their own gender identity and self-esteem and manage feelings of fear, isolation, and anger. One way to observe the importance of these online groups is by looking at what and how participants communicate in these forums. For example, on one of the online support groups Schrock, Holden, and Reid observed, a newcomer posted the following message:

> Subject: Weeeeeeeeeee!
> just couldn't resist sharing my *elation* at having found you! i stumbled across the group by accident during lunch today and my heart skipped, then skipped again, and again. i've been a t-something as long as i can recall, but never had much hope of meeting anyone else. it's so*good*to see you all out there.[50]

What this quote, and the many others like it, reveal is that individuals are conscious of how important online community is to them, and that its unique features of geographic and temporal flexibility, and anonymity, are key components of why the Internet is instrumental for individuals' identity and body work.

Online Identity Development

Societal changes and new technologies are facilitating the development and disbursement of new gender scripts and personal identities. Although I have largely focused on the social changes for transgender people facilitated by the Internet, change on the societal level is happening as well. Knowledge about transgenderism in the public sphere has increased, access to information is greater than ever before, and outspoken activists and allies have challenged transphobia in the workplace, in law, and in popular culture. The development of a national transgender movement and the ensuing publicity, advocacy, support, and validation that the movement created have changed the social context within which we all live.

A product of these contextual changes has been a shift in dominant gender paradigms. And, as I have been discussing, much of this ideological change was fueled by new Internet technologies. As transgender individuals have participated in more community organizing they have taken a more prominent place within GLBT organizing, have come out in greater numbers, and have advocated for social recognition. Simultaneously it is not just transgender individuals who have increased access to information about gender non-conformity; cisgendered[51] individuals have also benefited from easier access to information regarding gender non-conformity. While I traveled through my undergraduate education with no exposure to transgenderism, most of my students now have a working knowledge of it and many report developing this knowledge, at least in part, online. These new technologies and ideological changes have altered the landscape within which gender non-conforming individuals negotiate their lives and identities. Internet use has helped individuals learn, practice, and adopt new gender identity scripts, learn about whether and how to shape their body as authentic transgender individuals, and has offered new—and often more accepting—social gender paradigms with which people make sense of the world. In turn, the increased diversity of gender identities and bodies visible in real life and online fuel ongoing transgender-inclusive social and cultural change, technological development, and acceptance of transgender individuals and communities. Each component has worked in concert with other elements to change the range of possibilities available for transgender individuals and the set of acceptably gendered bodies and identities in our society.

Narrative Identity and Computer-Mediated Communication

The motor driving these changes in individual and social gender identity scripts is narrative identity. Applying Holstein and Gubrium's theory of narrative identity to computer-mediated communication illustrates how the Internet, viewed as an institutional setting, provides individuals a new space within which to narrate new identities. This theory of narrative identity can help explain *how* contextual and technological changes intersect with new individual identities and bodies, as well as how social identity scripts direct and respond to these changes. Let us begin by analyzing how the Internet shapes individuals.

The increased communication among transgender people, a product of computer-mediated communication, allows the sharing and refining of discourses-in-practice and discursive practices. For example on many public transgender blogs and public journals,[52] the types of information individuals share run the gamut from tips for gaining medical treatment and GID diagnoses to life histories in which they produce and police appropriate discourses-in-practice. This practice of sharing life histories is an opportunity for individuals to learn and deploy the discourses-in-practice required to construct an acceptably authentic transgender self. It also offers the transgender community at large a place to refine, challenge, and change the discursive practices used within communities to construct authentic transgender identities.

This identity work, in turn, challenges social paradigms of gender identity. Our societal conflation of gender and sex, and our cultural belief that these are fixed, stable components of self, stand in stark contrast to the discursive practices of transgender individuals. In actuality, the ongoing narrative construction of all gendered selves, both gender conforming and non-conforming, contradicts these social beliefs. Through expectation and naturalization, however, we render invisible the constructed nature of normative identities. In fact, the power of hegemony is ubiquitous such that the daily work of living up to social norms is so hidden that it appears inevitable. Just as the development of heterosexual sexual identities is normalized such that they appear inevitable, natural, and biological, so too does the ongoing construction of normative gender identities disappear. Moreover, individuals are held accountable for their gender; when it conforms to social norms they are rewarded and when it contradicts norms they are punished (what West and Zimmerman term 'doing gender').[53] While we expect and reward the development of normative genders (from girl to woman, for example), we treat the development of non-normative ones with suspicion and critique.

Similarly, while *everyone* engages in discursive practices and uses discourses-in-practice in the process of continually constructing and refining gender identities, these acts are rendered invisible when they match normative social scripts because of their mundane expectedness. It is possible, however, to tease out how gender paradigms lead to particular discourses-in-practice by engaging a sociological analysis that attends to paradigms, scripts, technologies, and embodied identities at the same time. For example, as a society we have a set of accepted narratives for moving from girl to woman or boy to man. There are narratives of becoming a woman at menstruation, and a man through sexual intercourse, feeling like a woman through dress-wearing, make-up and polished nails and like a man in the process of wearing a suit, acting chivalrously, and weight-lifting. But, Marshall McLuhan, a twentieth-century literary critic who philosophized about how technology would change society said it best, perhaps, when he commented, "Fish don't know water exists till beached."[54] In other words, social scripts for gender are so pervasive, so naturalized, that they disappear. It is only when we focus attention directly on these dynamics that they are visible.

When Identity Work Produces New Gender Identities

Just as coming to retell my own life story as a 'sociologist' where once I had told it as a 'theater person' was neither deceptive nor untrue to my identity, the process of learning and adopting new gender identities—both normative and non-conforming—is an identity change born of intentional narrative construction. What the Internet brings to the table is not the ability to create false, disembodied identities, but rather a new institutional context and set of technologies that support identity work. The gender identity work that individuals do online is really no different from the work previously done in support groups. The differences lie only in the number of individuals who can participate, the freedom to act differently because of the anonymity of virtual communication, and the ease of access to new groups and communities online. In online and real-life forums, as Schrock, Holden, and Reid conclude, "members collectively foster[ed] solidarity and authenticity by creating and telling self narratives . . . newcomers learn how to tell authenticating stories by modeling and be[ing] guided by seasoned group members."[55]

A number of other researchers have documented similar dynamics in other online spaces and have come to the same conclusions regarding the role and importance of online forums for identity work. Daryl Hill collected life histories from members of the Toronto, Canada transgender community and found that the majority of them thought the Internet played a crucial part in their own gender identity development. One example of the type of stories that Hill recorded comes from 'Melissa,' an individual who reflected that she learned who she was through the Internet.

> I got on the Internet, and the first thing I did, you know, was talk to anybody I could talk to about it [transgenderism] . . . I wanted to talk to anybody or anything I could, just to get some kind of rationale behind it, the vocabulary, do something with it . . . To build a story, to build a way to talk about it . . . it was something I could never do before.[56]

What is so interesting in this quote is that Melissa actually talks about looking for the vocabulary and available scripts to help her build her own story of transgender-ness. What individuals like Melissa described to Hill were the active and intentional construction of new personal, and ultimately societal, discursive practices and discourses-in-practice for gender identity construction. Now, certainly not everyone online and not all online communities are focused on or foster identity work. But for those that are, computer-mediated communication is clearly a new and important medium.

Collective Identity Work Online: Negotiating Social Scripts

The impact of developing and acquiring social scripts for gender online goes beyond the basic elements of ease, anonymity, and collectivity. The Internet has enabled the transgender community to assert new transgender ideologies, reframe existing pathological narratives of transgender selfhood, and develop new or transformed gender scripts outside of medical and psychological control. That is, it has provoked change in societal norms and scripts as well as in individual identity. While the last 75 years of gender non-conformity in North America have been dominated by medical and psychological discourse, the last 10 years have seen the most successful resistance to those pathologizing narratives. Online, individuals can share personal narratives that counter dominant medicalized scripts, share information about doctors and treatments, and advocate for changes in medical and social rights. The Internet has allowed transgender people to challenge medical identity scripts and to answer back to power-holders who control access to hormones and sex reassignment surgery, and police legitimate transgender narratives. The result has been that online transgender communities have been able to broaden the available identity narratives for transgendered people. It is with Internet use, for example, that we have seen the rise and solidification of gay FTM communities, genderqueer groups, and other marginalized transgender groups. The key here is not that transgender communities could not talk back to power-holders before the Internet, but rather that the Internet has made the personal and collective impact of these engagements exponentially greater. The case study that follows this chapter elaborates these dynamics.

Let us compare two protests, similar in most respects other than that one took place without Internet organization and the other used the Internet to mobilize; the differences in the results are striking. In 1993 the American Psychiatric Association (APA), which is the governing body that sets diagnostic and treatment standards for psychiatric practitioners, held its convention in San Francisco. This was a moment in time rife with social movement activism among gay and lesbian communities, including anti-assimilationist queer and transgender organizing.[57] The APA meetings inspired protest from within the transgender community around transgender inclusion in the Diagnostic and Statistical Manual.[58] While a number of transgender rights activists spoke with APA attendees inside the conference, a direct-action group named Transgender Nation[59] simultaneously took responsibility for organizing an anti-GID action that generated a vibrant protest outside and culminated in the arrest of several activists. The protesters' message was exceedingly clear; a spray-painted message on the side of the convention center put it succinctly: "APA go away, transgender liberation now."[60]

This 1993 protest against pathologization was modestly significant; certainly for San Francisco-based transgender activists it was a moment of solidarity, empowerment, and community building, and the protest garnered limited media coverage.[61] Activists like Jamison Green suggest that the protest helped transgender people inside the conference hall initiate discussion about GID and advocate for changes directly with practitioners.[62] That being said, the direct impact of the protest was limited for both transgender communities and transgender individuals. As far as change in how the psychiatric community approached GID, the APA did not even issue a formal response.

Comparing the 1993 APA protest to a more recent one casts into relief the impact of new information technologies on transgender activism. In the spring of 2008 (trans)gender activists sought to intervene in the appointment of Kenneth Zucker as chair of the American Psychiatric Association's Sexual and Gender Identity Disorders working group for the Diagnostic and Statistical Manual of Mental Disorders (DSM-V). A Toronto-based clinician, Zucker advocates for aggressively pursuing cures for gender non-conformity in childhood, in contradiction with the APA's rejection of reparative therapy (at least in terms of sexual orientation).[63] Zucker's methods, examined in a 2006 *New York Times* story, include removing 'wrong-gender' toys, forcing single-gender play and peer groups, and encouraging self and peer policing of behavior, desire, presentation, and identity.[64] The mother of one of Zucker's patients reflected in a recent NPR interview on the effect of the reparative therapy on her son, Bradley; she said, "He really struggles with the color pink. He can't even really look at pink." "He's like an addict. He's like, 'Mommy, don't take me there! Close my eyes! Cover my eyes! I can't see that stuff; it's all pink!'"[65]

This child appears to be in incredible pain as a direct result of Zucker's recommended treatment for his condition: that Bradley's desires are not in line with normative gender scripts. For Zucker, liking pink portends gender disaster for young boys, and clearly the extent to which parents and children are encouraged to fight against any inkling of desire for 'wrong gender' toys, colors, desires, and lives can be quite phenomenal. Beliefs such as pink being 'naturally' a girls' color and more generally that gender norms need to remain rigidly dimorphic underlie this compulsive resistance. Perhaps the most menacing judgments fundamental to this approach are that being 'normally' gendered is more important than comfort and desire, and that being gender non-conforming is pathological.

Given Zucker's efforts to 'cure' gender non-conformity in children, it is no surprise that gender activist and scholarly communities organized to oppose his appointment as chair of the APA's Sexual and Gender Identity Disorders working group. As part of this opposition, online networks were quickly abuzz with discussions about how to challenge Zucker's appointment. Discussion groups debated different approaches and shared information about Zucker and his practices, and individuals wrote and posted articles, essays, and reflections on their own blogs and in a diverse array of transgender and GLBT community forums online as well as in print media.

Organizations with strong online presences jumped to write and circulate petitions targeted at the APA for signatures, which were circulated rapidly and prolifically.[66] The largest petition generated more than 3,500 signatures in the first week, and almost 10,000 in a three-month period. When I ran a search for the petition in September 2008, I found more than 80,000 websites that discuss it. As the protest grew, it expanded to an attempt to exclude Zucker and his compatriots from other GID-focused conferences and events. While transgender activists and allies posted YouTube videos about Zucker, the APA, and the petition, news outlets including NPR and the *New York Times* ran stories about Zucker and debates about GID in the APA.[67] GLBT organizations released press statements against Zucker's appointment, and non-transgender blogs and communities posted information about the petition. In other words, the response to Zucker's appointment began online and spread rapidly and meaningfully to a diverse set of communities. In fact, outcry was loud enough to elicit a response from the APA.[68]

While it is too soon to tell whether this outcry will shape whether and how GID appears in the DSM-V, this mobilization has affected the debate. The APA amended the information it distributed about the working group and Zucker, and issued a press release about his limited influence. The activist and ally networks that mobilized around the petition continue to attend to these issues. A number of scholars and activists have publicly critiqued the August 2008 document produced by the working group, "Report of the [APA] Task Force on Gender Identity and Gender Variance" online, in print sources, and directly to the APA.[69] Key here is the size and impact of these protests and the centrality of the Internet. It is hard to imagine that the same mobilization could have occurred without the online dissemination of information, petition distribution, or networking.

Comparisons of these two protests offer a clear example of how individuals use technologies to shape dominant gender ideologies and available social scripts for gendered bodies and identities. Transgender activists used online technologies, and the unique assets they provided, to influence the medicalization of gender non-conformity. Simultaneously, these new ideologies, disseminated through technology by individuals and groups, influence the social context within which transgender movements and individuals advocate for rights and recognition. More people were able to learn about and participate in debate over GID and its presence in the DSM in 2008 than in 1993, in part because technologies were available that lessened the impact of geographical isolation, stigma, and medicalization. At the same time, transgender-positive social changes—partly facilitated by technological advances— over the last 15 years have created an environment more receptive to transgender issues, and community organizing. This is, again, facilitated by technological advances and has expanded available cultural gender scripts of who individuals can be.

The identity work that transgender individuals do online is visible more broadly, and has helped to decenter psycho-medical authorities like the APA in the processes of identity formation. A sociological analysis highlights how shifting gender paradigms—what debates about GID are about at their core—are the result of interaction with new technologies, (trans)gendered bodies and identities, and contemporary social scripts for who you can be. Simultaneously technologies, changing bodies, and dominant gender paradigms all come together to produce and disseminate new gender scripts.

Another arena where active gender identity negotiation takes place is in online web chat rooms. We can look to these sites for examples of how masculine gender scripts are negotiated and reproduced. A number of sociologists have studied how men negotiate and assert masculinity within online discourse.[70] Lori Kendall found that men in a social chat room actively worked to (re)produce hegemonic masculinity in online discussions by objectifying women, talking about sex and sexual prowess, and by displaying knowledge about typically masculine endeavors like sports and mechanics. Given what we know about identity work we would expect these discussions both to reflect dominant gender ideology and to participate in the construction of men's gender identities, and this is what research suggests. In a variety of different studies researchers found that hegemonic masculinity (i.e. the dominant gender ideology) and gendered social scripts for interaction (for example how men and women tend to communicate) are both the most common forms of discourse online.[71] Displays of hegemonic masculinity and the use of masculine interaction styles pervade online social spaces, and these discourses are as racialized and gendered as real-world hegemonic masculinity.

This research reiterates that online spaces are not characterized by an absence of socially significant embodied characteristics (like race or gender), but rather that the use of technology works interactively with social scripts and dominant gender and racial ideologies. Just as transgender individuals use online spaces to do identity work, cisgender and transgender men use web chat rooms and discussion boards to construct and substantiate masculine identities.[72] Lori Kendall examined how self-identified nerds negotiated hegemonic masculinity and asserted positive gender identities within the 'BlueSky' chat room. For men whose masculinity is suspect because of 'nerdiness' (often characterized as a lack of physical ability and a focus on intellectual or technical pursuits), constructing a normative masculinity online is one way to counter real-life gender non-conformity. The way many 'nerds' did this was by drawing on dominant discourses-in-practice for heterosexual masculinity. Kendall recounts one instance where several regulars used sexual prowess and the sexual objectification of women to establish themselves as men. She highlights this exchange:

> Mender says "did I mention the secretary babe smiled at me today"
> Roger Pollack WOO WOO
> Jet says "cool Mender"
> Jet says "did you spike 'er"
> Mender says "no, sir, I did not spike 'er."

In this interaction, talking about women as babes, turning immediately to a sexual question and objectifying women in the process are all tactics used by Mender, Roger, and Jet to assert masculine identities. As Kendall concludes, "The ironic sexism of much BlueSky discourse maintains 'the order of gender domination' (Lyman 1998: 172), almost irrespective of other aspects of BlueSky men's activities and behaviors with and toward the women in their lives."[73] What her research suggests is that commonplace interactions online are sites of identity work in ways that often reinforce hegemonic gender ideologies. Analyzing Kendall's research from a sociological perspective, established gender scripts pair with dominant gender paradigms to shape how technologies are used (in this example to engage in sexist discourse) and shape the identities cultivated through these computer-mediated communications. However, as I have demonstrated with all the other examples, the interaction of these elements—paradigms, scripts, technologies, and embodied identities—is never uniform.

While Kendall found the reproduction of hegemonic masculinity in 'BlueSky,' the creation of new counter-hegemonic scripts exists as well, scripts that will ultimately facilitate new counter-hegemonic identities. For example, a recent study of girls aged 13–15 in Vancouver, Canada, found that girls use online chat rooms, role-playing games, and social networking and messaging to try on new femininities before enacting them in real life.[74] In their study of both gender conforming and non-conforming girls Deirdre Kelly, Shauna Pomerantz, and Dawn Currie "found girls bending and switching gender to improvise nonconformist femininities and learning to express parts of themselves (e.g. aggression, sexual desire) that they had been made to feel were taboo offline." Girls described learning to take romantic initiative with boys, resist sexual harassment, and do non-normative femininity.[75] For example,

> Shale and her friend Rose used Internet chat rooms to challenge emphasized femininity and perform a rebellious femininity. They delighted in annoying girls with ultra-feminine online names like Sweet Flower Petal and dreamed of hacking onto "small Web sites with the Hello Kitty buttons and saying, 'You've been hit by Cookie the Bloody WhaHaHa'."[76]

What Kelly, Pomerantz, and Currie conclude is that while online spaces can be sexist alongside real-life ones, many girls felt more empowered to try on new and non-normative identities online, and more able to speak back to sexual harassment and sexist behavior.

These varied examples reveal how gender is being done—and undone—by people and groups in a variety of technologically mediated locations. Support groups, romance/dating websites, and a myriad of other sites of gendered identity work offer examples of how individuals are using information technologies to engage in gendered identity and body work. Sometimes this engagement is intentional and transformative (as in transgender support groups) and sometimes it serves to reinforce existing gender identities (as in romance/dating sites) or assert positive reformulations of marginalized identities (as in girls' identity work online). Regardless of focus, it is clear that these are active and agentic sites of both personal identity development and social script elaboration and extension. And yet, alongside the creation of new social scripts and identities, individuals continue to reproduce social inequalities that are written into established scripts for behavior, identity, and embodiment.

Rewriting and Reproducing Social Scripts

Many early utopian theories of computer-mediated communication asserted that as people "moved online" they would cast off gender, race, class, and body limitations to exist as undifferentiated equals. But the suggestion that race, gender, class, and nation or any other embodied characteristics will cease to matter online ignores the fact that biases such as racism, sexism, and 'ableism'[77] are not only individual prejudices but also structural inequalities.[78]

> **STRUCTURAL INEQUALITY**
>
> Unequal opportunities, outcomes, or rewards on the basis of group membership or individual identity and built into social institutions.

When people assert that prejudice disappears in cyberspace, they inadvertently naturalize its occurrence offline by suggesting that the inequalities that exist in real life are inevitable. The fact is, however, that race, class, and gender hegemony are manifest both through intentional discrimination and through social structures that reproduce inequality and construct default assumptions about what is normal, good, and desirable.

One of the first things I noticed when I began wandering around in *Second Life* was that almost all avatars in Lindenland were thin, tall, and White. It is unlikely that this is an accurate reflection of the real-life identities and bodies of participants, given the demographics of North America and the self-reported participation rates within gender, race, and age categories. I was intrigued and began to do some asking around in *Second Life* and some informal research outside of it to figure out what was going on. The first thing that became clear was that the ability to construct non-White avatars was limited; many 'skins,' which are literally skins for your avatar either purchased or selected from the *Second Life* library, are only available in light skin tones. Many skins do not allow you to adjust facial features to reflect phenotypically non-White characteristics such as a broad nose, for example, or lack of an epicanthic eyelid fold. In the early versions of *Second Life* it was almost impossible to create non-White avatars, and while the set of available choices has expanded greatly over the last few years, the domain is still set up in a way that reinforces hegemonic beliefs that White features and skin tones are normal and natural, and non-White features are atypical, outside of the norm, undesirable, and perhaps even proscriptive.

What does this limited availability to portray non-White identities say about how deeply racialized hegemonic norms are integrated into our identities and beliefs as individuals and as a society? If you can be anyone online, why would people independently but intentionally produce only a narrow range of hegemonically ideal bodies? And when creating a world in which people are encouraged to expand their identities and horizons, why would designers limit the choices for non-conformity? When I asked friends, students, colleagues, and other *Second Life* participants this question, most people responded that if you could be anyone, why not be what everyone desires—why not be the ideal? At its most basic, this offers a clear example of how hegemonic gender and racial identity paradigms shape the things people desire and the identity choices people make. There is another layer of significance, though; if the ideal—who we *should* want to be—is thin, White, tall, able-bodied, and normatively gendered, what does this say about racism, sexism, ableism, etc. in our society? Are we really leaving prejudice behind and charting new identity territory online?

Lisa Nakamura, one of the foremost scholars of race and racism online, thinks not. In a recent essay on the geographies of virtual reality she theorizes that, "when players choose blackness, whiteness, or brownness ... users *voluntarily* create racialized space."[79] What Nakamura suggests is that in the process of constructing online avatars people are reproducing racialized inequalities. Again, the utopian/ dystopian argument about information technologies is revealed as overly simplistic and as one that elides how new technologies both enhance and constrain social change. Online forums provide spaces for both individual identity work and for the reproduction of social inequalities and hegemonic norms.

Reproducing Inequality Online

It is not just individual choice that encourages this racial homogeneity, however. Just as in real life, there are sanctions for deviating from the racialized norm. One way individuals may be penalized is through harassment; for example, many people of color who participate in *Second Life* report experiences of overt racism including name calling and refusal to engage in conversation. Similarly, many feminine avatars possessing non-normative characteristics such as portliness, small breasts, or short stature report misogynist interactions. The limited research that has been conducted so far on the influence of race in online virtual worlds supports these individual experiences. In a recent study Paul Eastwick and Wendi Gardner examined interaction in a virtual world similar to *Second Life* and found that there was a statistically significant decrease in the willingness of participants to help dark-skinned avatars, "implying that reciprocity concerns took on greater importance when the requesting avatar was light-skinned." In other words, Eastwick and Gardner found that race mattered online in much the same way it does in real-life and that, "real-world racial biases, as they are inextricably intertwined with the rest of the human social mind, may also emerge in virtual environments."[80]

In addition to personal harassment, the very structures of most virtual worlds reinforce the hegemonic beliefs that normal equals White, thin, able-bodied, etc. Not only is it more difficult to find realistic looking dark skins, for example, but when you do, many of the details and life-like features of avatars disappear. Similarly, most of the available skins and clothing fit poorly on fat or disabled bodies. In one blog discussion about body size in *Second Life*, a participant reflected incredulously that:

I don't consider my avatar to be plus size, let alone fat, but apparently many of the content creators in SL must . . . I have to edit skirts so much it's not worth the effort. Boots are almost impossible to fit on my calves. So many fabulous pants and shirts look terrible once the texture is stretched over my shape. Even animations and poses can cause my hands to be imbedded in my body.[81]

The inability to find skins, clothing, or even gestures that accommodate larger avatars reinforces the idea that normal equals thin and that no one should or would want to be fat. One *Second Life* participant, Marissa Ashkenaz, decided to do an informal study in Lindenland for an academic panel at the 2008 National Popular Culture Association/ American Studies Association conference.[82] She asked eight people to spend one week in *Second Life* as fat avatars and to keep a journal about their experiences in Lindenland. What Ashkenaz found was that not only were individuals unable to find hair, skins, or clothing that fit their bodies, they had a hard time getting others to engage in social interactions, were often ignored, and even experienced significant overt harassment from other *Second Life* participants. These experiences confirm that, like race, participants in *Second Life* bring social scripts for normative body size and attractiveness into *Second Life* and scorn bodies that fall outside of these norms.

Again, in a social space not bound by real-life bodily limitations, people are working very hard to reproduce hegemonic bodies. Instead of reflecting the diversity of body sizes found in North America, the average height for both men and women in *Second Life* is more than six feet and almost all bodies are underweight. This offers another example of the reproduction and even refinement of hegemonic ideals and attendant prejudice in online virtual worlds. In other words, although online spaces can and do facilitate identity negotiation and transformation, they can also reproduce the inequalities and stereotypes that are written into existing identity paradigms and social scripts.

Lisa Nakamura calls the reproduction of stereotypes online 'cybertyping' and suggests that existing racial and gendered inequalities are written into information technologies in a variety of ways. Not only do people practice prejudicial behavior online, the structures of online spaces themselves (for example, the racial categories that are available in surveys) construct and reproduce racial difference and inequality. Most significantly, however, Nakamura highlights how the Internet can be used for "identity tourism" wherein people reduce race to skin color and take on highly stereotypical racialized characters (a popular one, for example, is the Japanese geisha).

IDENTITY TOURISM

Taking on racialized, gendered, classed, or national identities in cyberspace without recognizing the 'real-life' circumstances and disadvantages of these identities.[83]

Nakamura's critique is that just as real-life tourists in 'exotic' places see a sanitized view of 'native' life, online identity tourists "use race and gender as amusing prostheses to be donned and shed without 'real-life' consequences."[84] This leads to the reduction of race and other embodied social statuses to seemingly meaningless features devoid of real consequence, which in turn perpetuates social beliefs that racism, sexism, and other bigotries do not exist. These exact circumstances are evident in blogs about race in *Second Life*. Many of the online blog responses to an essay on racism in Lindenland, for example, attested to the lack of racism by noting that they (White individuals) put on Black skins on occasion. One commentator wrote, "I myself recently purchased an absolutely beautiful black skin which I wore almost constantly for over a week. (And I change skins almost hourly, so that's saying something!)."[85] One danger of the Internet, then, might be the ability to play at other identities without an awareness of the lived experiences and inequalities that are part of that real-life identity. How do we make sense, then, of the immense breadth of possibilities that computer-mediated communication opens up juxtaposed against the simultaneous presence of narrow, limiting social scripts and racialized, cisgender ideologies that shape identity work online?

Navigating Gendered Identities and Bodies Online

Eastwick and Gardner end their article on racial bias in virtual inter-action by quoting a participant at a real-world 'reunion' for members of *There.com*, an online virtual world akin to *Second Life*. This group member, reflecting on the significance of the community stated, "It may be a virtual environment, but the interaction is real."[86] The scholarly research presented throughout this chapter supports this analysis; much like gender, online interaction might not be real, but it is clearly real in its effects. These effects are shaped by social ideologies and identity scripts, sometimes mimicking and sometimes expanding those found in real life.

New online technologies do not, all of a sudden, allow us to cast off the shackles of hegemonic gender, race, class, or sexuality and redefine ourselves in any way imaginable. While so much early Internet hype hoped this would be the case, when we step back and think critically about entering a virtual realm it is no surprise that people bring their baggage with them. Gender, race, and other embodied characteristics are more than personal identities; they are structural components imbedded in all interaction. They are the means through which indi-viduals know who they are and who they are communicating with and as such they guide all real-life or computer-mediated communication. Instead of casting them off and becoming free floating entities, in the absence of their bodies people work even harder to substantiate themselves, and reconstruct normative identities in the process.[87]

More holistic sense can be made of this by engaging a sociological analysis that accounts for ideologies, scripts, technologies, and embod-ied gender identities. While new technologies do shape bodies and identities, they do so within a social and historical context. Available scripts and identity paradigms mediate the production of new selves, and even when our bodies are not visible our experiences of them continue to house and provide authenticating resources for these iden-tities. Our ability to use technologies to produce new identities, even when those identities are made available by new social scripts, is always filtered through our own experience. If, for example, our life experi-ences have produced a deep moral investment in the idea that gender is a natural expression of sex, then our awareness and acceptance of new gender scripts will likely be constrained. In contrast, if our biography has encouraged the interrogation of gender, perhaps because of our own gender non-conformity or exposure to people who question binary gender categories, we will likely be more receptive to expanded social scripts. It is still unclear, though, what the long-term effects of online social spaces will be on our real-world gendered bodies and selves. After all of this interrogation, I still wonder how we might create new ways of being that work outside of these normalizing forces.

In her groundbreaking essay about gender online, Jodi O'Brien takes up the question of whether and how online communication will complicate gender dichotomies. She offers a more complex analysis than many early utopian visions, which suggested that the Internet would be a place where physical markers no longer mattered. O'Brien asserts that because the gendered body is the means by which we make sense of social interaction it remains an organizing principle even in its absence. This means that while online communication may allow individuals to categorize their self and others in the absence of physical cues, it is not a space where the self and body cease to be mutually constitutive. Indeed, we do imagine an embodied self even when the body is not physically present.

Earlier in this chapter I discussed research which suggested that online identity work was both constrained by existing gender scripts, and generative of new ones; Jodi O'Brien's theoretical elaboration affords us another approach to make sense of that empirical research. As O'Brien elaborates,

> Even if it is possible for me to conceive and author characters that defy categorization along conventional lines, others cannot engage in meaningful interaction with me ('meaningful' being defined here as mutually comprehensible and generative) unless they too know something about the 'script' through which I am representing myself and/or characterizing the situation.[88]

Because we cannot proceed in interaction until we have been able to categorize the other person in a recognizable way,[89] the ability to 'be anything' online is limited by the ability to fit those new selves into agreed upon social scripts. O'Brien concludes that,

> It is possible to mentally transgender or ungender oneself in one's own imagination. It is possible to enact and negotiate this re/ungendering through interactions with others. And it may be the case that this is easier to accomplish online. But this does not mean that an institutionalized gender binary—and its consequences—will necessarily cease to exist.[90]

Like other scholars I have looked at in this chapter, O'Brien argues that new information technologies have the possibility to be, but are not necessarily, sites of counter-hegemonic identity work.

In the late 1990s, when O'Brien was writing this essay, online transgender communities were just coming together. The cautions she suggests in our approach to online communication are critical for making realistic sense of the radical gender potential—or lack thereof—in computer-mediated communication. That being said, the evolution of online communication over the last ten years suggests that there is a middle ground between utopian visions of a gender-free society, and O'Brien's "state of the 'net'" at the close of the twentieth century.

Recent scholarship demonstrates that these online forums do matter in people's real lives; although there are no guarantees, online community can mediate lack of support in the real world, can provide tools to produce more legible gendered selves, and over time, can change the real-life cultural context within which we all live. What current research suggests is that the cumulative effect of all this may be the alteration and expansion of social gender scripts. Intentional identity work within gender-oriented communities was significant in the lives of the transgender individuals that Daryl Hill and others spoke with, in part because the expectation of individuals in these communities was that gender work was being done. Participants assumed that the gender of online compatriots was being intentionally negotiated and presented in ways that would transcend the online interactions and spill over into embodied lives. In other words, this research suggests that while the Internet is not a utopian site of gender fluidity and play, it is a site where identity work can happen in meaningful ways. It is also a site where societal gender paradigms and scripts can be rewritten; in the case study that follows this chapter I examine how this has taken place for transgender social movements.

My examination of online technologies in this chapter suggests that these forums are sites of new and transformed gender identity scripts, and that these scripts are changing individuals' gender identities. The next question to ask might be, what about gendered bodies? In the next chapter I take a closer look at this question and ask whether new technologies are truly creating new social scripts for gender, and how these are manifesting in and through people's bodies.

CASE STUDY: FOCUS ON TRANSGENDER ORGANIZING

Many scholars and activists have argued that the mass movement online over the last ten years has been particularly meaningful for marginalized populations. There has been, for example, a huge growth in information clearinghouses, support services, and online community development sites within gay, lesbian, bisexual, and transgender communities.[1] The explosion of Internet participation occurred in the late 1990s, and by 2002 an Internet search for 'transgender' pulled up more than 800,000 websites, and over 1,000 listserves, news services and chat rooms. The same search in 2008 culled 12,900,000 websites and 2,766 listserves on Yahoo alone, more than 15 times as many sites in the span of just 6 years; if sites emerged evenly over these 6 years, that would mean more than 200,000 new sites a year. The emergence of a public transsexual presence in North America started with Christine Jorgensen's 1952 public coming out. There has been a dramatic shift in the transgender community from a pathologized transsexual population that existed around support and informational groups to a politicized transgender movement that advocates for treatment changes and lobbies for social protections since then. The past 50 years have seen a dramatic rise in the number of individuals who are coming out as transgender, accessing services, and demanding social recognition and rights.

While transgender people have been present in organizing and activism since the beginning of gay liberation in the 1970s, transgender issues and people have been sidelined in the mainstreaming of the gay and lesbian movement. Recent decades have witnessed the emergence of a vibrant public discourse in mainstream and community media, as well as in transgender conferences and organizations about transgender movements. This discourse can be seen in transgender publications, public debates between the transgender community and the feminist and gay and lesbian movements, and among activists. While state-focused activism is relatively recent (state and national lobbying has emerged as a central tactic only within the past 15 years), there is a collective movement identity firmly entrenched within the community and vibrant and focused activism around issues of social and cultural change through education, media, and legal rights work.

In 2002 I set out to understand how and why transgender activism had grown in the mid 1990s. I thought I would discover a story involving the gay and lesbian movement, changes within medical treatment, and the fruits of 50 years of individuals' isolated activism, advocacy, and transgender writing. What I found, however, was quite different. Included in every answer to my interview question, "what changed in the 1990s to make a national transgender movement possible?" was a clear response that the Internet was central, critical, and transformational. One of the first people I spoke with was Dr. Sandra Cole, a sexologist, 20-year activist, and founder of the University of Michigan Health System Comprehensive Gender Services Program. When I asked her what happened to produce the rise in transgender activism at the end of the twentieth century, she did not hesitate to answer that:

> The strongest impetus of the trans movement happened with the Internet. It's not exclusively responsible because individuals and some small pockets of advocacy in the U.S. already had a few clubs and social gatherings in an effort to help, but that was a very quiet and private, somewhat underground kind of outreach and activity . . . The information available through the Internet, and the publications that have been simultaneously produced, have done an enormous amount to educate transgendered people that they are not alone and isolated, not the only one . . . You can just see the expansion and spreading of information dramatically influencing the social presence of transgendered individuals in our culture.[2]

While it did not occur to me at the beginning of my research, this answer is not surprising; the Internet has become one of the primary ways many of us access new information. In fact, when I began working on this case study, one of the first things I did was to open up *Firefox* on my computer so that I could use web search engines to browse the current goings-on in leading transgender advocacy organizations, read recent academic journal articles and double check some of my facts. While my early academic career was spent in the university library looking through books and print journals, I now do much of that same work from the comfort of my office.

This shift away from text-based knowledge acquisition toward computer-mediated interrogation is one of several aspects of the Internet that has benefited the transgender community. In the view of transgender activists, the use of websites, listserves, and online community spaces has provided a critical mass of information, guidance, and virtual public spaces in which transgender people can connect, share knowledge and social scripts, and assert new gender identities. The Internet has facilitated contact in ways that helped to organize and focus community building, increased the ability to outreach and recruit members, and created an interpersonal community that allows for the sharing of information and experience. Sociological analysis suggests that new technologies work interactively with other social forces to change the social scripts individuals have for gendered identity. They also provide information about bodily interventions (surgery and hormones) to individuals outside of real-world transgender communities, and help to build a social movement focused on changing existing (trans)gender paradigms. Building upon the foundations laid by older support groups, organizations, conferences and publications, the Internet became the central site of transgender organizing and personal and community growth in the late 1990s. This technological innovation has shaped individual transgender bodies and identities as well as societal gender paradigms and scripts.

The Internet was not the start of transgender community support groups, or even activism. A variety of technologies emerged in the second half of the twentieth century that served as catalysts for increased transgender mobilization, although a number of factors inhibited widespread organizing until the mid-1990s. Beginning in the 1960s, transgender support groups existed in connection with the gender clinics that were built up in the wake of public frenzy over Christine Jorgensen's transition from male to female. The demand for transgender and transsexual treatment in North America grew after media coverage of Jorgensen, and the medical community struggled to make sense of and respond to requests for treatment by transsexuals. This led to the development of gender clinics across North America in universities such as Johns Hopkins, the University of Minnesota, Stanford, and UCLA, and at the Clarke Institute of Psychiatry in Toronto, Ontario (now the Center for Addiction and Mental Health) among others.[3] These clinics, while they did bring transgender people together, actually inhibited community development and even the development of interpersonal relationships. The strictly enforced scripts for changing one's sex and/or gender, which included going 'stealth,' i.e. disappearing into 'normal' society and severing ties to any transgender community, worked to prevent community development. Dallas Denny, a long-time transgender activist and founder of one of the oldest transgender information clearinghouses, the American Educational Gender Information Service (AEGIS), elaborated that, "transsexuals weren't in contact with one another under the medical model, because of confidentiality issues. There were few if any transsexual support groups, and there was just one little magazine published by Phoebe Smith out of Atlanta called *The Transsexual Voice*."

After a series of scandals in the late 1970s that were intended to discredit 'sex reassignment surgery' and target 'Gender Identity Disorder' clinics, the whole system of transsexual medical service providers crumbled. Not only was access to medical services shattered, but the social support networks (limited as they were) built up around them were destroyed as well. Over the next 15 years a variety of print magazines, information clearinghouses, and support groups developed to meet the needs of the mostly closeted transgender community in North America. Local transgender support groups provided a space to talk with other transgender people and perhaps to present in one's chosen gender. If only for those individuals lucky enough to live near one, even if it was just once a month, the ability to present oneself as desired in a safe space was invaluable. This was often the only place transgender people were able to fully disclose their identities, however, and other support group members were often their only confederates. These publications, organizations, and support groups also provided access to otherwise unavailable information about transgender surgery, medical, legal, and employment issues. It's hard to imagine what it was like then, at a time when, except for Christine Jorgensen's autobiography and scarce medical texts, there were no books about transgenderism available to the public, no television shows, magazine articles, or websites from which individuals could learn about or even observe gender non-conformity. Before the Internet, the primary sources of information and education were a few periodicals, remote organizations, and local support groups—and often knowledge about the first two rested on involvement with the latter.

With the rise of the Internet, we have seen the work of information, education, and support move from unconnected local groups to the online resource pages of national transgender organizations. While support groups remain an important source of community and identity development, much of the introductory work that had been managed by these real-life organizations is now done online, freeing support groups to focus on personal and community development. Indeed, many online support groups have emerged to complement or even take the place of real-life meetings. The significance of this is incredible, as the Internet has revolutionized the transgender movement in two fundamental ways. First, the Internet has allowed transgender people to connect with one another more easily, especially those who live in geographically isolated places. Second, these new communities have given individuals ways to experiment with defining their gender.

The Internet has given people in rural and isolated situations new access to information, community, and social scripts for transgender lives, and this has shaped individuals' embodied identities. Sadie Crabtree, a union organizer and leading transgender youth activist, explained in our interview that,

> The Internet opens doors for young people, for people in rural areas, and for people who are closeted. It gives them safe ways to connect with others, and even to do activist work . . . People have

been able to communicate with each other for quite a while but while there's mail, that's not a way to find people and you don't just dial a random [telephone] number. I think the Internet has revolutionized the way that people who are privileged enough to own computers and have Internet connections, connect with one another. Transsexual people got organized through the Internet; transgender came into its own because of the Internet.

Because the Internet can render geographical distance irrelevant, does not require simultaneous presence for communication, and is available all hours of the day, it is an invaluable activist resource for support, information distribution, and movement recruitment. A single activist can create a website, listserve, or email list that connects a diverse array of individuals who may be linked to each other solely by an informal and sparse social network, thereby fostering community and networking. Many examples of this type of community organizing exist today, such as the *Remembering Our Dead* website[4] created by Gwendolyn Anne Smith in 1999 in response to the murder of Rita Hester, a transwoman in 1998. The website memorializes the murder of transgender individuals and has led to the development of a real-life activist event, the Transgender Day of Remembrance. Since 2002 more than 80 cities around the world have held Transgender Day of Remembrance events and this type of organizing has contributed to a vibrant online and real-life activist community. Because of the lack of a geographical center for this movement, it would be difficult to orchestrate this type of mass activism without the online site to connect individuals.

As the Day of Remembrance suggests, the Internet assists in community development and networking in particularly salient ways for highly marginalized groups. Because outing oneself online does not carry the same risks, many more people are willing to inquire about and become active in the community and its informational and social networks. Nancy Nangeroni,[5] a longtime transgender activist, was clear about why the Internet was so important.

The Internet allows anonymous communication and so it allows people otherwise closeted to talk about things that they might not, and to talk about them with a stranger. Many cross-dressers fear discovery, they fear they'd lose their families, their jobs, or, at the very least, be socially humiliated. They can set up an email account through Hotmail or someplace like that and have anonymous communication or enter chat rooms.

The Internet, then, can serve to connect people who are still closeted and/or in unsafe situations who often need the most information, education, and support. As Sandra Cole highlighted, this is especially true for youth, who have even fewer resources available to them:

Youth now have grown up with the Internet, they're children of the Internet. So if they had any ideas about themselves or were just snooping around on the Internet they will run into transgender and they are able through all kinds of sources to find some relevance of social definition out there that might apply to them.

Research shows that the ability to access resources in private does not act as motivation to remain closeted, but rather helps individuals who do not have access to a local GLBT community or organization expand their knowledge about issues, meet other GLBT people, and solidify a positive identity.[6] This in turn helps build a support network and sense of community.

However, one must keep in mind that access to the community and support available on the Internet is mitigated by social class and race in North America.[7] It is important to temper utopian notions of the Internet's usefulness. While it is undeniable that the Internet has become a central arena for individual and community development, large segments of the transgender population are not online. This is particularly true for homeless, poor, and non-English speaking transgender individuals; while the technology of the Internet creates a nurturing community for those with access to it, this technology also widens the gap between those with that privilege and those without.

In sum, what emerged in my discussions with activists about transgender organizing is that with the rise of the Internet, access to information, social networks, and organizations developed, which brought the movement for transgender rights to critical mass. Not only has this interconnectivity allowed a highly marginalized community to advocate for change, it has changed the nature of the community itself. While individuals may be isolated physically, there is a vibrant online community that enables transgender individuals to share information and educational materials with each other, organizations to reach a wide variety of people, and allows the movement as a whole to build community. While the Internet is not a panacea, it has facilitated transgender individuals' and the community's growth.

3

NEW BIOMEDICAL TECHNOLOGIES, NEW SCRIPTS, NEW GENDERS

In 1939, soon after graduating from St Anne's College of the University of Oxford, England, Lawrence Michael Dillon became the first transsexual man to undergo physical transition from female to male. Dillon had lived as a masculine woman during college and experienced discrimination for years because of his gender presentation. While Dillon came to a masculine identity during his college years, he had long looked and acted masculine and expressed desires to be a man. Even though Dillon knew himself to be a man, albeit one hidden within a female body, he had no social support and no social scripts with which he could make sense of his situation. He was without any language to talk about gender non-conformity or transgenderism; indeed the word 'transsexual' had yet to be coined, and there was certainly no discussion of any difference between sex and gender. Dillon was unable to find anyone who would either support his gender identity or enable the physical changes he required to live as a man, and he struggled to make sense of these desires.

Michael Dillon's life story stands in stark contrast to the contemporary experiences of many young female-to-male transgender people. A feature article in the *New York Times Magazine* on March 16, 2008, for example, included a profile of Rey, an 18-year-old White female-to-male transgender college student.[1] In this *New York Times Magazine* article Rey reflects on growing up a masculine child, being mistaken for a boy, and coming out as transgender to himself at 14 and to his family at the age of 17.

Rey's story is similar in part to Michael Dillon's; both grew up masculine and developed a gender identity as a boy/man, at a young age. But while Michael Dillon negotiated an identity without a language for gender non-conformity, Rey not only gained language and learned social scripts to describe who he was from other transgender people, he was able to do so at a relatively young age. Specifically, he heard a transgender man speak at a Gay Straight Alliance meeting at his high school and immediately went home and ran a Google Internet search for the word 'transgender.' In another illustration of the online identity work that was discussed in the last chapter, Rey elaborated that, "The Internet is the best thing for trans people . . . Living in the suburbs, online groups were an access point [for me]."[2] Unlike Michael Dillon, who had no access to information about transgenderism, Rey was able to find and use a wide array of information and support resources to validate, define, and negotiate his own masculine identity and female body.

Much like Douglas Schrock, Daphne Holden, and Lori Reid demonstrated in their research on online transgender support groups (which I discussed in Chapter 2), the ability to communicate with other transgender individuals, learn about treatments for transsexualism, and engage with others as a boy online, all helped Rey redefine his identity. Advances in communication helped Rey understand and define his gender identity, while developments in medical technology, which will be dealt with in this chapter, allowed Rey to reshape his body to reflect his gendered identity. Whether and how new social scripts emerge in response to technological innovations in fields dealing with human anatomy can be illuminated by examining how individuals use biomedical means to know and construct their bodies. In the last chapter I examined how information technologies have produced new gendered identities and social scripts. I found that information technologies have facilitated identity work and that this identity work sparks changes in the lives and bodies of individuals. In order to fully understand how new technologies are changing individuals, it is also necessary to look at how biomedical technologies are being employed in a similar manner to shape gendered bodies in new and transformative ways. Here, I look at how technology is directly shaping bodies, and how this is relevant to the lives of individuals. If new information technologies are facilitating identity work, then new biomedical technologies are enabling—or sometimes inhibiting—individuals' embodiment of these new identities. Simultaneously new identity repertoires are emerging in response to these biomedically facilitated body changes.

New Body Technologies

Notwithstanding issues of transgenderism, the ability for and acceptability of body modification has also changed, as demonstrated by the rise and social acceptance of bodily transformation practices such as plastic surgery, use of pharmaceuticals, weightlifting, tattooing, shaving, and hair dyeing. More so now than ever before, it is common practice for individuals to produce and refine their gendered bodies in ways that both reinforce and contest normative social scripts for women's and men's bodies.

The approach taken in this book, and one that is increasingly used within studies of the body, is to make sense of the body as something that is in dynamic relationship to both society and personal identity.[3] Individuals are always acting in and through their body, and always within a social and cultural context. Bodily change can be the product of a variety of factors including chance (for instance, an accident might cause changes in one's mobility), social structures (for example, the military), and intentional manipulation (such as weightlifting or cosmetic surgery).

While body work is transformative and often purposeful on the part of individuals, these changes, whether by chance, social structure, or agency of the individual, are always already shaped by social norms and historical context.[4] When an individual chooses to get a tattoo, for example, they may do so for any of a variety of reasons including an effort to adorn their body, mark a significant event, or signal participation in a community or identity category. But this agentic choice is informed by and given meaning through gendered societal beliefs about tattoos and their significance, body and beauty scripts, and the dominant societal paradigms. Approaching the body from the perspective of being something both shaped by and actively shaping identity as well as society allows a better understanding of how new technologies are dynamically engaged with gendered bodies.

In this chapter I examine a number of case studies to make sense of how gendered bodies and identities both inform and respond to these new biomedical technologies. Using a sociological approach to map the intricate, multiple connections between embodied identities, technologies, and social gender paradigms, I examine how the ability to construct new bodies is changing who people think they are and can be.

By looking at the exponential growth of weight-loss surgeries in recent years, the relationship between beauty norms and plastic surgery, and transgender identities and sex reassignment surgeries I also explore the complex implications of these interventions. Once again we will see that while technologies themselves are impartial, neither liberating nor regressive, they are developed along lines and deployed in ways that produce both socially normative bodies and counter hegemonic ones. It is possible to map these changes to better understand whether and how new identities and bodies take shape alongside new technologies.

Somatechnics: Technologies and the Body

Biomedical technology has become the medium through which we know and intervene into our bodies, and genetic testing, body scans, surgery, and medication are just a few examples. A term that emerged in the 1970s to reflect the increasingly technological approaches to biology and medicine, 'biotechnology' brings engineering and technological theories in disciplines including agriculture, medicine, genetics, and physiology to bear on natural systems. In other words, biotechnology refers to any intentional manipulation of organic processes/organisms. The oldest forms of biotechnology—seed saving, pest management, and crop cultivation—mark the actual development of

BIOTECHNOLOGY

The United Nations defines biotechnology as "any technological application that uses biological systems, living organisms, or derivatives thereof, to make or modify products of processes for specific use."[5]

agriculture, while early experiments into immunization have been traced back to 200 B.C.E. Both technologically-informed farming and primitive medical efforts have shaped societies and individuals for thousands of years.[6] These interventions have taken on new significance in the last three decades, however, with the exponential growth of biological technologies and the advent of patents for living organisms, which turned biotechnology into a profit-making enterprise.[7]

Of particular relevance to this discussion is biomedical technology, or technologies that are directed at maintaining and/or transforming the human body. This includes genetic testing and manipulation, pharmacology, surgery including microsurgery, imaging, cloning, synthetic drugs, hormones and vaccines, prosthetics, and implants, to name a few. Moving beyond discovery for its own sake as a motivation for scientific research, the profitability of biotechnology has led to the development of numerous attendant industries centered on body work. Rates of plastic surgery, 'lifestyle drug' use, genetic engineering, and 'medi-spa' treatments have increased dramatically over the last 20 years. The hugely profitable biotechnological industry in the United States generated 58.8 billion U.S. dollars in health care revenue in 2006 alone.[8] In Canada biotechnology firms generated 4.2 billion Canadian dollars of revenue in 2005.[9]

This exponential growth in the techniques of biomedical intervention and their acceptance also signals a source of social change for institutions and individuals. Most research has failed to bridge the gap between social sciences and the natural sciences, however, to the detriment of both disciplines. Feminist scholars, as one example, have failed to interrogate the 'realness' of anatomical differences, even though the construction of clear binary sexes is a social and societal endeavor. In the past, sociology has taken biology for granted, and ignored how the meaning and significance of bodies and biology are social constructs.[10] By taking the body and bodily functions for granted, scholars have reified these concepts and turned something socially constructed into something that appears natural and inevitable.[11]

Let us take, for example, the general concept of 'illness.' While we think of illness as a straightforward matter of biology, it is deeply social; rates of sickness and death are strongly correlated to social class and gender. Working-class men and women are at much higher risk of illness than their middle-class compatriots are,[12] and women are more likely to be disabled by seemingly ungendered illnesses such as arthritis and strokes, than men are.[13] Moreover, social class and rates of diagnosis and treatment are positively correlated; as income increases, rates of diagnosis and treatment also increase. Similarly, race is highly correlated to health outcomes wherein people of color are less likely to be diagnosed with or recover from serious illnesses like cancer.[14] These findings highlight how gender, race and class paradigms, and social scripts for sickness all intersect with how bodies are understood, diagnosed, and treated.

What Is a Social Body?

The body is always *both* an individual product and an entity shaped by its social and physical context. This sociological approach views bodies as sites within which individuals can actively meet their own needs and affect change in their environment. This occurs within a particular social context shaped by dominant paradigms and using existing and shifting social scripts.

Over the past ten years social scientists have turned renewed attention to the relationship between human biology and theories of individual and societal identity. This has greatly increased scholars' understanding of the social body. Spurred on by recent changes in scientific technologies, scholars in a variety of disciplines have begun to refocus their inquiry on the body as a social construction to fill in serious gaps in scholarship. Many theorists have questioned the shifting meaning of the body in light of biomedical developments such as face transplants, stem-cell research, and in-vitro fertilization, all of which allow heretofore impossible manipulation of the body.[15] Feminist scholars in particular have paid new attention to how these affect gendered bodies and identities on the individual and societal level.[16] Although bodily manipulation has a long history, new scholarship suggests that the nature and pervasiveness of contemporary interventions have called into question core social beliefs about the body as unique, natural, and fixed.[17] The emergence and profitability of bio-technology, then, is altering the bodily landscape on individual and socio-cultural levels.

Recently, some scholars have used the term *somatechnics* to describe human-body focused technologies and to distinguish them from agricultural and/or animal-focused biotechnologies.

SOMATECHNICS

Technologies of the body. More specifically, an understanding that the body and technology are always and already interrelated and mutually constitutive. Technologies shape how we know, understand, and shape the body, and the body is always a product of historically and culturally specific transformative practices.

The word 'somatechnics' draws together the Greek words 'soma' meaning 'body' and 'techne' which we know from the definition of technology to mean 'craft;' it is used in an effort to express that the body is always known and shaped through the technologies of a particular society. Nikki Sullivan, one of the pioneers of this concept, has focused on body modification like tattooing to make sense of how body technologies are both shaped by and an intentional engagement with social scripts for gendered bodies.[18] Others have done work in a similar vein, including Susan Stryker, who has explored the social and technological history of transsexualism, and Samantha Murray, whose work focuses on fatness and the emergence of bariatric surgery.[19] Research by each of these scholars demonstrates that modern embodied identities are always already in dynamic relationship to technologies, and more specifically that technologies are used to construct, maintain, and transform gendered bodies and identities.

For example, in her study of women's body work Debra Gimlin found that women saw their bodies as reflections of their inner characters. Women believed that an imperfect body bespoke an imperfect self.[20] The women Gimlin interviewed turned to a variety of bodily manipulations including hairstyling, plastic surgery, and exercise to address the gendered body and character flaws they identified. Similarly, clothing can be selected to display class, personality, sexuality, and oppositional consciousness as documented by Dick Hebdige in his groundbreaking research on punk sub-cultural aesthetics.[21] What these scholars find is that a great deal of body modification such as plastic surgery, diets, hairstyles, and exercise regimens are efforts by people to change their body structure to reflect a current or desired inner identity. Individuals often assert that bodily flaws are mismatched with their true identities and mask "the people they truly are."[22] Simultaneously research on body modification has demonstrated how changes in the body spark identity shifts for individuals. Bodily manipulation, then, can be an effort to create alignment (or justify misalignment) between appearance and character, between identity and body.

Somatechnics and Social Norms

One very timely example of the dynamic relationship between somatechnics and social norms is bariatric (i.e. weight loss) surgery. With weight loss surgery, individuals—mostly women—are using biomedical technologies to reshape their bodies in dramatically increasing numbers.[23] Many individuals benefit from this surgery, which can reduce health problems, raise self-esteem, and facilitate alignment between body and identity. Like the other cases I have introduced, the phenomenon begs more critical analysis, however.

Even though versions of the surgery have been used for more than 50 years, widespread access to this biomedical technology was limited.[24] During the 11-year period from 1995–2006 bariatric surgery rates skyrocketed by 800 percent; estimates suggest that in 2008 more than

200,000 surgeries were performed in the United States alone.[25] What makes bariatric surgery such an interesting case study is that the highly contentious debates about the surgery engage directly with contemporary body and gender paradigms and social scripts. These debates take place within both medical circles and larger society as they manifest in and through the bodies and identities of individuals. Dominant body paradigms posit the idea that fat bodies are inherently unhealthy, undesirable, and a sign of internal character failings, which legitimates biomedical intervention.[26]

Societal body norms have a direct effect on what individuals do to reshape their bodies. Both men and women are pressured to change their bodies, and are stigmatized if they do not conform to these demands. Although the scientific research and development of weight loss technologies may be seen as unbiased, the emphasis on that objective revolves around contemporary body and gender paradigms. These societal forces are joined with contemporary advances in medical technology to form the foundation of a phenomenally profitable weight-loss industry—just think of how many diet and body shaping products you can name—and that industry puts even more pressure on individuals to conform to physical ideals.

The debate playing out around bariatric surgery is over the nature of the body. Dominant paradigms view thinness as natural and achievable through discipline and in turn discount the need for surgery. Slowly challenging this (aided by bariatric surgery, weight loss drugs like Alii, and the hunt for a 'fat gene') is a paradigm that views fatness as disease and therefore a malady worthy of medical intervention and treatment.[27] Finally, the recent emergence of fat-positive activism has challenged social paradigms regarding body size.[28] Groups like the National Association to Advance Fat Acceptance (NAAFA) take issue with dominant medical and social paradigms that link health to thinness and fat to disease. These organizations point toward historical and cultural variation in body size scripts,[29] and stress that research reveals a wide range of differences in health and body size; not all large bodies are unhealthy and not all thin bodies are healthy. For many individuals whose bodies do not conform to normative body scripts, the presence of a counter-hegemonic paradigm reinforces their own positive social body and identity scripts. In other words, the debate about 'normal' bodies is in fact a debate over the dominant body paradigm, and it is taking place in part through debates about biomedical 'treatments' for obesity. This new technology of bariatric surgery is reshaping individual bodies and identities while the application of the technology is simultaneously responding to and reshaping societal body paradigms (paradigms such as what constitutes a healthy body) and social scripts for 'normal' embodied identities.

A number of social scientists have studied this emerging soma-technical phenomenon and found that weight loss surgery is altering individual gendered identities and bodies.[30] For example, as Patricia Drew documents in her research, part of how bariatric advocates have tried to legitimize this new biomedical intervention has been to first create scripts for the ideal patient that draw on and reinforce hege-monic body paradigms and then require the adoption of these scripts in order to access bariatric surgery. This gate-keeping requires that indi-viduals adopt (or, at the very least, pretend to adopt) particular physio-logical, behavioral, and attitude scripts (much like transsexual scripts to access 'sex-reassignment surgery'). This ideal patient script is shaped by the controversial history of the technology, a history in which early versions led to high rates of complication and death. It is, in turn, reshaping dominant body paradigms and scripts, offering a fine example of how technological development can interact with social scripts and bodies. Paradigm shifts in the perception of fatness as a disease can both be shaped by the increase in bariatric surgery, and, simultaneously, further legitimize the biomedical intervention. Similarly, the dominant belief that the internal self is reflected in the body compels individuals to change their body to match their internal identity, and simultaneously reinforces body scripts that devalue fat bodies (often decreasing people's estimation of the worth of their own inner selves). These dynamics are also gendered; fat male bodies are viewed as feminized while fat female bodies are de-feminized, particu-larly in terms of sexuality. Body scripts shape the identities and bodies of individuals by demanding particular gendered scripts and body practices from individuals, as in turn the bodies and identities present in a context reinforce or challenge existing social scripts.

In her study, Patricia Drew found that the very public medical debates about weight loss surgery shaped the ways one could be an acceptable patient by constructing ideal patient scripts, while these same scripts shaped individuals in significant ways. Drew's interviews with patients revealed that most individuals incorporated into their own story the key narrative elements of the dominant script, elements such as viewing themselves as empowered through the use of weight loss surgery, and as responsible for their body. At the same time, those whose narrative did not contain the key elements of the acceptable script still used it strategically to access surgery.[31] What Drew concludes is that these ideal patient scripts, or discourses-in-practice, learned in part through mandatory support group meetings, which afforded discursive practice, helped individuals negotiate between larger social body paradigms and individual identity. Most patients adopted the ideal patient scripts in part or full, and in the process, hegemonic body paradigms. Concomitantly, the social scripts rooted in those ideologies shaped the bodies and identities of participants.

In addition to this clear example of how technologies are in dynamic relationship to social scripts, ideologies, bodies and identities, bariatric surgery is a compelling case study for another reason: it is deeply gendered. According to the U.S. Centers for Disease Control, while women make up 59 percent of the obese population they account for 85 percent of weight loss surgery patients.[32] If surgery was simply the product of obesity, then men and women would be accessing surgery at rates equal to the ratio of obesity in the general population, that is, statistically only 59 percent of patients should be women. These numbers suggest that people use this new technology of weight loss surgery based on gendered ideologies and gendered social scripts for ideal patients. Thus the technology is gendered and it produces gendered outcomes and societal changes.

Patricia Drew concludes that weight loss surgery is deeply gendered because of four intersecting gendered paradigms and scripts. First, as many scholars have documented, North American societies' gendered body and beauty paradigms place higher demands on women, and place more stringent sanctions on them for deviating from normative beauty standards.[33] Women are expected to go to greater lengths and exercise more discipline upon themselves and their bodies than men are.[34] Second, as Nelly Oudshoorn argued with regard to birth control, part of why women are held more accountable is that when the male body is held as a normal baseline, the female body is resultantly seen as more in need of intercession, and as a more legitimate target for biomedical intervention. Women are more likely to seek any medical care, which is, in itself, a product of gendered body and health paradigms, and this holds true for weight loss surgery. Third, weight loss surgery requires participation in support groups, groups that our society views as largely the domain of women.[35] Finally, these gendered dynamics shape the social scripts disseminated by medical and media sources about weight loss surgery. In her analysis of hundreds of brochures, advertisements, and websites about weight loss surgery, Drew found that publicity materials pictured women much more often than men. For example, in 21 issues of *Obesity Help*, with a total of 80 advertisements, only nine of the ads featured men as patients.[36] Patricia Drew concludes that not only do dominant ideologies shape the ideal patient scripts, but they also shape whether and how individuals use the new technologies. This, in turn, inspires change in both men's and women's bodies and identities, and reinforces the ideologies and scripts that produced these bodies and identities in the first place. These dynamically intertwined relationships are just one example of how individuals both reinforce and contest paradigms and scripts for femininity and masculinity as they use somatic technologies.

Technology and Body Work

In summary, somatechnics refer to the variety of new biomedical technologies that are allowing individuals to shape how their body looks and works in increasingly diverse ways. It is now possible to alter the look of one's body through myriad technologies, just a few of which are plastic surgery, steroids, growth hormones, hair dye, permanent makeup, hair transplants, sub-cultural body modification practices like

BODY WORK

The intentional manipulation of the body by an individual. This can include surface manipulation like spa treatments, makeup, hairstyling, and dress, as well as more substantial interventions like surgery, diet, and exercise. The term has also been used to refer to the manipulation of an individual's body for pay, or the effect of work on the body.

tattoos and scarification, laser hair removal, machine-enhanced exercise regimens, and spa treatments.

For individuals who want and have the means to engage in this transformative work, the ability to embody new identities, in order to either manifest what was previously consigned to one's existing inner selfhood or produce a body that matches a sought after inner identity, is increasingly possible. This holds true for both normative and non-normative bodily changes; individuals can become more masculine men (for example through steroid use or testosterone shots), more feminine women (through breast augmentation and laser hair removal, as examples), as well as transverse gender norms to become more feminine men, masculine women, or more androgynous male, female, or transgender individuals. All of this work is *body work*. 'Body work' refers to both the intentional nature of interventions into the body and to the technological and personal labor involved in those transformations.

For many scholars body work is tied to acknowledgement that societal power relations governing gender, social class, race, religion, and sexuality manifest in and through the body.[37] This means that whether and how individuals engage in body work is shaped by social pressures, norms, and expectations specific to their location and within the social matrices of power and privilege of their community. Moreover, individuals engage in body work as part of the dynamic relationship between body and identity, as both an impetus for and response to identity change. And they do so within biographical and societal contexts, using the technologies available to them. It is impossible to examine body work without situating it within a social context, informed by social paradigms and scripts. Most significant, perhaps, are the ways in which body work is deeply gendered and racialized in North America.

Gendered Selves, Gendered Bodies

Anne Balsamo published a groundbreaking book in 1996, *Technologies of the Gendered Body*, which explored how body technologies in the late twentieth century were shaped by, and in turn reproduced, dominant gender paradigms and inequalities.[38] Examining primarily media and cultural products, she analyzed technological interventions into the body, and concluded that these technologies are "ideologically shaped by the operation of gender interests, and consequently . . . serve to reinforce traditional gendered patterns of power and authority."[39]

In other words, what Balsamo is saying is that body technologies are developed and used in tandem with hegemonic gender paradigms to reproduce gender inequality and maintain the status quo. Later work has taken both a more empirical approach to studying gendered technologies by relying more on examination of individuals' lived experiences rather than on textual analysis, and a more liberatory view of technological intervention. However, Balsamo's scholarship captures the central connection between gender ideologies and scripts and somatechnics that I have been examining. In her analysis of body technologies and gender, she asserts that technologies shape and are shaped by dominant gender paradigms and that these together reshape gendered bodies and identities.

How Are Biomedical Technologies Shaping Gendered and Raced Bodies?

When scholars speak about biomedical technologies and gender, they are referring to a wide range of bodily interventions that are a subset of the range of biomedical technologies we discussed earlier. Gendered technologies include hormone manipulation (estrogen and testosterone for both men and women, birth control pills, hormone blockers, synthetic thyroid medications, steroids, etc.), non-surgical body modification (tattoos, hair dye, weight lifting, dieting, piercing, dress, etc.), and surgical body modification (plastic surgery, weight-loss surgery, sex-reassignment surgery, breast augmentation, etc.). These technologies can be used, as I explore below, in both liberating and regressive ways. In all of the cases that follow, many individuals benefit from biomedical technologies like plastic and bariatric surgery. My intent here is not to argue these technologies are good or bad, but to bring complexity to their analysis.

While both men and women are using gendered technologies to shape their bodies in a variety of ways, these changes are neither evenly distributed among men and women, nor gender neutral in their consequences. By way of illustrating this uneven distribution, consider the example of gender distribution among plastic surgery recipients. According to 2008 data from the American Society of Plastic Surgeons,[40] almost 11 million cosmetic procedures in the United States were performed on women, compared to 1.1 million procedures on men. This amounts to women comprising a staggering 91 percent of all plastic surgery cases. While the rates of invasive cosmetic procedures like liposuction have held relatively stable over the last few years, the rise in minimally invasive procedures such as Botox injection has been astronomical. This increase marks not only a remarkable increase in the overall number of cosmetic procedures, but also a significant statistical increase of women as recipients in proportion to men. In 2000, women comprised 86 percent of all procedures, but between 2000 and 2008 there was a 72 percent increase in procedures for women whereas there was only a 9 percent increase in rates for men.[41]

Examining this demographic data alongside ethnographic accounts of plastic surgery use, it is evident that plastic surgery is being used to construct explicitly gendered bodies and identities. These are products of social scripts, gender paradigms, and available technologies, and are often hyper-normative. For example, the most common surgical cosmetic procedures for women are breast augmentation and liposuction, both of which are invasive methods to produce hyper-normative femininity: thinness, and large breasted-ness. This gendered aspect is not lost on patients; in her interviews with women patients, Debra Gimlin found that plastic surgery was a deeply gendered endeavor deployed by women to "make do" within a sexist and beauty-obsessed culture.[42] In the personal narratives Gimlin collected, she found that the body work women engaged in was a conscious part of negotiating a gendered identity within the constraints of gender, class, and race norms.

The ability to produce socially valued bodies, bodies that possess the ideal skin color, facial features, and so forth, rests not only in the production of normative gender, but also requires race- and class-based privileges. Indeed, women of color in North America face unattainable expectations because social scripts include very racialized ideal beauty norms. As societies, North America prizes White features, and this list of prized features is limited to characteristics natural only in some White phenotypes. Similarly, body size is intertwined with social class; a well toned body is often a mark of wealth since cheap food is more fattening and promotes poor health, and the time and means to exercise is often a class-based privilege. When women use plastic surgery they are constructing a racialized, gendered, and classed body and they often do so in line with a narrow ideal characterized by features such as blond flowing hair, a thin nose, almond-shaped eyes, large breasts, a small waist, and broad hips. And as Balsamo pointed out, just as gender inequality affects somatechnics, racism affects the technologies that are developed and used.

Women of color are increasingly turning to cosmetic surgery; in 2008 White men and women made up 73 percent of patients, which was a significant decrease from 2000 when 86 percent of patients were White. In fact, while cosmetic procedures decreased 2 percent for White people in 2008, they increased 11 percent for men and women of color. Looking at trends over the last eight years, in the United States between 2000 and 2008 there was a 161 percent increase in cosmetic procedures among African-Americans, 227 percent among Hispanics, and 281 percent for Asian Americans compared to an increase of 63 percent among White individuals. Moreover, the most common cosmetic surgery procedures for people of color are nose reshaping, eyelid surgery, and breast augmentation, which are all procedures that alter racialized facial and body features to better match White norms.[43]

The racial disparities in the statistics among cosmetic procedures suggest a trend by women of color toward using these technologies to mediate radicalized gender beauty norms. In this process, these women reaffirm the hegemony of White body and beauty paradigms. Eugenia Kaw's 1991 study of plastic surgery and race in San Francisco is a strong example of these processes. Kaw interviewed Asian American women, asking questions about why they used plastic surgery and what it meant to them. In these interviews women described plastic surgery as a way to better meet societal beauty scripts. In her interviews it was also clear that, like Gimlin found in her study of mostly White women, these Asian American women were conscious about what they were doing and how it mattered. For example, 'Jane' commented,

> Especially if you go into business, whatever, you kind of have to have a Western facial type and you have to have like their features and stature—you know, be tall and stuff. In a way you can see it is an investment in your future.[44]

While the women Kaw spoke with were all vocal about their pride at being Asian, they also understood, as 'Jane' summarized, that White features were viewed more positively in society. The plastic surgeons that Kaw interviewed expressed very similar views, while also revealing how racialized gender scripts not only shape individuals, but whether and how technologies may be used. For instance, Kaw notes that doctors couched their racialized cosmetic procedures as efforts to help women achieve a look that is 'naturally' more beautiful, implying that White features are objectively more attractive. For example, one doctor stated that, "90 percent of people look better with double eyelids. It makes the eye look more spiritually alive."[45] Through these and other compelling examples Kaw builds a substantial analysis of how plastic surgery is being used to produce particular raced and gendered bodies concurrently.

Based on these interviews, Kaw suggests that social and ideological changes have coincided with the increased acceptance of plastic surgery in recent years to encourage surgical body work among Asian women and that this body work, in turn, constrains available scripts for femininity by erasing racialized differences among women's bodies. What Kaw concluded was that plastic surgery is, "a means by which the women can attempt to permanently acquire not only a feminine look considered more attractive by society, but also a certain set of racial features considered more prestigious."[46] In other words, experiences of body work were gendered and racialized in such a way that while plastic surgery was simultaneously liberating on the individual level, it was detrimental on the societal level as social scripts for normatively gendered bodies became even more ethnocentric.

Hegemonic Race and Gender Norms Are Reproduced Through Body Work

Across the board women's bodies are more subject to body work than men's are. This does not come as a surprise given the scholarship of researchers like Nelly Oudshoorn, who uses birth control trends to document how women's bodies are medicalized at higher rates (recall Chapter 1).[47] This fact does, however, raise serious questions about whether and how we as a society are producing increasingly normative gendered bodies in the process, and more specifically increasingly rigid racialized femininities. Many cultural critics have argued that new media technologies are creating unrealistic ideals for bodies and that these unattainable body scripts affect women disproportionately.[48]

Although photographic images are still commonly viewed as factual evidence, recent technological advancements in print and film now allow imperceptible alterations to these images. Because of the ability to alter media images to create features like smaller pores, bigger eyes, thinner legs, larger breasts, and more defined muscles, published and broadcast representations of idealized beauty are themselves fictions. Recent resistance to this manipulation on the part of some actresses has made public how even thin and normatively beautiful actresses are subject to body-editing. For example, Keira Knightley, whose breasts were digitally enhanced in publicity for the 2004 movie *King Arthur*, refused similar manipulation for the 2008 movie *The Duchess*, and the ensuing tension between the actress and the movie studio was played out in the media. Kate Winslet publicly critiqued the manipulated images of her legs in *GQ* magazine in 2003, an edit she was not consulted about.[49] These and similar examples point to how no bodies—not even famous ones prized for their sex-appeal—meet the ideal without somatechnic manipulation.[50]

Although beauty scripts place a greater burden on women to meet bodily expectations, men are also subject to gendered scripts that suggest the need to technologically enhance their masculinity. Recent revelations about the seemingly omnipresent use of steroids by male athletes are signs of scripts that declare that men's bodies are inadequate in their un-enhanced state. The use of steroids in U.S. Major League Baseball has become so expected that revelations of use do little to damage the careers of players like Alex "A-Rod" Rodriguez and Barry Bonds. The investigatory "Mitchell Report," submitted to the Commissioner of Major League Baseball, quotes National League Most Valuable Player Ken Caminiti as stating in 1992 that in his estimate, "at least half" of Major League players were using anabolic steroids.[51] This widespread use of steroids and the subsequent bodily changes in baseball players have shifted body scripts for athletes so much that un-enhanced bodies stand little chance of competing.

Similarly, the increasing attention paid to men's bodies and the rising rates of eating disorders among boys suggest that boys and men are increasingly subject to gendered body pressures. Television shows like "Queer Eye for the Straight Guy" and men's magazines such as *GQ* all capitalize on the rise of the 'metrosexual,' a masculinity rooted in high levels of body work. This body work encompasses not only pursuits of traditional male attributes by means such as working out and sculpting efforts, but also includes practices formerly confined to the pursuit of feminine ideals, such as shaving, waxing, dyeing, plucking, and renewed attention to clothing.[52]

These revelations taken together suggest the impossibility of constructing a body that meets the social ideal—because the ideal itself does not exist in reality. Computer manipulation of bodies in the media of print and film creates unreachable scripts for gendered bodies for both men and women, and these scripts have real consequences in the lives of individuals. Dominant beauty paradigms and body scripts, hand-in-hand with biomedical somatechnologies, are reshaping the human body. The combination of new media and body technologies is changing social body scripts and these together are impacting the gendered bodies and identities of individuals.

Recent scholarship by Jennifer Wesely offers a rich example of how individuals are intentionally using biomedical technologies to construct hegemonically gendered and raced bodies. Wesely interviewed 20 women in the southwest of the United States to examine how women working in a strip club used body technologies to construct profitable bodies, and to negotiate multiple identities: for example to demarcate their true self as separate from their stripper self. What she found was that the women engaged in a wide variety of often dangerous and painful technologies like drug use, plastic surgery, waxing, and diuretics in order to produce the idealized femininity they felt was expected of them. Moreover, this gendered body work became a central focus of their lives. Wesely found that, "As dancers, these women relied on their bodies in ways that necessitated their constant critique, attention, and maintenance, leading to more body technologies."[53] The pervasive use of these body technologies erased differences in bodies through implants, hair dye, tanning, and dieting, and reinforced hegemonic beauty scripts such that the ideal to which the women held themselves accountable was one which is now biomedically constructed. Samantha Kwan and Mary Nell Trautner summarize this process as it functions in society at large and conclude that, "Women's effortless authentic beauty is thus far from it. Beauty work is in large part this process of transforming the natural body to fit the cultural ideal, altogether while concealing the process and making it seem natural."[54] In the case of Wesely's study, the intentionally constructed nature of gendered bodies was rendered invisible and assumed to be natural because body work was ubiquitous at the strip club, and produced bodies that aligned with idealized femininities.

One particularly insightful part of Wesely's research is her investigation of how these bodily changes function in conversation with the multiple layers of identity that the dancers (and everyone else) construct and employ through body technologies. Wesely found that the dancers' bodies and identities were in dynamic relationship to one another. What is key here is the complexity by which this happens. First of all, these women are not dupes; they are intentionally crafting their bodies because it makes dancing more profitable. By the same token, however, these choices, which make sense within the world of strip clubs, set these women apart from mainstream society. The choices the strippers make about body work are shaped and constrained by their context. Further, their choices have meaning and import beyond the personal level; the more the women shape their bodies to match an unrealistic feminine ideal, the more masked the constructed nature of femininity becomes, and the more normative, or, rather, hyper-normative the feminine body and identity scripts supported at the clubs become. The technologically enhanced bodies that the women who work at the strip club construct, shaped in line with the particular norms within that narrow context, are more feminine, more sexual, and more gendered than our broader society's normative scripts demand.

Through her ethnographic research, Wesely is able to document how the women experienced identity changes as the product of these technological interventions. The more technologies the women used to produce ideal bodies, the more wedded they became to their 'stripper' identities. Even though the women often wanted to separate their 'true identity' from their 'dancer identity,' body technologies such as breast enhancement, genital piercing, and hair dyeing would not allow them to leave the dancer-life behind. As one dancer commented, "In real life, when we're dressing in clothes . . . if you've got huge tits you look awful during the day. They look good only in a G-string in a strip club."[55] In other words, some body technologies used by the women met beauty scripts only in the strip club, but the women had to 'wear' them all the time, which limited their ability to cast off a 'stripper identity' at the end of the day. Simultaneously, Wesely found that the women engaged in other technological interventions in an effort to cordon off their 'true' identities from their 'stripper' identities (for example through different clothing, by shaving, and through drug use).

Along with altering their bodies, then, the women tried to walk the line between producing a marketable body and maintaining a body that was a meaningful reflection of their internal sense of self.[56] The women made choices about their bodies, but did so within a context that limited their options and as a result often were unable to embody their 'inner selves.' As Wesely concludes:

> Although body technologies have the potential to destabilize or challenge constructions of gendered bodies and related identity, this is even more difficult in a context that capitalizes on very limited constructions of the fantasy feminine body. Indeed, the women in the study felt tremendous pressure to conform to body constructions that revolve around extreme thinness, large breasts, and other features that conform to a "Barbie doll" image.[57]

The consequences of these choices, as Wesely suggests, are significant. A number of scholars have documented how women who embody hege-monic femininity earn more money for stripping, and the women Wesely talked with acknowledged that normative gender scripts alongside finan-cial, peer, and managerial pressure, directly informed the changes they made in their bodies.[58]

On the personal level, this body work affects the identities of the women. They engage in body work that is encouraged within the context of their occupation, and which is aimed at producing feminini-ties in line with the dominant gender paradigms of the strip club. In due course, this body work, in tandem with each individual's personal biog-raphy, shapes their identity. On an institutional level, the outcome of the biomedical construction of hyper-normative femininities by the women was an erasure of difference. By producing a very narrow set of femi-ninities in line with hegemonic paradigms and gendered body scripts, the women naturalized a feminine body that was virtually unattainable without the use of body technologies, and in this process they erased the very real differences that had existed between each of their bodies. Predictably, the somatechnical changes the women manifested were not only gendered, but also raced; the women of color at the clubs Wesely studied spoke about how they had to look *more* sexy, and produce a *more* ideal femininity than White women to be seen as acceptable by both management and customers. These findings are in line with what Eugenia Kaw found in her study of Asian American women. A consequence of this body work, then, was the reproduction of racist beauty norms, and the re-entrenchment of phenotypically White bodies as the only ideal body type.

How Does a Sociological Perspective Illuminate the Meaning of Body Work?

The ways that individuals intervene into their own bodies—the technologies that are developed and used in a society—are shaped by dominant paradigms and social scripts within a social context and filtered through personal history. For example, whether and how people manipulate their bodies using biomedical technology is different in distinct communities of a single nation, not to mention in different countries. These differences are based on different social scripts, paradigms of gender and embodiment, identities, and available technologies within a particular micro (strip club) or macro (North American societies) context.

While plastic surgery may be the dominant way to construct larger breasts within middle and upper class communities in North America, individuals without the same social and economic capital are more likely to use prosthetics, growth stimulants, or even the very dangerous injection of liquid silicone into breast tissue.[59] Similarly, men in different race, class, and sexual communities engage a diverse array of somatechnics to manage hair loss. Some, particularly middle or upper class men, use hair transplants (now the fifth most common cosmetic surgery procedure for men), while other men use less expensive over-the-counter hair-growth stimulants, such as the U.S. brand 'Rogaine,' wigs, toupees, or hairstyling techniques. Not only do rates of baldness vary by race, but also the forms of treatment utilized vary across race, class, and community.

Biomedical technologies are in dynamic relationship to gender paradigms, scripts, bodies, and identities. What the case studies examined in this chapter suggest is that individuals deploy contemporary biotechnologies in order to shape both their physical self and their internal identity but that these endeavors are always and already informed and constrained by context, as well as guided by reigning gender and race paradigms and scripts. Analysis must mediate between viewing new technologies as tools for personal agency (such as when plastic surgery makes women feel more feminine), and the larger social implications of biomedical intervention (such as shifting norms for men's body size in light of steroid use).

It is no surprise that all of us engage in body work of various types daily, and that we do so for personal and societal benefit. The case studies in this chapter share the same dynamics as the more mundane body work that most individuals engage in every day. We do it because it matters. Large amounts of research have been done on body work, affirming that meeting or approximating hegemonic gender scripts leads to positive outcomes in individual lives, including increased work prestige, increased social status, higher income, and higher self-esteem.[60] More specifically, overweight people tend to earn less and garner less occupational prestige than thin people, and this dynamic is gendered in that the consequences are more severe for fat women than for fat men, who experience discrimination to a lesser degree.[61]

In another example, laser hair-removal treatments offer women a semi-permanent method of body work that, on a personal level, increases their ability to meet feminine beauty standards. However, on a societal level, this use of laser hair removal reshapes women's bodies in ways that reinforce and make 'natural' contemporary gendered beauty scripts that define women's bodies as unmarred by body hair—which in turn will place a stronger demand on women to conform to this ideal. Similarly, new biomedical techniques like injecting steroids or testosterone to boost muscle mass or hair transplants to reverse balding increase men's embodied masculinity as ways to help men meet hegemonic masculine norms. These interventions play a central role in reifying hyper-masculine bodies and naturalizing unattainable scripts, which may prove even more significant at a historical moment when men are increasingly subject to beauty and body norms.

It is important to remember, however, that while each technology may have the possibility of reifying gender scripts, it can also open up potential for new gendered bodies. Females can lift weights, play sports, and cut their hair; males can don makeup, wear high heels, and dance ballet. Multiple mundane technologies can be, and are, deployed to create new masculinities and femininities. Technologies can and do have multiple, contradictory personal and social implications. For instance, hair removal and surgical technologies are used by members of the transgender community in order to manipulate public perception of their bodies so that this perception matches their gender identities. Plastic surgery is neither good nor bad; it is a technology engaged by individuals in complex ways within particular social contexts.

What the cases in this chapter suggest is that while we could make gendered, embodied selves in a multitude of ways, hegemonic body paradigms and gendered social scripts lay out a constrained set of gendered bodies that are intelligible, in other words, that 'make sense' to others and ourselves. This 'making sense' is a social and interactional process that is shaped by dominant paradigms and social scripts within particular contexts and shaped by personal history and socializing agents. And, when culturally inscribed somatechnologies change who we can be, social scripts adapt to new ways of being that reflect these new identities and bodies. As Victoria Pitts summarizes, "new practices for the body respond to, are shaped by, and are limited by the larger social and historical pressures that regulate bodies."[62]

The Complexities of Body Work

In the preview to this book I suggested that people transform their public and private identities and bodies using the technologies available in any given moment. This process is both intentional and unintended; the use of technologies both shapes individual bodies and identities by chance, and they are deployed by individuals to directly and purposefully shape their bodies and lives. For example, working on computers for extended periods of time causes changes in eyesight and posture, being right or left handed will increase the size and musculature of the dominant arm, sports create particularly gendered/muscled bodies, wearing masculine or feminine clothing changes the shape of bodies (think back to high heels). And there are countless other examples.

Alongside these circumstantial changes, new technologies are allowing people to intervene into the shape, function, and appearance of their bodies in transformative ways. The ability to manifest, in an embodied fashion, chosen identities and/or appearance norms is significant, and these technologies are working hand-in-hand with existing body and gender paradigms and scripts to refashion people's lives. Returning to the stories of Michael Dillon and Rey demonstrates how these dynamics bear on the lives of individuals; these two men came of age in two very different historical moments, and the gender paradigms, scripts, and technologies of their day and the social contexts within which they were situated crafted radically different paths for each of them.

Michael Dillon came of age in the early 1930s, in England. At the same moment that Michael Dillon was struggling to make sense of his own gender non-conformity Radcliffe Hall was embroiled in an obscenity trial that catapulted language and knowledge of lesbianism and gender non-conformity into the public sphere. In Radcliffe Hall's *Well of Loneliness*, the gender and sexuality of the main character, Steven, are conflated such that Steven was understood as lesbian because of his gender non-conformity. This became one of the only places Dillon saw himself reflected and it was through this public debate that he learned about gender non-conformity. But, just as Radcliffe Hall's *Well of Loneliness* was about gender non-conformity that was culturally understood as homosexuality, Michael Dillon was told to make sense of his own gender non-conformity as homosexuality by the few people in whom he confided.

Michael Dillon spent years trying to situate himself within society and ultimately sought medical intervention so he could manifest socially his internal gender identity. His quest for help, however, was thwarted, in part because there was no gender paradigm within which transgenderism could fit. When Dillon's search for medical help failed, he became a doctor in his own right in order to support his own and others' bodily changes. He began taking testosterone in 1939 and by 1944 had legally changed his gender after both hormonal and surgical 'sex-reassignment' efforts. Just eight years after Lili Elbe's publicized sex-reassignment surgery (she is credited with being the first male-to-female person to medically change her sex) and 11 years before Christine Jorgensen's public coming out after her surgery, Dillon became the first female-to-male (FTM) person on record to change his sex. He was finally able to bring his gender identity as a man into more alignment with his public role and body. Over the next 20 years, Dillon wrote about what would eventually be termed transsexuality (see, for example, his book *Self: A Study in Endocrinology and Ethics)*, and struggled to make a life for himself. Dillon intentionally cultivated a heteronormative life, and in fact took on a misogynist persona as part of constructing his masculinity. After being publicly outed as transsexual in 1958, Dillon retreated to a life of monasticism in Tibet, and died in 1962 aged 47.[63]

Rey's story is not yet fully written—he is, after all, only 18—but already there is much more to tell about his path toward social masculinity than there was for Dillon. At age 18, after coming out to his family and starting college, Rey pursued hormone therapy and began to live his life in his chosen gender. Within a few months he began taking testosterone to produce masculine secondary sex characteristics like facial and body hair and a deeper voice. He also had 'top surgery' which included a double mastectomy alongside the construction of a male-appearing chest. Compared to Michael Dillon's long wait and multiple surgeries (surgeries which were often failures—Dillon endured more than 13), Rey was able to engage in body-altering procedures with relative ease. Rey is part of a growing population of young transgender and transsexual individuals who have both the ability and social support to reshape their bodies and identities.

A number of things are significant about Rey's experience and the magazine article that profiled it. First, Rey's ability to manifest his chosen gender, in a bodily fashion, is remarkable. Compared to Michael Dillon's multi-year struggle to physically change his sex, Rey's ability to do so as soon as he turned 18 (the point at which he no longer needed parental consent) marks a significant shift in accessibility, education, and legitimacy. Second, the respect and acumen with which Alissa Quart constructed her story on Rey and other young transgender individuals is heartening. In the span of 50 years, social scripts have expanded significantly such that they reflect a familiarity with the language and complexity of gender non-conformity; for example the *New York Times Magazine* used terms like transgender, transmale, and genderqueer that were unfamiliar or non-existent during Dillon's lifetime.

These changes suggest that the possible ways of being sexed and gendered in the world have expanded. While I am not claiming that transgenderism has been incorporated as normative into North American cultures, I am suggesting that progress has been made. New technologies have been developed that range from the simple expansion of language to cutting edge surgeries that allow and facilitate precise bodily changes. Dominant gender paradigms have shifted to include transgenderism as a possibility hand-in-hand with these technologies. Alternative gender scripts have proliferated making it possible for individuals—including young people like Rey—to access information about transgenderism more readily and to construct more diverse gender identities and sexed bodies than ever before. Indeed, the life-stories of Michael Dillon and Rey reveal significant change in gender scripts over the past 50 years. And, Dillon's and Rey's experiences reveal how these changes in gender paradigms, scripts, technologies, and embodied selves matter in the everyday lives of individuals.

Like the stories of Dillon and Rey, all of the case studies I have discussed in this chapter have demonstrated significant relationships between social scripts, individual bodies and identities, and social paradigms. As embodied gender continues to change, I suspect that it will fuel ongoing transformation of social scripts and paradigms. I would expect, for example, a shift in gender norms alongside more diversity of bodies. But, as established in Chapter 1, technology is neither utopian nor regressive. Technologies are being used to transform bodies in both non-normative ways and in ways that reinforce expectations about gendered bodies. Further, new bodies and identities can both support and inhibit social change, provoke normative identity re-entrenchment and spark an expansion in social scripts, regardless of the desire or intention of individuals. Personal meaning making around one's body or identity does not exist in a vacuum.

These intentions are only part of the impact of body work; historical context, social norms, and power relations all shape the reception, meaning, and import of new technologies, bodies, and identities. Victoria Pitts, a scholar of the body, talks about body work as a 'project' and draws on theorist Elizabeth Grosz to elaborate that:

> No body projects limitlessly expand the range of possibilities for human subjectivity, nor do they 'invent' the self as a matter of personal choice. Body projects may appear to be productions of the self, but they are historically located in time and place, and provide messages that "can be 'read' only within a social system of organization and meaning" (Grosz 1997: 239).[64]

This system of organization within which people are situated is bounded by social statuses like gender, sexuality, and race, all of which shape one's ability to engage in body work and achieve socially valued embodied identities; in other words, body work is always both a social and political endeavor where individuals negotiate between social norms, power relations, and individual desires. The elements of this complex and dynamic set of relations between identity, body, social scripts, dominant ideologies, and technologies are all part of how new embodied identities come to be. Just as is true of identity change, technologically spurred body work is both liberating and regressive. This runs contrary to both utopian visions of body-agency wherein people can remake their embodied self as they wish, and disciplining narratives that suggest that individuals are rigidly constrained by a set of already available, static scripts for body and identity.

We are clearly living in a moment where gender paradigms, scripts, bodies, and identities are all being simultaneously refined and renegotiated. New technologies are being deployed to re-entrench hegemonic masculinities and femininities and erase race and gender differences in bodies. Hormonal birth control places the burdens of sexual decisions on women and genital surgeries such as 'hymenorrhaphy' (hymen reconstruction) reinforce the importance of virginity in women.

Conversely, these same biomedical technologies such as testosterone and estrogen regimens and genital construction methods are allowing individuals to shape their bodies in new ways that create more diverse pairings of sex and gender, and these new embodied genders are significant.

We must recognize the social gender paradigms and scripts tied up with biomedical innovation and attune ourselves to whether, and how, these new technologies are disciplining, regulating, and transforming the gendered body in new ways. Are we on the brink of a new gender order? Somatechnic frontiers are certainly reshaping the body in previously unknown ways, and this process challenges gender norms and scripts to make space accordingly. The documented expansion of gender possibilities—for both transgender and cisgender individuals—certainly suggests that gender ideologies and scripts are being reworked. But just as information technologies are not moving North American societies uni-directionally toward expanded identity possibilities, biomedical technologies are used in some ways that encourage expansion of gender possibilities while in others they help to resist this process. If, however, we take as true the dynamic and reciprocal relationships between technology, ideology, scripts, bodies and identities, then gender is now and will continue to transform itself alongside technological innovation.

CASE STUDY: FOCUS ON THE 'TREATMENT' OF INTERSEX AND TRANSGENDER INDIVIDUALS

The construction of binary genders that correspond to binary sexes is a social endeavor that, while not universal, has dominated North American and European thought since the nineteenth century. Researchers have increasingly documented, however, that this model is inadequate; it does not reflect the diversity of human bodies and lives. The hegemonic sex equals gender paradigm in North American societies asserts that male and female bodies are clearly, dimorphically distinguished by chromosomes (specifically XX for females and XY for males), internal and external biology (the presence of testes or ovaries, penis or vagina), as well as by naturally corresponding secondary sex characteristics (whether breasts or an adam's apple, and the appropriate presence or absence of body hair). In this idealized model all bodies clearly fit into one and only one of two possible sex categories, in which each individual's genetic information matches his or her genitals and those genitals are the visible key that decodes his or her sex and attendant gender.[1]

This two sex/two gender paradigm so strongly structures our social scripts and meaning making that even scientists describe male biological attributes and processes as aggressive, violent, and strong and female biological functions as passive, soft, and receptive.[2] In both medical and lay publications, for example, descriptions of conception typically depict sperm that compete, race, burrow, and hunt while eggs wait patiently to be inseminated. This is held as true even though a more accurate description of biological processes would cast the egg as far more active and the sperm as more receptive.[3] As Anne Fausto-Sterling, a biologist who has written extensively about the social construction of sex, summarizes, "reading nature is a socio-cultural act."[4] The scripts for what 'normal' bodies are and the dominant paradigm for sex and gender shape what we see when we look at the human body from a scientific perspective.

Reality is much more complex, however. Fausto-Sterling estimates that between 1 and 2 percent of infants are born intersex, possessing ambiguous genetic and/or physiological sex characteristics, but many of these cases are undiagnosed until something precipitates closer inspection. For example, in 1996, eight female bodied women, classified, raised as, and identifying as women their whole lives, failed the International Olympics Committee's chromosomal testing used to prevent men from competing as women.[5] This technologically advanced method of verification replaced the 'primitive' method of genital inspections for women athletes, which was required until 1968. Instead of clarifying the 'real' sex of athletes, however, these 'advanced' technological methods only muddied the waters, so much so, in fact, that the International Olympics Committee dropped genetic testing for sex in 2000. Instead it returned to a reliance on lived experience and presentation. In this case, instead of offering clarity into competitors' 'true' sex, new technologies highlighted the very instability and constructed nature of sex and gender.

Human bodies are not as clearly distinct in terms of sex or gender as most think. There are more physical and mental similarities than differences between men and women, and the considerable presence of intersex bodies challenge the veracity of a bipolar model of sexed bodies. This variation is viewed as disordered, however, and doctors—and the sciences that underlie their practice—impose a binary imperative on biological variation. Until very recently, the constructed binary was so naturalized that this diversity of sexed bodies was not allowed to exist. Instead, parents of intersex infants were pushed into surgical 'correction' of their children's bodies, even when the surgical intervention served no purpose whatsoever outside of the construction of clear bodily distinction between male and female.

We as a society are so invested in this binary sex system, this notion that bodies come in only two forms, male and female, that we surgically alter bodies that do not fit this model *simply because they do not fit*. Indeed, decisions about whether to make intersex infants male or female have as much to do with social beliefs as any biological truth. Shaped by gendered beliefs (for example men need sexual satisfaction, women do not), infants are much more likely to be 'made' female, in part because medical guidelines sway surgeons away from selecting maleness unless the child will have a 'large enough' penis. Simultaneously, 'feminizing' surgeries often permanently destroy sexual sensation for the girl child.[6] This profound commitment to a sex/gender paradigm is a clear example of how dominant social paradigms for sex and gender inform technological intervention into and personal experiences of bodies. Only in recent years has activism on the part of intersex individuals (often through advocacy groups like Intersex Society of North America [ISNA]) begun to change the treatment of intersex infants.

ISNA has worked for many years now to educate doctors and parents about intersex conditions and to advocate for delaying surgical or hormonal intervention. Driven by their own experiences of dishonesty on the part of parents and doctors, surgeries that scarred their bodies and removed pleasure (often surgeries on intersex children result in the loss of sexual sensation or function), and gender identities mismatched to their surgically assigned sex, intersex activists have protested, advocated, and fought for new treatment protocols. Most significantly, activists have argued that medically unnecessary treatment should be delayed until intersex children develop their own gendered sense of self and can participate in the decision-making.

And they have been reasonably successful; increasingly hospitals have intersex advocates on call so that when intersex children are born an advocate can come in alongside doctors to offer support and counseling. In the past parents were pushed by doctors to make quick decisions about treatment, often without access to any information about intersexuality in general or their child's condition more specifically. Now, the increased access to information and support has resulted in more parents choosing to delay or refuse surgical intervention. ISNA's work is just a fraction of what must be done to refashion our sex/gender paradigm in line with the diversity of human bodies, however.

Why might we as a society reinforce a two-sex system even though evidence supports a more diverse conceptualization of sex? Answers to this question reveal a lot about the power of sex and gender as a social institution. To begin with, our social order is based around two sexes: marriage laws and norms assume only men and women; buildings are required to have single-sex male and female bathrooms and locker rooms but not private or unisex ones; schools and organizations divide individuals by male/female; and official forms all offer only two distinct sex-categories. The binary sex/gender paradigm works interactively with other social institutions such as marriage, medicine, education, and sport to structure and direct our society, bodies, and identities. In this binary system, non-conforming bodies must be 'disciplined,' as Foucault would say, into place by available technologies of power. Although this discipline does not work perfectly, these societal forces are so powerful that diverse bodies are forced to conform, at least on the surface. As a consequence, the social invisibility of intersex contributes to the naturalized belief in a binary gender model.

As social context shifts and communities advocate for change, these same technologies can be used in new and non-normative ways. Groups like ISNA have been increasingly successful in changing how intersex infants are treated at birth, counseling parents to leave them to develop their own gender identities and then decide whether to avail themselves of any available technological interventions later in life. In many cases, intersex individuals are now choosing to leave their bodies as they are, and in the process are manifesting new sexed bodies. Meanwhile, transsexual and gender non-conforming individuals are also using the same technologies to intentionally construct differently gendered and sexed bodies.

In response to changes in societal gender paradigms and scripts, brought on by transgender and intersex activism, medical gate keepers such as psychiatrists and surgeons are slowly relaxing medical barriers to breast and genital (re)construction surgery. These changes are creating a diverse array of gendered and sexed bodies as individuals may solicit some but not all sexed/gendered bodily modifications. For example, an individual may choose to have breast augmentation or reduction ('top' surgery), genital (or 'bottom') surgery, hormones, a combination of these biomedical interventions, or none of them.

Based on evidence discussed so far in this book, it will come as little surprise to discover that rates of surgery, hormone use, and cross-gender dress and bodily comportment vary dramatically across racial, economic, geographic, and sexual communities. We can begin to understand why hormone use dominates transsexual treatment in North America, for example (as opposed to primary reliance on hair removal or transplant, social role changes, or dress), by examining dominant paradigms of sex and gender and paying close attention to the central role of hormones in defining sex, the need for distinct physical sex characteristics, and the naturalization of gender.[7] The United States and Canada have legislated the validity of these types of differences—but not others—by requiring irreversible bodily changes in order to legally change one's gender status on official documents like driver's licenses, birth certificates, and bank records. As discussed in Chapter 1, while the requirements vary by state, those states that do allow changes in legal status tend to require significant bodily transformations as opposed to less invasive ones like a change in personal identity or social role. This is one of many reasons that transgender women and men with class privilege in North America are more able to gain recognition for their chosen identities than poor individuals; the ability to deploy legitimized gender change scripts requires the financial and social capital to afford the required transformations.

The set of surgical procedures aimed at changing an individual's body to match a gender identity have traditionally been called sex-reassignment surgery (and before that sex-change surgery). In recent years, however, as the transgender movement has grown and activists have received more attention, this term has fallen into disfavor by some. Some activists argue that they are not changing their gender or sex, but rather correcting the alignment between their body and their internal sense of self. Many of these individuals have come to use the terminology 'gender confirmation surgery' to reflect these beliefs. Similarly, some transgender individuals bristle at the term 'gender identity disorder,' claiming that their gender—their internal sense of self—has never changed, that only their ability to manifest this self by having their body match it has.[8]

As this debate plays out in media and press materials, in transgender activist and organizational statements, and among scholars and medical professionals, it is clear that the debate is really about sex and gender ideologies. These new technologies and attendant new scripts for what gender individuals can be are challenging the gender paradigms utilized to structure the dominant sex/gender system. If power is the ability to have one's own knowledge count as true, then this debate reflects the growing power of transgender individuals and communities to set the terms of their own lives, in the face of hegemonic gender paradigms, and the medical institutions empowered to maintain this system. In response to this diversity it is likely we will see more shifts in hegemonic paradigms and sex/gender scripts.

Debates over sex and gender identity reflect how language and attendant explanations for gender non-conformity change alongside ever-broadening gendered and sexed selves. Shifts in dominant gender and transgender paradigms have allowed for more diverse gender and sex scripts, and in turn individuals have advocated for visibility, support, and somatechnic interventions in line with these scripts. As examined in Chapter 1, medical gate keeping was routinely used to police transgender body work by demanding that after gender/sex changes people live in line with hegemonic gender and sexuality scripts. Now, however, increasing numbers of endocrinologists and surgeons are willing to perform surgery or prescribe hormones even when individuals do not match heteronormative identity scripts, something that was highly unlikely only ten years ago. As these doctors allow the expansion of appropriate discourses-in-practice, there is less pressure on individuals to construct their own narratives within prescribed boundaries; at the same time the language of gender itself is broader and more readily available. Whereas most individuals identified as transsexual or trans-gender in the past, contemporary surveys find a multitude of gender non-conforming identities including genderqueer, bi-gender, and androgene.[9]

These differences are also generational, which suggests that younger transgender individuals are constructing identities and coming out with very different gender paradigms, social scripts, and technologies at their disposal. For example, young transgender individuals are significantly more likely to claim a diversity of gender non-conforming identities. As Rey, the young FTM who was profiled in Chapter 3, commented in a 2008 *New York Times Magazine* article,

> Some transmen want to be seen as men—they want to be accepted as born men . . . I want to be accepted as a transman—my brain is not gendered. There's this crazy binary that's built into all of life, that there are just two genders that are acceptable. I don't want to have to fit into that.[10]

Moreover, there is a strong correlation between age and when individuals report meeting another transgender person for the first time (and presumably when they came to know about transgenderism and gain exposure to transgender identity and body scripts). In Beemyn and Rankin's National U.S. study, 76 percent of individuals under 22 years old had met another transgender individual by the age of 19, while only 32 percent of individuals between the ages of 23 and 32, and only 5 percent of people 63 years old and older had. That is, the lower the age-cohort a person is in, the more likely they are to have met a transgender person at a young age. In the same study, Beemyn and Rankin found that 27 percent of individuals age 63 or older were totally closeted about their transgender status, while only 10 percent of individuals 22 or younger were, and only 9 percent of people age 23–32 were. Similarly, 34 percent of individuals age 23–32 described themselves as out to all their friends, while only 17 percent of people 63 and over were (other age groups ranged between 26 percent and 30 percent).[11] These statistics alone do not imply any causality; however, this data suggests that who people think they can be, and how able they are to manifest that identity in their body are changing significantly and these changes have everything to do with shifting gender paradigms and social identity and body scripts.[12]

While there has been positive change, it is important not to romanticize transgender lives or choices without grounding them within the lived reality of transgender people. Rey experienced significant levels of harassment and institutional resistance that caused him to move out of the dormitories at Barnard and even take a leave of absence from college. Rates of violence for transgender youth are significantly higher than for their cisgender[13] peers, as are rates of poverty and homelessness.[14] Some studies report that 60 percent of transgender youth experience physical violence.[15] Researchers also find that lack of social support from family, GLBT peers, teachers, and school administrators leads transgender youth to disproportionately high rates of suicidal thoughts, loneliness, and homelessness.[16] Moreover, class and race both affect outcomes for young people and adults, and transgender people of color experience more violence, higher rates of homelessness, and lower social status than their White peers do.[17]

Social change continues to be a slow process. Transgender social movements have brought transgender advocacy into the public sphere, and gender scholars across a variety of disciplines have documented the complexity of gender and the inadequacy of binary sex/gender systems. However, hegemonic paradigms and scripts have not yet caught up and gender non-conformity remains pathologized. That said, even though transgender individuals face tremendous discrimination and prejudice, transgender youth are more visible and more accepted now than at any other time in modern Western history.[18] As individuals live in more complex bodies and with more diverse gender identities, these paradigms will likely continue to loosen, and social gender scripts will likely expand. The biomedical technologies being used to produce embodied gender differently will slowly shape public knowledge and discourse about gender and gender non-conformity.

REVIEW
SOCIOLOGICAL ANALYSES OF GENDER AND TECHNOLOGY

In the film *Kinky Boots,* when Charlie Price introduces his new business plan of producing shoes for drag queens to the workers in his shoe factory, he tries to ease the transition with a proclamation that, "The factory that started the century providing a range of footwear for men will go into the next century providing footwear for . . . a range of men."[1] Charlie's humorous comment is a strikingly simple way to explain his proposition, a proposition that reveals both ingenuity and a significant reframing. High-heeled shoes for drag queens are, at their most basic, a new technology for male bodies doing femininity.

Steve Pateman, the real-life factory owner upon whom Charlie Price is based, did manufacture shoes for a broader range of men, women, and transgender individuals. By doing so, Pateman facilitated the embodiment of more diverse genders by creating shoes that allowed male-bodied femininities; that is, he developed a new technology and, in doing so, produced new gender possibilities.

As I have explored throughout this book, changes in embodied identities, social scripts, technologies, or societal paradigms are elements of larger dynamic and interactive relationships between all of these components. I return, then, to the questions that I began this book with: how are new technologies reshaping gendered bodies and identities, and what does this mean for us as individuals and as a society?

The Impact of Contemporary Biomedical and Information Technologies

One of the first concepts I introduced in this book was that technology is employed in the service of making meaning and doing gender. Moreover, gender technologies are shaped by the prevailing gender paradigms and scripts within a society. Consider, for example, a 1968 advertisement in which a woman in a spacesuit holds a bottle of the cleaning solution *Lestoil* while the advertisement copy reads, "Women of the future will make the moon a cleaner place to live."[2] Advertisers in 1968 could imagine living on the moon, but, apparently, not without Earth's cleaning products and gender inequalities. While this light-hearted example minimizes the complex individual and social gendering processes discussed so far, it does provide a good example of how gendered social scripts manifest in society and work in concert with paradigms, technologies, and embodied individuals.

Extending this example to encompass a broader social context, we see that our beliefs and social ideologies about gender shape how we interpret all aspects of the world around us and describe the realm of possibilities we can imagine for our lives and society. Furthermore, social institutions, socializing agents and individual gender identifications all, in turn, shape the array of gendered bodies and identities rendered legible in a particular context.

Like the *Lestoil* advertisement, many of the examples analyzed thus far have provided an opportunity to make sense of gender in a way that accounts for these social and individual forces. For example, our inquiry into new information technologies found that technologies are being deployed to simultaneously re-inscribe, resist, and rewrite social gender scripts. These gendered changes are meaningful in the lives of individuals as well as on institutional and societal levels. Marginalized individuals use online community forums and discussion boards, for instance, to discover and refine identities and to rewrite gendered body scripts. New biomedical technologies reshape gendered bodies in both normative and non-normative ways; steroids and plastic surgery can be used to construct hyper-masculine men and hyper-feminine women, but they can also be deployed to manifest gendered bodies outside of the recommended strictures of male men and female women.

All of these examples demonstrate in detail that new technologies are neither regressive nor utopian. Rather, technologies are actively and purposefully deployed on individual and institutional levels, in the service of gender, body, and identity work. This is done within particular social contexts, and is shaped by attendant gender paradigms and scripts.

Have We Become Cyborgs?

In the mid 1980s feminist philosopher Donna Haraway began to argue that we increasingly live in a cyborg society characterized by the hybridization of bodies and technology, creating a blurred line between human and machine, mixing natural and constructed realms.[3] She asserts that this hybridization is transforming the ways that gender, race, sexuality, and nation are written onto the body and integrated into the self on the individual level. In addition, this hybridization works at a societal level by influencing how these categories of oppression, and identity, are located within relations of power. Haraway's argument about technology foretold many of the contemporary issues that are taken up in this book.

Like Haraway I began my analysis by addressing the question, "How is technology reshaping contemporary bodies and identities?" And I endeavor to answer this question, as Haraway did, through the lens of gender. In the end, I have drawn similar conclusions but with a less celebratory note. Technologies are reshaping the most intimate aspects of individuals' bodies and selves. Furthermore, technologies are doing so in conversation with gendered paradigms and scripts. That is to say, people are using information and biomedical technologies to help construct, define, and manifest new complex embodied identities; in the process, social scripts and gender paradigms are shifting. These changes in individual identities, social scripts, and paradigms are not producing an unbounded utopia, however. Technology has the potential to both facilitate progressive body and identity possibilities and re-entrench oppressive ones. I began this book with the premise that while technology is changing who we are as gendered individuals, how gender changes is complex and variable.[4]

By building this analysis on an understanding of gender as both socially constructed and real in its effects, or what Stuart Hall calls a 'discursive approach' to bodily difference, I have avoided both a utopian construction of technology as an egalitarian liberator, and a pessimistic one that casts technology as reproducer of racial and gender inequalities.[5] Instead, I approach technology as a force of social change that has potential to do both. If core identities like gender and race are 'floating signifiers'—systems of classification without biological bases—then we must examine them "more like a language than a way in which we are biologically constituted."[6] That is, we, as scholars, must approach identities as social projects around which institutional support, including that of scientific theory, is built or denied. This book has endeavored to do just that by examining, through specific case studies, how technological change has challenged who people think they can be as gendered beings and how these transformed identities are manifested in the bodies of individuals.

A Sociological Analysis of Technology and Gender

This book began with an examination of the relationship between the histories of gendered bodies and identities (both conforming and non-conforming) and technological innovation. People of every era produce gender using the technologies available to them. As the mutual construction of gender and technology change over time, the criteria for appropriate and inappropriate gendered bodies and identities also change. Just as Bernice Hausman suggests (as covered in Chapter 1), the technologies available in a given historical moment work to develop particular subjectivities. Simultaneously, changes in technology alter what kinds of body work are available and required for different genders, and which body codes are necessary to communicate a particular gender effectively. While hegemonic ideology suggests that our gender flows directly from natural sex differences in the body, gender is, in fact, a construct. It is based on biological and physical processes, influenced by gendered scripts and norms, seen through the lenses of contemporary paradigms, policed by technologies of power, and finally defined and constructed by the individual, whose embodied gender will be enhanced and limited by available technologies.

The social scripts that shape how individuals think about, portray, and perceive gender, work to create the constructed but seemingly natural gender/sex binaries. These 'recipes for behavior'—these scripts—teach us how to make sense of our own and others' bodies and identities, and they teach us how to experience them as sexed (designated as male or female according to hegemonic scripts) as well as gendered (limited to men or women according to hegemonic scripts). As explored in this book, however, these scripts are neither always proscriptive, nor stable. They are constantly re-entrenched, contested, transformed, and challenged. And individuals continuously navigate the complex terrain of conformity and resistance, of hegemonic scripts, and of assertions of new ways of being in the world.

What a Sociological Approach Illuminates

Each of the cases examined in this book offers evidence that new technologies are in dynamic relationship to societal paradigms and social scripts, and that these relationships result in the reshaping of gendered bodies and identities. I also find that gendered bodies and identities are affecting the development of technologies, social scripts, and gender paradigms within individual groups and communities, and in society as a whole. In other words, the five aspects of social life to which we have directed our attention appear to be intricately interconnected. A sociological analysis that accounts for this complexity allows us to make visible the hidden processes of socialization and identity and body work. Through all of these processes, technology, paradigms, and scripts interact and transform our social and individual lives and bodies.

Bringing all of these elements—paradigms, scripts, technologies, bodies and identities—to bear on the question of gender in this technological age sheds light on a number of important dynamics. Most significantly, it offers a way to analyze the nuanced and ever-changing relationships between aspects of individual and societal gender. The relationships between paradigms, scripts, technologies, bodies, and identities vary across context and time, and this analytical approach clarifies these relationships without eliding their differences, contradictions, or specificities. Moreover, a sociological analysis accounts for social context and individual difference. A sociological analysis highlights individual (personal experience), local (subculture, group, or community) and society-wide dynamics.

Holstein and Gubrium's theory of narrative identity (as discussed in Chapter 2) helps explain how social scripts are deployed and negotiated in the process of identity construction and reconstruction online. When this theory of identity is brought into conversation with a sociological analysis of technology we can better recognize how technologies are opening up new arenas of identity work, such as blogging, online diaries, and *Second Life*, and how new collective stories are being developed and deployed in forums including online discussion groups, chat rooms, and electronic bulletin boards. Theories of technological innovation and bodily change are similarly clarified when analyzed sociologically. This approach, then, does not replace existing empirical models and conceptual theories; rather, it extends these elaborations of gender, identity, body, and technology by accounting for a broad range of social forces simultaneously.

A sociological analysis enables us to decipher how social and individual change processes are intertwined. It reveals how gender paradigms and social scripts can vary across social contexts (for example in drag troupes and strip clubs) and how these differences offer particular ranges of possibilities for gendered bodies and identities. Similarly, this approach offers insight into how technological innovation (for example birth control pills) is both shaped by dominant paradigms and influential (for example, how the rise of sexology changed meaning making around sex and gender). Finally, a sociological analysis charts a path toward answering whether and how information and biomedical technologies can have real-life effects on bodies and identities.

New Areas of Inquiry

Using a sociological analysis to elaborate the social processes that underlie changes in gendered bodies and identities casts light on a number of key contemporary social changes. Simultaneously, it raises many new questions to be taken up in future scholarship. The analysis I have undertaken in this book has highlighted how social forces overlap and interact in social contexts to produce a wide array of lived experiences; however, it does not conclusively settle on how individuals consciously or unconsciously navigate normative and non-normative social scripts— in fact, it raises provocative questions. How do people actively negotiate between existing social scripts and novel ones? How do they choose to accept, resist, or rewrite socially sanctioned discourses? And how do these choices impact social institutions? While offering clarity regarding the interaction of social forces, my analysis also fosters new questions about how individuals make sense of the social scripts available to them, negotiate their personal relationship to these scripts, and assimilate available scripts into lived embodied identity. Future empirical research on these questions could be wonderfully illuminating.

Another area of inquiry for study is the mechanisms by which embodied identity and body changes take place, both on the individual and societal level. Some of the empirical studies and gender theories discussed in this book offered insight into these mechanisms, but further research is needed. While the sociological analysis I undertook allowed us to look under the hood, as it were, of embodied identity to make sense of how paradigms, scripts, and technologies interact with bodies and identities in the production of new embodied selves, it did not chart the particular processes by which this happens. Additionally, how can we better understand the meaning and import of new body and identity forms? And what happens when we tease out the re-entrenchment of hegemonic gender paradigms and scripts with their resistance and transformation? As research on this area of social change is elaborated, new analytical models and theoretical frameworks will emerge that will help make better sense of these and similar changes.

What we have found to be true for gender using a sociological approach can also be used to make sense of other embodied identities and forces of social change. An analysis focused on race could elaborate how new technologies are being used to revive and contest the biology of race, such as in the search for racial markers within the human genome. Similarly, a focus on sexuality would enable us to look at how new technologies are reshaping the meaning and practice of sex and sexuality. Analyses focused on sexual, racial, or class identity would illustrate the interactive relationships between new technologies affecting those identities and related paradigms, scripts, existing technologies, bodies, and identities. Finally, we may also anticipate that future research will explore the connections between gender and sexuality scripts in more detail and help scholars map how the development and deployment of technology is implicated in these relationships.[7]

Making Sense of the Technologically Saturated World Around Us

The central questions that I have taken up in this book—and the issue I have returned to in each of the case studies mentioned herein—is whether and how the development of new technologies is reshaping who people are as gendered individuals, and what the importance of these changes is. Certainly the many examples I explored suggest that technological development is intimately tied up with changes in gendered bodies and identities. In support of this analysis, scholars argue that increased deviation from established social body norms marks moments of intense social change and this social change often manifests in new identity schemas.[8] We, as scholars, then, can make sense of body work as a significant phenomenon, one that is tied to larger social and cultural changes. All of the cases I have examined suggest that social changes have made room for more diverse bodies and identities. How, then, do we take the concepts and analyses developed throughout this text and use them to make sense of the world at large? One situation in which these changes can be examined is when they manifest in public debate and discourse. Let us consider, for example, how these embodied changes are affecting dominant gender paradigms and social scripts in one final case study: the very public pregnancy of Thomas Beatie, a transgender man.

Transgender Pregnancy and Thomas Beatie

We can witness how bodies are being shaped by new technologies and how social scripts and gender paradigms are being challenged and changed in the process by turning our attention to a current site of social change and debate. The case of transgender pregnancy highlights how gendering happens in concert with social institutions and gender paradigms as well as how these processes shape the lives and bodies of individuals.[9] Because removal of reproductive organs is not always part of changing one's sex or gender, many male-to-female (MTF) individuals still have the biological capacity to impregnate and many female-to-male (FTM) people retain the ability to become pregnant. This usually requires temporary cessation of hormones, but does not necessarily halt, set back, or divert individuals' body or identity changes.

Transgender men in particular are caught in a bind in terms of pregnancy. While the desire for children is not restricted to women, the state of pregnancy is deeply gendered in our society. In fact, it is one of the primary ways that we differentiate women from men. For female-to-male transgender individuals who choose to bear children, however, their embodied identity rests on disengaging pregnancy from womanhood. In one of the only studies of FTM biological parents, Sam Dylan More interviewed nine German FTM individuals. He found that FTM individuals had to engage in significant identity and body work to mitigate the impact of societal pregnancy scripts that gendered them as women. For example, in an interview one participant, Del, commented,

> I did not feel more feminine, but still the feminine image was imposed upon me externally . . . Sitting in the doc's office who delivered me . . . was also humiliating in an (en)gendered way: that space was woman's space and fundamentally at the surface of my skin I didn't fit in.[10]

What Del highlights in his interview, and what the scholarship explored throughout this book suggests, is that individuals are intentionally negotiating complex gendered body and identity scripts, and this holds particularly true for individuals whose gender identification and bodies stray from hegemonic norms.

While a number of transgender individuals have had children either before or after changing their sex or gender, this issue was catapulted into mainstream North American consciousness for the first time in 2008. Thomas Beatie, a transgendered man, announced in an April 2008 issue of the gay and lesbian news magazine, *The Advocate,* that he was pregnant.[11] In his first-person account, Beatie shared his story of coming out as transgender and, a number of years later, deciding to have a child. His narrative focuses on the discrimination and prejudice he and his wife, Nancy, had experienced thus far and asserted that what they chose to do was moral, natural, and logical. About his choice to bear children Beatie acknowledged his wife's infertility but iterated that, "Wanting to have a biological child is neither a male nor female desire, but a human desire."[12] Moreover, he saw no conflict between his gender and his pregnancy. He wrote: "Despite the fact that my belly is growing with a new life inside me, I am stable and confident being the man that I am."[13] That is, for Thomas Beatie being a man and being pregnant are not mutually exclusive. In the process of navigating his gendered body through pregnancy he redefines what it means to be a man. He is embodying a new gendered identity and body that conflicts with social scripts and challenges social gendered body scripts in the process.

Beatie is not the first transgender person to have a child after changing his sex;[14] however, his story was the first to garner widespread attention from the mainstream media. Reactions have been mixed both within and outside of the transgender community. Beatie's coming out, as it were, generated both praise and anger within transgender communities.[15] In a *Salon.com* article, for example, Thomas Rogers spoke with leading transgender activists and scholars about Beatie. Some activists, like Mara Keisling, felt that Beatie's actions pushed what might be considered a more pressing transgender issue such as workplace protection and access to healthcare to the margins. Others expressed fears that this tabloid-style attention has put the validity of all transgender identities at risk and compromised the safety of individuals. In contrast, Jameson Green, a longtime transgender activist and author, felt that the attention generated by Beatie's disclosure would help to educate mainstream society.

In the mainstream media, stories have revealed attitudes that are as mixed as they are within the transgender community. For example, a particularly transphobic television report involved MSNBC's Joe Scarborough repeatedly commenting that he was "going to be sick" when reporting the story. Notably, however, most news media have been positive and respectful. Certainly the specials run by Oprah Winfrey and Barbara Walters displayed compassion and at least a superficial understanding of transgenderism, as did a cover story in *People Magazine*. All told, the media attention and public response was neither wholly progressive nor wholly regressive. While it is too soon to assess public consensus about transgender pregnancy or draw clear conclusions about the meaning and import of Beatie's coming out, I can make some cursory observations.

Making Sense of Transgender Pregnancy

The first and most obvious effect of Beatie's news article was that it generated a new wave of public discussion about transgenderism, some of which was educational and some reactionary. The anonymous responses posted in online blogs were very lukewarm, tending toward hostility. Paisley Currah, a transgender-rights scholar summarized the range of public responses:

> Some bloggers felt that 'she' was still a woman; others thought transitioning should mean Beatie had forfeited his right to give birth; still others (usually women) expressed annoyance at all the attention the first 'pregnant man' was getting. A small proportion seemed to have no problem getting their mind around the idea.[16]

It is undeniable, however, that more people now know about transgender lives and possibilities, and it is very likely that more transgender individuals are thinking about pregnancy; research shows that these changes in consciousness matter in fundamental ways. For instance, Beatie has given birth to his second child, and this news has generated much less uproar and attention than it did only a year ago.

While I could make sense of this shift in a multitude of ways, one possibility is that our social scripts for pregnancy are indeed changing. At the very least, the idea that a man can be pregnant is fathomable to more individuals than it was just a year ago. The range of sociological analyses I have engaged in this book suggest that this varied public discussion will likely produce *both* new possibilities for individuals and a societal retrenchment of hegemonic gender scripts. That is, the impact of transgender pregnancies and the debate that surrounds them are likely as complex as the matrices of forces at play in shaping their manifestation and meaning.

Second, by situating Beatie's case within a sociological framework we can analyze how institutions participate in the production and enforcement of gender paradigms and scripts. For example, Beatie reported having difficulty finding doctors and hospitals willing to treat him.[17] The lack of institutional support or procedures for non-normative pregnancies is one way to control who is seen as a legitimate pregnant person, i.e. who is a legitimate woman or a legitimate man. In fact, a number of European countries and several states in North America place sanctions on transgender individuals who bear children by limiting or revoking legal gender status changes.[18] There is a variety of structural constraints hindering treatment for pregnant transgender individuals, such as the lack of maternity spaces for men, as well as narrative ones, for instance the dearth of language for men who bear children. This offers a clear example of how gender ideologies and existing social scripts shape the range of possibilities for gendered bodies, identities, and practices. We can also imagine, however, the impact of changes to these paradigms and scripts; the more scripts for pregnancy expand to include men, the less gendered pregnancy will become, and the more flexibility for gendered bodies and selves there will be.

Finally, examining the public experience of Thomas Beatie raises many questions about the 'nature' of sex and gender in this time of increased technological intervention into the body. Shortly after Thomas Beatie's coming out, an editorial appeared in the science journal *Nature*, that highlighted the shifting of body scripts. Responding to critiques that a pregnant man was 'unnatural,' the editors took up the question of sex and gender in a technological age. They wrote,

When we consider this story [of Thomas Beatie] with the reasoning parts of our brains, exactly what was so 'unnatural'? The
longing to have a baby? That is a profoundly human desire,
whether the prospective parents are male, female or transgendered.
Or is it that Beatie has acted on his certainty that he is a man
who happened to be born without a Y chromosome? Biologists
have found that gender-straddling and gender-switching behav-
iours are not at all uncommon in the 'natural' world, either for
humans or non-human animals.[19]

This editorial is an example of how scientific data is being deployed to
challenge existing gender and sex paradigms in an explicit effort to
expand the legitimate ways for individuals to be in the world. The
editors of *Nature* continue by connecting these changes in gendered
bodies and identities to technological development. They write:

True, modern biotechnology has considerably raised the stakes,
and is allowing humans to manipulate their biological make-up to
an ever-increasing degree. But it hasn't fundamentally changed the
game. And its applications, however unsettling they may be to
some people, are not, by definition, 'unnatural.'

This quote demonstrates deployment of new and transformed gender
scripts for who can bear a child, and what it means to be a man, a
woman, or even a parent. It also establishes the negotiation of a new
gender paradigm rooted less in biological determinism and more in
both social and technological logics.

The case of transgender pregnancy raises a whole host of new questions about gender on the individual and institutional level. If pregnancy is one of the key markers of womanhood in our society, what does
it mean for pregnancy to be divorced from femaleness, and womanhood? How does the use of fertility treatments to extend the reproductive lives of women past menopause raise many of the same gender
questions? How will the ability to control those futures more through
in-vitro fertilization, genetic screening, and sex-selection challenge

dominant gender paradigms and scripts for embodied womanhood? Similarly, how are testosterone therapies, hair transplants, penis enlargements, and steroid use changing the meaning and embodiment of maleness and manhood? And what does it tell us about our social norms to observe that many of these questions are raised only when we are confronted by the case of a transgender pregnancy?

All of the questions above center on the realities of gendered bodies and identities within a technologically saturated society. And these are questions that can only be answered with further empirical and theoretical inquiry across scientific and social scientific disciplines. For now, the analytical tools engaged in this book enable a robust understanding of the social forces that have produced these changes, and their significance on the individual and institutional levels.

Gender Circuits: Where Do We Go From Here?

As I draw to a close, then, I return to the questions that began this book: how are new technologies changing who we are as gendered beings, and what does this suggest about where these changes are leading us as individuals and as a society? The many cases I have explored point toward dramatic changes in the gendered bodies and identities of twenty-first century individuals. New technologies are being engaged on individual and institutional levels to create, reinforce, and rewrite what it means to be a male, female, or transgendered individual in our society. Contrary to post-modern claims that identities will cease to matter, our inquiry has revealed active negotiation and substantiation of gender identity on the part of individuals and a high social investment in particular identities on the institutional level.

It is also clear from our inquiry that the body continues to play a central role in individual experience, even as technology enables more 'virtual' possibilities. As Holstein and Gubrium remind us, "the body continues to be an omnipresent material mediator of who we are or hope to be."[20] The body plays a central role in our lives, acting as the canvas upon which we can display 'who we are,' and the means by which we interact with the world around us.[21] Sociological analysis can help us make sense of the diverse social and individual changes that result from technological innovation, and of how these changes, in turn, spur further technological development. This approach offers a way to understand how social paradigms, scripts, technologies, bodies, and identifications are in dynamic relationship to one another and how these social and individual forces, together, are remaking gender.

The conclusions I can draw open as many new doors of inquiry as they close. While I have established that technology is impacting individuals in significant and transformative ways, I have also documented that technology is neither a utopian field of unbounded possibility, nor does it flatly reproduce hegemonic scripts for identity. Rather, it offers both liberating and regressive opportunities that respond to and enable a diverse array of changes. The possibilities are not infinite, but they are as yet tantalizingly open.

ENDNOTES

Preface
1 Frangos 2006.

Preview
1 Bijker and Law 1992; Franklin 2007; Mackenzie and Wajcman 1999; McGinn 1991; Turner 2007.
2 Bryant 2007; Futter 2006; Zipern 2001.
3 Holstein and Gubrium 1999; Kendall 2002; Rheingold 1993b; Shilling (ed.) 2007; Turner 1997.
4 McLuhan 1994.
5 Heidegger 1977.
6 Turner 2007: 23.
7 Gabe, Bury, and Elston 2004: 73.
8 Eugenics movements were early twentieth-century social movements that advocated for the active cultivation of particular characteristics in society by encouraging some people to reproduce and curbing (by influence or force) the reproduction of others. Eugenics drew on Darwin's concept of 'survival of the fittest' and asserted that only the fittest members of society (i.e. White, Western, Christian, heterosexual, and able-bodied) should bear children.
9 Ensler 2000: 13.
10 Gimlin 2002.
11 Lorber 1996.
12 Connell 2002.
13 Fausto-Sterling 2000.
14 Pragmatism is a theoretical tradition focused on the process of how ideas, meaning, and truth come to be, and how they work in practice.
15 Cooley 1902; Goffman 1959; Mead 1934.
16 Mead 1934. For scholarship on situational identity theories see: Becker 1953; Blumer 1969; Denzin 1987; Fine 2001; Sandstrom, Martin, and Fine 2006. For scholarship on identity development through narrative practices/discourses see: Charmaz 1994;

Collins and Blot 2003; Gimlin 2007; Holstein and Gubrium 2000; Reagan 1996; Ricoeur 1991; Sandstrom 1998.

17 O'Brien 1999.

18 Kimmel 2007.

19 Dworkin and O'Sullivan 2007: 115.

20 Dworkin and O'Sullivan 2007.

21 Goffman 1959.

22 Archer 1992.

23 Kessler and McKenna 1978; Lorber 1996.

24 Preves 2003.

25 Lamb and Watson 1979.

26 Pääbo 2003.

27 Pääbo 2003.

28 Gramsci 1971.

29 Zammuner 1987.

30 McGlen and O'Connor 1998.

31 Clothing (Turbin 2003), toys (Messner 2000; Schwartz and Markham 1985; Zammuner 1987), schooling (Jacobs 1996; Orenstein 1995; Thorne 1993), careers (Padavic and Reskin 2002), love and desire (Kimmel 2005; Tolman 1994), political participation (McGlen and O'Connor 1998), employment (Reskin and Roos 1991), and family (Brines 1994; Coltrane 2004; Hochschild 1989).

32 Crawley, Foley, and Shehan 2007:4.

33 Crawley, Foley, and Shehan 2007; Lorber 1996.

34 Cafri et al. 2005; Stanford and McCabe 2005.

35 Crawley, Foley, and Shehan 2007: 1, emphasis theirs.

36 Lexis Nexis search March 11, 2008, for 'transgender' and 'transsexual' in US news sources.

37 Gamson 1998.

38 DeGregory and Helfand 2007.

39 Stratton 2007.

40 DeGregory 2007.

41 DeGregory 2007.

42 DeGregory 2007.

43 Fausto-Sterling 2000; Feinberg 1996; Foucault 1990.

44 Gender Identity Disorder, or GID, has been listed as a mental illness in the Diagnostic and Statistical Manual since 1980, and is considered a psychological disorder warranting psychological or medical intervention.

45 Shapiro 2007.

46 Holstein and Gubrium 2000.

47 "Professor Assigns Students to 'E-Fast'" 2007.

48 Walker 2007.

49 Many scientists, philosophers, and scholars have been thinking about how new technologies are shaping our world. See, for example, Adas 1989; Alkalimat, Gills, and Williams 1995; Bijker and Law 1992; Cowan 1997; Featherstone and Burrows 1995; Hacker 1989; Lyon 1995; Morley and Robins 1995; Rheingold 1993b; Shields 1996; Turkle 1994 and 1995; Webster 1996.

50 Kleinman 2008.

51 O'Brien 2005: 502–503.

52 Active participants are participants who have logged in at least once in the past 60 days. See http://lindenlab.com/pressroom/releases/22_09_09 for additional metrics

53 "Maxim's 2007 Hot 100."
54 Haraway 1991.
55 Haraway 1991: 164.
56 Balsamo 1996.
57 Park 2007.
58 In the United States 86 percent of eyelid surgeries are performed on women according to 2008 statistics (American Society of Plastic Surgeons 2009a).
59 Goering 2003.
60 Bartky 1988.

Case Study: Focus on Tattooing and Masculinity

1 Giddens 1991.
2 Kosut 2000.
3 Kosut 2000: 80.
4 DeMello 2000; Fisher 2002; Sanders 1989.
5 "The Tattooing Fad" 1897.
6 Fisher 2002.
7 Armstrong and Murphy 1997; Braithwaite et al. 1999; Koch et al. 2005.
8 Janssen 2005.
9 Halnon and Cohen 2006.
10 Govenar 2000.
11 Cumming 1943: 38.
12 Coe et al. 1993.
13 DeMello 2000.
14 Janssen 2005: 185.
15 Phelan and Hunt 1998
16 Fisher 2002.
17 Hawkes, Senn, and Thorn 2004.
18 Pew Research Center for People and the Press 2007.
19 Armstrong and Pace-Murphy 1997; Laumann and Derick 2006.
20 Steward 1990.
21 Copes and Forsyth 1998.
22 Laumann and Derick 2006; Pew Research Center for People and the Press 2007.
23 Hawkes, Senn, and Thorn 2004.
24 Fisher 2002: 100.
25 Gill, Henwood, and McLean 2005.
26 Gill, Henwood, and McLean 2005: 38.
27 Sweetman 1999: 53.

Chapter 1

1 *Kinky Boots* 2005.
2 Strauss 2004.
3 Carr 2006.
4 de Lauretis 1987; Hausman 1992; Halberstam 1991; Irvine 1990.
5 As I explore later, this is not to say males who identify and live as women, or females who live as men, are a modern phenomenon. Rather, the creation of a pathologized medical identity, 'transsexual,' is new.
6 Hausman 1992: 275.

 7 Derry and Williams 1993.
 8 Gebhart et al. 1979, as cited in UNESCO 1985: 4.
 9 Borgmann 2006.
10 Cordaux and Stoneking 2003.
11 Park argues that dissection of the female body was undertaken to confirm reproductive function, and to verify the divinity of holy women by locating religious relics embedded in their bodies (Park 2006).
12 The dominant ontology of Western societies through the mid sixteenth century suggested that royalty was divinely chosen by God to lead hand in hand with the church. This ontology granted legitimacy and omnipotence to rulers.
13 Kleinman 2005: 4.
14 Embryonic sex selection is the process of selectively choosing embryos cultivated in-vitro for implantation on the basis of desired sex (male/female).
15 Moscucci 1990; Oudshoorn 2000, 2003.
16 Fausto-Sterling 2000: 146–147.
17 Oudshoorn 1994.
18 Oudshoorn 2003: 5.
19 Oudshoorn 2003.
20 MacKenzie and Wajcman 1999.
21 Ritzer 1993; Weber 1947, 2005.
22 Ellul 1964; Heidegger 1977.
23 While Karl Marx saw the Industrial Revolution as devastating for workers, the problem lay not with the technological developments that led to the Industrial Revolution, but in the economic system (capitalism) that put new technologies to particularly exploitative uses.
24 Hughes 2004; Marx 1977.
25 Segal 1986; Kling 1996.
26 Foucault 1965, 1979.
27 Foucault names these: technologies of production, technologies of sign systems, technologies of self, and technologies of power (Foucault 1988).
28 Gimlin 2002.
29 Foucault 1988.
30 Foucault 1979.
31 Foucault's argument can be extended to the contemporary lack of gender-based workplace protection for individuals or the psychological definition of Gender Identity Disorder as a mental illness. These are logical products of technologies of power that reinforce normative gender scripts and marginalize non-normative genders; by pathologizing gender non-conformity and legitimating discrimination on the basis of gender power-holders maintain and reify existing gender ideologies.
32 Epstein and Straub 1991: 17.
33 Foucault 1979.
34 Rooney 1997: 403.
35 Thompson 1999.
36 Daldry 2000.
37 West and Zimmerman 1987; West and Fenstermaker 1995.
38 Bourdieu 1968.
39 Feinberg 1996.
40 It is important to both recognize histories of gender non-conformity and keep in mind that we make sense of these stories from the past from within contemporary ontological viewpoints, theories of gender and sex, and vocabularies of gender

difference. While some scholars have argued that we can make sense of past gender non-conformity using contemporary concepts (Bullough 1975), others have argued that because subjectivities are the product of the ideologies and technologies of the time, it is ahistorical to make sense of historical gender non-conformity as transgender/transsexual (Hausman 1992).

41 Foucault 1990: 152.

42 Stryker 2006: 13.

43 Lorber 1993: 578.

44 Fausto-Sterling 2000: 22.

45 Epstein and Straub 1991: 19.

46 Park and Nye 1991: 54. The doctrine of humors was the dominant ontology from the 400s B.C.E. (theorized by Hippocrates) through the 1700s. It posited that all matter was comprised of fire, earth, water, and air and that each of these humors had specific qualities—hot and dry, dry and cold, cold and wet, and wet and hot respectively. The doctrine fell out of favor with the development of cell-based pathological models and microbial sciences in the mid 1800s. See Arikha 2007 for more information on the doctrine of humors.

47 Laqueur 1990: 4–6.

48 Lorber 1993.

49 Soemmerring, 1796.

50 Stolberg (2003) argues that this estimate is off by several hundred years, and offers evidence that the first drawing of a female skeleton was published in 1583.

51 Laqueur 1990.

52 Schiebinger 1987.

53 This is similar to the shifts in how mentally ill individuals were treated, which Foucault documented in *Madness and Civilization* (1965). His study began by asking why, over fewer than 100 years, insane individuals went from being tolerated and included in society, to being confined within asylums. What Foucault found was that as medicine gained authority over illness and the body, madness came to be seen as a social failure and consequently individuals were observed, diagnosed, confined, and treated.

54 This term, coined by early sexologist Havelock Ellis, pays homage to Chevalier [Knight] D'Eon (Charles Genevieve Louis Auguste Andre Timothee d'Eon de Beaumont), a famous eighteenth century ambassador (and spy) for French King Louis XV, who, while born male, lived as a woman for a large part of her life. While serving Louis XV D'Eon lived as both a man and a woman, and her 'true' sex was hotly debated throughout her life (at one point betting took place on the floor of the London Stock Exchange). After a series of espionage-related fiascos in London, D'Eon petitioned Louis XVI to be able to return to France from exile. The king agreed on the condition that D'Eon live and dress as a woman for the rest of her life. It was only after her death in 1810 that her male birth sex was revealed. For a more detailed discussion, see De Beaumont et al. 2001.

55 Summers 2003: 2

56 Chicago Corset Company 1881: 3.

57 Summers 2003: 7.

58 Freedman 1974.

59 As many scholars have argued (Foucault 1990; Katz 1996), an identity based on sexual practice is a relatively new phenomenon that emerges in the nineteenth century alongside the rise of capitalism, urbanization, and "regimes of normalization" (Foucault 1990). Before this sexual practices were acts devoid of an associated identity

category. Terms like homosexual were not invented by Kertbeny until 1869 (Stryker 2008: 35).

60 See for example, Feinberg 1996, who includes detailed histories of non-binary gender possibilities around the world, including Xanith of Oman, Mahu of Tahiti, Travesti of Central and South America, Sworn Virgins of Eastern Europe, and Hijras of India. See also, Blackwood and Wieringa 1999.
61 Epstein and Straub 1991: 19.
62 Bullough 1975.
63 Hausman 1992.
64 Ries 2004: 168.
65 Rupp 2001.
66 Coming, a number of scholars suggest, from a derogatory Persian term for slave boy (Reis 2004: 169–170).
67 Muñoz 2009.
68 Bullough 1975.
69 Meyerowitz 2002: 5.
70 Meyerowitz 2002: 5.
71 Meyerowitz 2002: 1.
72 Gender dysphoria is the feeling of dissatisfaction/wrongness with one's assigned sex or gender.
73 For a review of Harry Benjamin's work and roots see Pfäfflin 1997.
74 American Psychiatric Association 1994.
75 Jeffreys 2003.
76 Vidal-Ortiz 2002, 2008.
77 Stryker 2008: 35.
78 Feinberg 1996.
79 Feinberg 1996: 101.
80 Heyes 2003: 1094.

Case Study: Focus on Bloomers and Nineteenth-Century Womanhood

1 Crane 2000.
2 Crane 2000: 112.
3 Crane 2000.
4 "Against Bloomers and Bicycles" 1897.
5 "Divided Skirts" 1881. Emphasis mine.
6 "Women's Emancipation" 1851.
7 Ewing 1978: 63.

Chapter 2

1 Nakamura 2002: xiii.
2 Pew Internet and American Life Project 2009.
3 Linden Research, Inc. 2009.
4 Pew Internet and American Life Project 2007.
5 Stryker 2008: 146.
6 Madden 2006: 3.
7 All data is from Pew Internet and American Life Project. All surveys prior to March 2000 were conducted by the Pew Research Center for People and the Press.

 8 Middleton and Sorensen 2005.
 9 Gattiker 2001; Mansell and Steinmueller 2000; Smith and Kollock 1998.
10 William Gibson 1982.
11 Hine 2000; Shostak 1999.
12 Fisher 1998: 158–159.
13 Meyers 1994.
14 Agger 2008: 4.
15 Donath 1997; Jones 1995.
16 Bruckman 1992; Kendall 2000; Kollock and Smith 1996; Mackinnon 1995, 1997, 1998; Phillips 1996.
17 Baudrillard 1990.
18 Haraway 1991.
19 Snow and Anderson 1987: 1348.
20 Loseke 2001.
21 Gergen 1991; Gottschalk 1993; Hill 2005.
22 Bruckman 1993; Burris and Hoplight 1996; Dickel 1995; Poster 1995; Turkle 1995.
23 Broad and Joos 2004: 926.
24 Rheingold 1993b.
25 Hill 2005: 28.
26 Bruckman 1992.
27 Gauthier and Chaudoir 2004; Hill 2005; McKenna, Green, and Smith 2001; Shapiro 2004.
28 Kendall 2000; Rheingold 1993a.
29 Stone 1991: 113.
30 Stone 1995; Turkle 1995.
31 Goffman 1959, 1963, 1974; Gergen 1991; Holstein and Gubrium 2000.
32 Plummer 1995.
33 Loseke 2001: 121.
34 Holstein and Gubrium 2000: 177–186; Denzin 1987.
35 Holstein and Gubrium 2000: 94.
36 Many more examples of this narrative process can be found in recent scholarship on coming out processes among children with LGBT parents (Joos and Broad 2007), narrative stories of midwives (Foley 2005), and construction of race and class identities (He and Phillion 2001).
37 Holstein and Gubrium 2000: 103.
38 Mason-Schrock 1996: 177.
39 Mason-Schrock 1996: 186–187.
40 Cooper 2007.
41 Devos and Banaji 2003; Eagly and Chaiken 1993, 1998; Festinger 1957; Fiske and Taylor 1991; Harmon-Jones and Mills 1999.
42 Cooley 1902; Goffman 1959; Mead 1934; Snyder, Tanke, and Berscheid 1977.
43 McKenna and Bargh 2000; Postmes, Spears, and Lea 1998.
44 Yee and Bailenson, 2007.
45 Yee and Bailenson, 2007: 25.
46 Turkle 1995.
47 Seale 2006: 355.
48 Seale 2006: 348.
49 2004.
50 Schrock, Holden, and Reid 2004: 66.

51 Cisgender refers to individuals whose birth gender matches their birth sex. Refer back to Chapter 1 for a more detailed definition.

52 See for example *LiveJournal* (http://www.livejournal.com).

53 West and Zimmerman 1987.

54 McLuhan 1970: 191.

55 Schrock, Holden, and Reid 2004: 66.

56 Hill 2005: 44.

57 Stryker 2008.

58 Recall from the last chapter that the inclusion of Gender Identity Disorder (GID) in the DSM both marks it as a mental disorder and functions to police access to transgender treatment and surgery. Simultaneously some people see GID's inclusion as evidence that gender non-conformity needs to be taken seriously and that it deserves medical treatment and intervention. The inclusion of Gender Identity Disorder in the DSM, then, has been both praised and condemned by individuals within and outside of the transgender community. For a longer discussion of this debate, see Bryant 2008.

59 Transgender Nation was founded in 1992 as a focus group of Queer Nation and primarily focused on transphobia within the gay and lesbian community. Its name pays homage to and grew out of the same direct-action political ideology of Queer Nation and ACT-UP (Green 2004; Stryker 2008).

60 Green 2004: 79–80; Stryker 2008: 135–136.

61 Olszewski 1993.

62 Green 2004: 79–80.

63 Ex-gay groups such as the "National Association for Research and Therapy of Homosexuality" have used Zucker's work to assert that gender non-conformity can, even *should*, be treated in childhood because of its ties to homosexuality in adulthood. This practice reinforces heteronormative and gender reductionist ideologies, and relies on the idea that homosexuality and/or gender non-conformity is wrong and *should* be cured. This argument rests firmly on solid ground only if we understand and accept heterosexuality and the sex/gender binary to be exclusively natural, biological, and ahistorical.

64 Brown 2006.

65 Spiegel 2008.

66 "Objection to DSM-V Committee Members on Gender Identity Disorders" 2008. The petition reflects both the strengths and weaknesses of online organizing, though. On the one hand it mobilized huge numbers of people and garnered significant attention beyond the transgender community. On the other hand, the petition included misleading and false information about Zucker and the APA. For example, the petition states that Zucker himself advocates for reparative therapies, which is incorrect.

67 Spiegel 2008.

68 American Psychological Association 2008.

69 APA Task Force on Gender Identity and Gender Variance 2008; Conway 2008.

70 Cook and Stambaugh 1997; Kendall 2000.

71 Herring 1999; Soukup 1999.

72 Bruckman 1993; Herring 1996; Rodino 1997.

73 Kendall 2000: 264.

74 Kelly, Pomerantz, and Currie 2006.

75 Kelly, Pomerantz, and Currie 2006: 22.

76 Kelly, Pomerantz, and Currie 2006: 11.

77 As used in Garland-Thomson 2005: 1,557–1,587.

78 Kendall 2000: 220.
79 Nakamura 2008: 73.
80 Eastwick and Gardner 2008: 12.
81 Au 2008.
82 Ashkenaz 2008.
83 Nakamura 2002: 14–15.
84 Nakamura 2002: 14.
85 http://anya.blogsome.com/2007/02/03/big-fat-lily-white-second-life/
86 Eastwick and Gardner 2008: 29.
87 Herring and Martinson 2004; O'Brien 1999.
88 O'Brien 1999: 85.
89 Langer 1989; O'Brien 1999.
90 O'Brien 1999: 99.

Case Study: Focus on Transgender Organizing

1 Cooper, McLoughlin, and Campbell 2000; Smith and Kollock 1999.
2 Unless otherwise noted, quotes from activists come from the interviews I conducted.
    For a more detailed discussion see Shapiro 2004.
3 The first of these gender clinics was the Johns Hopkins Gender Identity Clinic,
    established in November 1966, which provided the entire range of medical services to
    transsexual individuals including sex reassignment surgery. The success of this center
    led to the development of numerous other university affiliated centers around the
    country in the 1960s and 1970s.
4 http://www.gender.org/remember/#
5 Nancy Nangeroni ran an award-winning weekly radio talk show for more than 10
    years called *Gendertalk* (http://www.gendertalk.com). The radio show covered a wide
    array of issues important to transgender communities and was broadcast online to a
    wide audience.
6 McKenna and Bargh 1998.
7 Horrigan and Smith 2007; Xavier, Bobbin, Singer et al. 2005.

Chapter 3

1 Quart 2008.
2 Quart 2008: 34.
3 This is an approach rooted in pragmatism and built on the same theories we have used
    to understand the social self, including those of George Herbert Mead, William James,
    Charles Cooley, and Irving Goffman.
4 Pitts 2003; Shilling 2008.
5 United Nations 1992.
6 International Medical Congress 1913.
7 The defining U.S. Supreme Court case was Diamond v. Chakrabarty in 1980. (444
    U.S. 1,028 1980).
8 Guilford-Blake and Strickland 2008.
9 Lonmo and McNiven 2007.
10 Pitts 2003; Shilling 2007, 2008; Turner 1984, 2007.
11 Armstrong 1983; Morgan and Scott 1993.
12 Link et al. 2008.
13 Morgan and Scott 1993.

14 Johnson 2008.
15 Archer 2000; Butler 1990, 1993; Featherstone 1982; Turner 1984. For a longer discussion of this body of work, see Shilling 2007: 8.
16 Franklin 2007; Grosz 1994.
17 For example, plastic surgery dates back to ancient Egypt. For an in-depth history of plastic surgery see Morgan and Scott 1993; Santoni-Rugiu and Sykes 2007.
18 Sullivan 2005, 2006.
19 Murray 2008; Stryker 2008.
20 Gimlin 2002.
21 Hebdige 1979.
22 Gimlin 2002: 84.
23 Murray 2008.
24 The first intestinal bypass was performed by A. J. Kremen in 1954.
25 American Society for Metabolic & Bariatric Surgery 2007.
26 Not only do the legacies of Enlightenment thought draw connections between self and body (Pitts 2003; Sullivan 2006), but a number of scholars have documented how individuals in our society try to manifest their identities in their bodies (Goffman 1959; Schlenker 1980; Swann 1987). Individuals intentionally use identity cues to assert or confirm their self-identification, and when absent work to create them.
27 Murray 2008.
28 Gimlin 2002.
29 For example body norms in the West African nation of Mauritania prize fatness in women, just as Western norms have historically, because fatness is/was seen as a sign of wealth, social class and health.
30 Drew 2008a; Joanisse 2005; Throsby 2007.
31 Drew 2008b.
32 Drew 2008a.
33 Bartky 1988; Bordo 1993; Davis 1995.
34 McKinley 1999.
35 Krizek et al. 1999.
36 Drew 2008a. All issues of *Obesity Help* between July 2003 and January/February 2008 were coded.
37 Gimlin 2002; Kang 2003; Wolkowitz 2006.
38 Balsamo 1996.
39 Balsamo 1996:10.
40 ASPS has collected national level data on plastic surgery since 1992. For more information see: http://www.plasticsurgery.org/Media/Statistics.html.
41 American Society of Plastic Surgeons 2009a.
42 Gimlin 2002: 109.
43 American Society of Plastic Surgeons 2009b.
44 Kaw 1993: 78.
45 Kaw 1993: 81.
46 Kaw 1993: 80.
47 Oudshoorn 1994.
48 Bordo 2003; Davis 1995.
49 Albright 2007.
50 For a great example of how images are manipulated see the Dove Campaign video, *Evolution*. Available at: http://www.campaignforrealbeauty.com/home_films_evolution_v2.swf (Staav and Piper 2006).

51 Mitchell 2007: 60–61.
52 Coad 2008.
53 Wesely 2003: 655.
54 Kwan and Trautner 2009: 59.
55 Wesely 2003: 662.
56 Wesely 2003: 666.
57 Wesely 2003: 665.
58 Ronai and Ellis 1989; Sweet and Tewksbury 2000; Wood 2000.
59 Kulick 1998; Xavier et al. 2005.
60 Kwan and Trautner 2009.
61 Conley and Glauber 2005; Hamermesh and Biddle 1994.
62 Pitts 2003: 44.
63 Kennedy 2008.
64 Pitts 2003: 34.

Case Study: Focus on the 'Treatment' of Intersex and Transgender Individuals

1 Kessler and McKenna 1978.
2 Allen 2007.
3 Tomlinson 1995.
4 Fausto-Sterling 2000: 75.
5 Fausto-Sterling 2000.
6 Allen 2007.
7 Fausto-Sterling 2000.
8 Bryant 2008; Waszkiewicz 2006.
9 Beemyn and Rankin, forthcoming.
10 Quart 2008: 37.
11 Beemyn and Rankin, forthcoming.
12 Grossman and D'Augelli 2006.
13 Cisgender, as we discussed in Chapter 1, refers to a somatic state where one's birth gender (gender assigned at birth) matches one's birth sex (sex assigned at birth).
14 Namaste 2006; Shilling 2008.
15 Moran and Sharpe 2004.
16 Pardo 2008; Pardo and Schantz 2008.
17 Xavier et al. 2005.
18 For more information about rates of violence see Beemyn and Rankin, forthcoming. More information can also be accessed through a related website: http://www.umass.edu/stonewall/translives.

Review

1 Jarrold 2005.
2 Lestoil 1968.
3 Haraway 1991.
4 Nakamura 2002.
5 Hall 1996.
6 Hall 1996.
7 See for example Ingraham's (1994) concept of 'heterogender.'
8 Shilling 2008.

 9 More 1998.
10 More 1998: 322.
11 Beatie 2008.
12 Beatie 2008: 24.
13 Beatie 2008: 24.
14 Califia-Rice 2000.
15 Rogers 2008.
16 Currah 2008: 330.
17 Beatie 2008.
18 More 1998: 320.
19 "Defining 'Natural:' Visceral Reactions to an Act Should Not Distract from the Real Ethical Issues." 2008.
20 Holstein and Gubrium 2000: 197.
21 Swann 1987.

REFERENCES

Adas, Michael. 1989. *Machines as the Measure of Men: Science, Technology and Ideologies of Western Dominance.* Ithaca, NY: Cornell University Press.

"Against Bloomers and Bicycles." 1897. *New York Times.* January 11, p. 1.

Agger, Ben. 2008. *The Virtual Self: A Contemporary Sociology.* Boston, MA: Blackwell Publishing.

Albright, Julie M. 2007. "Impossible Bodies: TV Viewing Habits, Body Image, and Plastic Surgery Attitudes among College Students in Los Angeles and Buffalo, New York." *Configurations* 15(2): 103–123.

Alkalimat, Abdul, Doug Gills, and Kate Williams. 1995. *Job-Tech: The Technological Revolution and Its Impact on Society.* Chicago: Twenty-First Century Books.

Allen, Caitilyn. 2007. "It's a Boy! Gender Expectations Intrude on the Study of Sex Determination." *DNA and Cell Biology* 26(10): 699–705.

American Psychiatric Association. 1994. *Diagnostic and Statistical Manual of Mental Disorders,* 4th Edition, Revised. Washington, DC: American Psychiatric Association.

American Psychological Association Task Force on Gender Identity and Gender Variance. 2008. "Report of the Task Force on Gender Identity and Gender Variance." Washington, DC: American Psychological Association. Retrieved August 7, 2008. (www.apa.org/pi/lgbc/transgender/2008TaskForceReport.pdf).

American Psychological Association. 2008. "APA Statement on GID and the DSM 2008," May 9. Washington, DC: American Psychological Association.

American Society for Metabolic & Bariatric Surgery. 2007. "Fact Sheet on Metabolic & Bariatric Surgery." Retrieved October 30, 2009 (http://www.asbs.org/Newsite07/media/asmbs_fs_surgery.pdf).

American Society of Plastic Surgeons. 2009a. "2009 Report of the 2008 Statistics: National Clearinghouse of Plastic Surgery Statistics." Arlington Heights, IL: American Society of Plastic Surgeons. Retrieved May 26, 2009 (http://www.plasticsurgery.org/Media/stats/2008-US-cosmetic-reconstructive-plastic-surgery-minimally-invasive-statistics.pdf).

American Society of Plastic Surgeons. 2009b. "Cosmetic Procedures Up in All Ethnic Groups Except Caucasians in 2008." Arlington Heights, IL: Society of Plastic

Surgeons. Retrieved May 26, 2009 (http://www.plasticsurgery.org/Media/
   Press_Releases/Cosmetic_Procedures_Up_in_All_Ethnic_Groups_Except_
   Caucasians_in_2008.html).
Archer, John. 1992. "Childhood Gender Roles: Social Context and Organisation." Pp.
   31–62 in *Childhood Social Development: Contemporary Perspectives*, edited by Harry
   McGurk. East Sussex, England: Psychology Press.
Archer, Margaret S. 2000. *Being Human: The Problem of Agency*. Cambridge, England:
   Cambridge University Press.
Arikha, Noga. 2007. *Passions and Tempers: A History of the Humours*. New York, NY: Ecco
   Press.
Armstrong, David. 1983. *Political Anatomy of the Body: Medical Knowledge in Britain in the
   Twentieth Century*. Cambridge, England: Cambridge University Press.
Armstrong, Myrna L. and Kathleen Pace Murphy. 1997. "Tattooing: Another Adolescent
   Health Risk Behavior Warranting Health Education." *Applied Nursing Research* 10:
   181–189.
Ashkenaz, Marissa. 2008. "You Mean You Chose to be Fat?: Body Image in a Virtual
   World." Retrieved March 10, 2009 (http://marissaracecourse.com/2008/06/03/you-
   mean-you-chose-to-be-fat-body-image-in-a-virtual-world/).
Au, Wagner James. 2008. "Can A Female Avatar Be Too Thin?" *New World Notes*.
   Retrieved May 30, 2008 (http://nwn.blogs.com/nwn/2008/05/can-a-female-av.html).
Balsamo, Anne. 1996. *Technologies of the Gendered Body: Reading Cyborg Women*. Durham,
   NC: Duke University Press.
Bartky, Sandra. 1988. "Foucault, Femininity and the Modernization of Patriarchal Power."
   Pp. 61–86 in *Feminism and Foucault: Reflections on Resistance*, edited by Irene
   Diamond and Lee Quinby. Boston, MA: Northeastern University Press.
Baudrillard, Jean. 1990. *Seduction*, translated by Brian Singer. Basingstoke, England:
   Macmillan.
Beatie, Thomas. 2008. "Labor of Love." *The Advocate*, April 8, p. 24.
Becker, Howard. 1953. "Becoming a Marihuana User," *American Journal of Sociology* 59:
   235–242.
Beemyn, Brett-Genny and Sue Rankin. Forthcoming. *Understanding Transgender Lives*.
   New York, NY: Columbia University Press.
Bijker, Wiebe E. and John Law. 1992. *Shaping Technology/Building Society*. Cambridge,
   MA: MIT Press.
Blackwood, Evelyn and Saskia E. Wieringa. 1999. *Female Desires: Same-Sex Relations and
   Transgender Practices Across Cultures*. New York, NY: Columbia University Press.
Blumer, Herbert. 1969. *Symbolic Interactionism: Perspective and Method*. Englewood Cliffs,
   NJ: Prentice-Hall.
Bordo, Susan. 1993. *Unbearable Weight: Feminism, Western Culture, and the Body*. Berkeley,
   CA: University of California Press.
Bordo, Susan. 2003. "The Empire of Images in Our World of Bodies." Pp. 105–114 in
   Beyond Words: Reading and Writing in a Visual Age, edited by John Ruszkiewicz,
   Daniel Anderson and Christy Friend. Upper Saddle River, NJ: Pearson Education.
Borgmann, Albert. 2006. "Technology as a Cultural Force: For Alena and Griffin." *The
   Canadian Journal of Sociology* 31(3): 351–360.
Bourdieu, Pierre. 1968. "Outline of a Sociological Theory of Art Perception." *International
   Social Science Journal* 20(4): 589–612.
Braithwaite, Ronald L., Torrance Stephens, Claire Sterk, and Kisha Braithwaite. 1999.
   "Risks Associated with Tattooing and Body Piercing." *Journal of Public Health Policy*
   20: 459–470.

Brines, Julie. 1994. "Economic Dependency, Gender, and the Division of Labor at Home." *American Journal of Sociology* 100: 652–688.

Broad, Kendal L. and Kristin E. Joos. 2004. "Online Inquiry of Public Selves: Methodological Considerations." *Qualitative Inquiry* 10(6): 923–946.

Brown, Patricia Leigh. 2006. "Supporting Boys or Girls When the Line Isn't Clear." *The New York Times*, December 2, A1, A11.

Bruckman, Amy S. 1992. "Identity Workshop: Emergent Social and Psychological Phenomena in Text-Based Virtual Reality." Unpublished Manuscript. Retrieved October 30, 2009 (http://www.cc.gatech.edu/~asb/papers/old-papers.html).

Bruckman, Amy S. 1993. "Gender Swapping on the Internet." *Proceedings of INET 1993*. Retrieved October 30, 2009 (http://www.cc.gatech.edu/~asb/papers/old-papers.html).

Bryant, Adam. 2007. "iSee Into the Future, Therefore iAm." *New York Times*, July 1.

Bryant, Karl. 2008. "In Defense of Gay Children? 'Progay' Homophobia and the Production of Homonormativity." *Sexualities* 11(4): 455–475.

Bullough, Vern L. 1975. "Transgenderism in History." *Archives of Sexual Behavior* 4(5): 561–571.

Burris, Beverly and Andrea Hoplight. 1996. "Theoretical Perspectives on the Internet and CMC." Paper presented at the annual meetings of the American Sociology Association, August 17, New York.

Butler, Judith P. 1990. *Gender Trouble: Feminism and the Subversion of Identity*. New York, NY: Routledge.

Butler, Judith P. 1993. *Bodies That Matter: On the Discursive Limits of 'Sex.'* New York, NY: Routledge.

Cafri, Guy, J. Kevin Thompson, Lina Ricciardelli, Marita McCabe, Linda Smolak, and Charles Yesalis. 2005. "Pursuit of the Muscular Ideal: Physical and Psychological Consequences and Putative Risk Factors." *Clinical Psychology Review.* 25(2): 215–239.

Califia-Rice, Patrick. 2000. "Family Values: Two Dads With a Difference—Neither of Us Was Born Male." *The Village Voice,* June 20. Retrieved June 5, 2009 (http://www.villagevoice.com/issues/0025/califia-rice.php).

Carr, Coeli. 2006. "If the Shoe Fits, You're Lucky." *The New York Times*, April 9, Section 9, p. 2.

Charmaz, Kathy. 1994. "Identity Dilemmas of Chronically Ill Men." *The Sociological Quarterly* 35(2): 269–288.

Chicago Corset Company. 1881. "After Wearing Ball's Corsets Madame Adelina Patti Says …" Chicago, IL: Shober & Carqueville Lithograph Company.

Coad, David. 2008. *The Metrosexual: Gender, Sexuality, and Sport*. New York, NY: SUNY Press.

Coe, Kathryn, Mary P. Harmon, Blair Verner, and Andrew Tonn. 1993. "Tattoos and Male Alliances." *Journal of Human Nature* 4(2): 199–204.

Collins, James and Richard Blot. 2003. *Literacy and Literacies: Texts, Power, and Identity.* New York, NY: Cambridge University Press.

Coltrane, Scott. 2004. "Household Labor and the Routine Production of Gender." Pp. 186–206 in *The Gendered Society Reader,* edited by Michael S. Kimmel. New York, NY: Oxford University Press.

Conley, Dalton and Rebecca Glauber. 2005. "Gender, Body Mass and Economic Status." NBER Working Paper No. W11343. Retrieved March 14, 2009 (http://ssrn.com/abstract=727123).

Connell, R.W. 2002. *Gender.* Cambridge, MA: Polity Press.

Conway, Lynn. 2008. "Falsification of GID Prevalence Results by the APA Task Force on Gender Identity and Gender Variance." Retrieved August 7, 2008

(http://ai.eecs.umich.edu/people/conway/TS/Prevalence/APA/Falsification_of_GID_
   prevalence_results_by_the_APA_Task_Force.pdf).
Cook, Kimberly J. and Phoebe M. Stambaugh. 1997. "Tuna Memos and Pissing Contests:
   Doing Gender and Male Dominance on the Internet." Pp. 63–84 in *Everyday Sexism
   in the Third Millennium*, edited by Carol Rambo Ronai, Barbara A. Zsembik and Joe
   R. Feagin. New York, NY: Routledge.
Cooley, Charles Horton. 1902. *Human Nature and the Social Order.* New York, NY:
   Charles Scribner's Sons.
Cooper, Al, Irene P. McLoughlin, and Kevin M. Campbell. 2000. "Sexuality in
   Cyberspace: Update for the 21st Century." *CyberPsychology & Behavior* 3(4):
   521–536.
Cooper, Robbie. 2007. *Alter Ego: Avatars and Their Creators.* London, England: Chris Boot
   Ltd.
Copes, John H. and Craig J. Forsyth. 1998. "The Tattoo: A Social Psychological
   Explanation." *International Review of Modern Sociology* 23: 83–89.
Cordaux, Richard and Mark Stoneking. 2003. "South Asia, the Andamanese and the
   Genetic Evidence for an 'Early' Human Dispersal Out of Africa." *American Journal of
   Human Genetics* 72(6): 1,586–1,590.
Cowan, Ruth Schwartz. 1997. *A Social History of American Technology.* New York, NY:
   Oxford University Press.
Crane, Diana. 2000. *Fashion and Its Social Agendas: Class, Gender and Identity in Clothing.*
   Chicago, IL: University of Chicago Press.
Crawley, Sara L., Lara J. Foley, and Constance L. Shehan. 2007. *Gendering Bodies.*
   Thousand Oaks, CA: Rowman & Littlefield Publishers.
Cumming, Helen. 1943. "War Booms the Tattooing Art." *New York Times* September 19,
   p. 38.
Currah, Paisley 2008. "Expecting Bodies: The Pregnant Man and Transgender Exclusion
   from the Employment Non-Discrimination Act." *WSQ: Women's Studies Quarterly*
   36(3–4): 330–336.
Daldry, Stephen (dir.). 2000. *Billy Elliot.* Universal Studios.
Davis, Kathy. 1995. *Reshaping the Female Body: The Dilemma of Cosmetic Surgery.* New
   York, NY: Routledge.
De Beaumont, Charles d'Eon, Roland A. Champagne, Nina Claire Ekstein, and Gary
   Kates. 2001. *The Maiden of Tonnerre: The Vicissitudes of the Chevalier and the Chevalière
   d'Eon.* Baltimore, MD: Johns Hopkins University Press.
"Defining 'Natural:' Visceral Reactions to an Act Should Not Distract from the Real
   Ethical Issues. (Editorial)." 2008. *Nature* 452(7,188): 665–666.
DeGregory, Lane. 2007. "The Ripple Effect of Transformation." *St. Petersburg Times,*
   December 31, 1E. Retrieved August 11, 2008
   (http://www.sptimes.com/2007/12/31/Life/Susan_Stanton_s_lonel.shtml).
DeGregory, Lane and Lorri Helfand. 2007. "His Second Self." *St. Petersburg Times,* March
   11, 1A.
de Lauretis, Teresa. 1987. *Technologies of Gender: Essays on Theory, Film, and Fiction.*
   Bloomington, IN: Indiana University Press.
DeMello, Margo. 2000. *Bodies of Inscription: A Cultural History of the Modern Tattoo
   Community.* Durham, NC: Duke University Press.
Denzin, Norman K. 1987. *The Recovering Alcoholic.* Newbury Park, CA: Sage
   Publications.
Derry, T. K. and Trevor I. Williams. 1993. *A Short History of Technology: From the Earliest
   Times to A.D. 1900.* New York, NY: Dover Publications.

Devos, Thierry and Mahzarin R. Banaji. 2003. "Implicit Self and Identity." Pp. 153–175 in *Handbook of Self and Identity*, edited by Mark R. Leary and June Price Tangney. New York, NY: Guilford Press.

Diamond v. Chakrabarty. 1980. 444 U.S. 1,028.

Dickel, M. H. 1995. "Bent Gender: Virtual Disruptions of Gender and Sexual Identity." *Electronic Journal of Communication* 5(4). Retrieved August 11, 2008 (http://www.cios.org/www/ejc/v5n495.htm).

"Divided Skirts." 1881. *New York Times*, October 31, p. 4.

Donath, Judith. 1997. *Inhabiting the Virtual City: The Design of Social Environments for Electronic Communities*. Boston, MA: MIT Press.

Drew, Patricia. 2008a. *Surgically Altered Self: How Patients' Negotiations of Weight Loss Surgery Discourses Shape Self Conceptions*. PhD. Dissertation, Department of Sociology, University of California, Santa Barbara.

Drew, Patricia. 2008b. "Weight Loss Surgery Patients' Negotiations of Medicine's Institutional Logic." Pp. 65–92 in *Research in the Sociology of Health Care*, Volume 26, edited by Jennie Jacobs Kronenfeld. Bingley, England: Emerald Group Publishing.

Dworkin, Shari and Lucia O'Sullivan. 2007. "'It's Less Work For Us and It Shows Us She Has Good Taste:' Masculinity, Sexual Initiation, and Contemporary Sexual Scripts." Pp. 105–121 in *The Sexual Self: The Construction of Sexual Scripts*, edited by Michael Kimmel. Nashville, TN: Vanderbilt University Press.

Eagly, Alice H. and Shelly Chaiken. 1993. *The Psychology of Attitudes*. Fort Worth, Texas: Harcourt Brace Jovanovich College Publishers.

Eagly, Alice H. and Shelly Chaiken. 1998. "Attitude Structure and Function." Pp. 269–322 in *Handbook of Social Psychology*, edited by Daniel Gilbert, Susan Friske and Gardner Lindsay. New York, NY: McGraw-Hill.

Eastwick, Paul W. and Wendi L. Gardner. 2008. "Is It a Game? Evidence for Social Influence in the Virtual World." *Social Influence* 4(1): 18–32.

Ellul, Jacques. 1964. *The Technological Society*, translated by John Wilkinson. New York, NY: Vintage Books.

Ensler, Eve. 2000. *The Vagina Monologues*. New York, NY: Dramatist's Play Service.

Epstein, Julia and Kristina Straub. 1991. *Body Guards: The Cultural Politics of Gender Ambiguity*. New York, NY: Routledge.

Ewing, Elizabeth. 1978. *Dress and Undress: A History of Women's Underwear*. New York: Drama Book Specialists.

Fausto-Sterling, Anne. 2000. *Sexing the Body: Gender Politics and the Construction of Sexuality*. New York, NY: Basic Books.

Featherstone, Mike and Roger Burrows. 1995. "Cultures of Technological Embodiment: An Introduction." *Body & Society* 1(3–4): 1–19.

Featherstone, Mike. 1982. "The Body in Consumer Culture." *Theory, Culture & Society* 1(2): 18–33.

Feinberg, Leslie. 1996. *Transgender Warriors: Making History from Joan of Arc to Dennis Rodman*. Boston, MA: Beacon Press.

Festinger, Leon. 1957. *Theory of Cognitive Dissonance*. Evanston, IL: Row Peterson.

Fine, Gary Alan. 2001. *Gifted Tongues: High School Debate and Adolescent Culture*. Princeton, NJ: Princeton University Press.

Fisher, Dana R. 1998. "Rumoring Theory and the Internet: A Framework for Analyzing the Grass Roots." *Social Science Computer Review* 16(2): 158–168.

Fisher, Jill. 2002. "Tattooing the Body, Marking Culture." *Body & Society* 8(4): 91–107.

Fiske, Susan and Shelley Taylor. 1991. *Social Cognition*. 2nd edition. New York, NY: McGraw-Hill.

Foley, Laura. 2005. "Midwives, Marginality, and Public Identity Work." *Symbolic Interaction* 28(2): 183–203.

Foucault, Michel. 1965. *Madness and Civilization.* New York, NY: Pantheon Press.

Foucault, Michel. 1979. *Discipline and Punish: The Birth of the Prison.* New York, NY: Vintage.

Foucault, Michel. 1988. "Technologies of the Self." Pp. 16–49 in *Technologies of the Self: A Seminar with Michel Foucault,* edited by Luther H. Martin, Huck Gutman, and Patrick H. Hutton. London, England: Tavistock Publications.

Foucault, Michel. 1990. *The History of Sexuality: An Introduction.* New York, NY: Vintage Books.

Frangos, Maria. 2006. "Embodied Subjectivity and the Quest for Self in Televised Narratives of Body Modification." Pp. 54–62 in *Bodies in the Making: Transgressions and Transformations,* edited by Nancy N. Chen and Helene Moglen. Santa Cruz, CA: New Pacific Press.

Franklin, Sarah. 2007. *Dolly Mixtures: The Remaking of Genealogy.* Durham, NC: Duke University Press.

Freedman, Estelle B. 1974. "The New Woman: Changing Views of Women in the 1920s." *The Journal of American History* 61(2): 372–393.

Futter, Ellen V. 2006. "Failing Science." *New York Times,* November 26, Section 14: 11.

Gabe, Jonathan, Michael Bury, and Mary Ann Elston. 2004. *Key Concepts in Medical Sociology.* Thousand Oaks, CA: Sage Publications.

Gamson, Joshua. 1998. *Freaks Talk Back: Tabloid Talk Shows and Sexual Nonconformity.* Chicago, IL: University of Chicago Press.

Garland-Thomson, Rosemarie. 2005. "Feminist Disability Studies." *Signs: Journal of Women in Culture and Society* 30(2): 1,557–1,587.

Gattiker, Urs E. 2001. *The Internet as a Diverse Community. Cultural, Organizational, and Political Issues.* New York, NY: Routledge.

Gauthier, DeAnn and Nancy Chaudoir. 2004. "Tranny Boyz: Cyber Community Support in Negotiating Sex and Gender Mobility Among Female to Male Transsexuals." *Deviant Behavior* 25(4): 375–398.

Gergen, Kenneth. 1991. *The Saturated Self: Dilemmas of Identity in Contemporary Life.* New York, NY: Basic Books.

Gibson, William. 1982. "Burning Chrome." *OMNI* 4 (July): 72–82.

Giddens, Anthony. 1991. *Modernity and Self-identity: Self and Society in the Late Modern Age.* Stanford, CA: Stanford University Press.

Gill, Rosalind, Karen Henwood, and Carl McLean. 2005. "Body Projects and the Regulation of Normative Masculinity." *Body & Society* 11(1): 37–62.

Gimlin, Debra L. 2002. *Body Work: Beauty and Self-Image in American Culture.* Berkeley, CA: University of California Press.

Gimlin, Debra L. 2007. "Discourses of Ageing and Narrative Resistance in a Commercial Slimming Group." *Ageing & Society* 27: 1–19.

Goering, Sara. 2003. "Conformity through Cosmetic Surgery: The Medical Erasure of Race and Disability." Pp. 172–188 in *Science and Other Cultures: Issues in Philosophies of Science and Technology,* edited by Robert Figueroa and Sandra G. Harding. New York, NY: Routledge.

Goffman, Erving. 1959. *The Presentation of Self in Everyday Life.* New York, NY: Doubleday.

Goffman, Erving. 1963. *Stigma: Notes on the Management of Spoiled Identity.* New York, NY: Simon & Schuster.

Goffman, Erving. 1974. *Frame Analysis: An Essay on the Organization of Experience.* Boston, MA: Northeastern University Press.

Gottschalk, Simon. 1993. "Uncomfortably Numb: Countercultural Impulses in the Postmodern Era." *Symbolic Interaction* 16: 351–78.

Govenar, Alan. 2000. "The Changing Image of Tattooing in American Culture, 1846–1966." Pp. 212–233 in *Written on the Body: The Tattoo in European and American History,* edited by Jane Caplan. Princeton, NJ: Princeton University Press.

Gramsci, Antonio. 1971. *Selections from the Prison Notebooks.* London, England: Lawrence and Wishart.

Green, Jamison. 2004. *Becoming a Visible Man.* Nashville, TN: Vanderbilt University Press.

Grossman, Arnold H. and Anthony R. D'Augelli. 2006. "Transgender Youth: Invisible and Vulnerable." *Journal of Homosexuality* 51(1): 111–128.

Grosz, Elizabeth. 1994. *Volatile Bodies: Toward a Corporeal Feminism.* Bloomington, IN: Indiana University Press.

Guilford-Blake, Roxanna and Debbie Strickland (eds.). 2008. "The Guide to Biotechnology." *Biotechnology Industry Organization.* Retrieved January 29, 2009 (http://bio.org/speeches/pubs/er/BiotechGuide2008.pdf).

Hacker, Sally. 1989. *Pleasure, Power and Technology: Some Tales of Gender, Engineering, and the Cooperative Workplace.* Boston: Unwin Hyman.

Halberstam, Judith. 1991. "Automating Gender: Postmodern Feminism in the Age of the Smart Machine." *Feminist Studies* 17(3): 439–459.

Hall, Stuart. 1996. "Race: The Floating Signifier." Lecture at Goldsmiths College.

Halnon, Karen Bettez and Saundra Cohen. 2006. "Muscles, Motorcycles and Tattoos: Gentrification in a New Frontier." *Journal of Consumer Culture* 6(1): 33–56.

Hamermesh, Daniel S. and Jeff E. Biddle. 1994. "Beauty and the Labor Market." *The American Economic Review* 84(5): 1,174–1,194.

Haraway, Donna. 1991. "A Cyborg Manifesto: Science, Technology, and Socialist-Feminism in the Late Twentieth Century," Pp. 149–181 in *Simians, Cyborgs and Women: The Reinvention of Nature.* New York, NY: Routledge.

Harmon-Jones, Eddie and Judson Mills. 1999. *Cognitive Dissonance: Progress on a Pivotal Theory in Social Psychology.* Washington, DC: American Psychological Association.

Hausman, Bernice L. 1992. "Demanding Subjectivity: Transsexualism, Medicine, and the Technologies of Gender." *Journal of the History of Sexuality* 3: 270–302.

Hawkes, Daina, Charlene Y. Senn, and Chantal Thorn. 2004. "Factors That Influence Attitudes Toward Women With Tattoos." *Sex Roles* 50(9/10): 593–604.

He, Ming Fang and JoAnne Phillion. 2001. "Trapped In-between: A Narrative Exploration of Race, Gender, and Class." *Race, Gender & Class* 8(1): 47–56.

Hebdige, Dick. 1979. *Subcultures: The Meaning of Style.* London, England: Methuen.

Heidegger, Martin. 1977. *The Question Concerning Technology,* translated by W. Lovitt. New York, NY: Harper & Row.

Herring, Susan C. 1999. "Posting in a Different Voice: Gender and Ethics in Computer-Mediated Communication." Pp. 241–265 in *Computer Media and Communication: A Reader,* edited by Paul Mayer. New York, NY: Oxford University Press

Herring, Susan C., 1996. "Gender and Democracy in Computer-Mediated Communication." Pp. 476–489 in *Computerization and Controversy: Value Conflicts and Social Choices,* edited by Rob Kling. San Diego, CA: Academic Press.

Herring, Susan C., and Anna Martinson. 2004. "Assessing Gender Authenticity in Computer-Mediated Language Use." *Journal of Language and Social Psychology* 23(4): 424–446.

Heyes, Cressida. 2003. "Feminist Solidarity After Queer Theory: The Case of Transgender." *Signs: Journal of Women in Culture and Society* 28(4): 1,093–1,120.

Hill, Darryl. 2005. "Coming to Terms: Using Technology to Know Identity." *Sexuality and Culture* 9: 24–52.

Hine, Christine M. 2000. *Virtual Ethnography.* Thousand Oaks, CA: Sage Publications.

Hochschild, Arlie. 1989. *The Second Shift.* New York, NY: Avon.

Holstein, James A. and Jaber F. Gubrium. 2000. *The Self We Live By: Narrative Identity in a Postmodern World.* New York, NY: Oxford University Press.

Horrigan, John B. and Aaron Smith. 2007. "Home Broadband Adoption 2007." *Pew Internet and American Life Project.* Retrieved October 30, 2009 (http://www.pewinternet.org/PPF/r/217/report_display.asp).

Hughes, James. 2004. *Citizen Cyborg: Why Democratic Societies Must Respond to the Redesigned Human of the Future.* Boulder, CO: Westview Press.

Ingraham, Chrys. 1994. "The Heterosexual Imaginary: Feminist Sociology and Theories of Gender." *Sociological Theory* 12(2): 203–219.

International Medical Congress. 1913. *The History of Inoculation and Vaccination for the Prevention and Treatment of Disease: Lecture Memoranda.* London, England: Burroughs Wellcome.

Intersex Society of North America. (n.d.) *Intersex Society of North America.* Retrieved April 14, 2008 (http://www.isna.org).

Irvine, Janice M. 1990. *Disorders of Desire: Sex and Gender in Modern American Sexology.* Philadelphia, PA: Temple University Press.

Jacobs, Jerry A. 1996. "Gender Inequality and Higher Education." *Annual Review of Sociology* 22: 153–185.

Janssen, Janine. 2005. "Tattoos in Prison: Men and their Pictures on the Edge of Society." Pp 179–192 in *Spaces of Masculinities*, edited by Bettina van Hoven and Kathrin Hörschelmann. New York, NY: Routledge.

Jarrold, Julian (dir.). 2005. *Kinky Boots.* Miramax Films.

Jeffreys, Sheila. 2003. "FTM Transsexualism and the Destruction of Lesbians." Pp. 122–143 in *Unpacking Queer Politics: A Lesbian Feminist Perspective*, edited by Sheila Jeffreys. Cambridge, England: Polity Press.

Joanisse, Leanne. 2005. "'This is Who I Really Am:' Obese Women's Conceptions of the Self Following Weight Loss Surgery." Pp. 248–259 in *Doing Ethnography: Researching Everyday Life*, edited by Dorothy Pawluch, William Shaffir and Charlene E. Miall. Toronto, Canada: CSPI/Women's Press.

Johnson, LaShaune. 2008. "Opening Remarks." *Annual Audre Lorde Cancer Awareness Brunch and the Black Women and Breast Cancer Conference: Prevention, Disparities and Wellness*, October 18, Simmons College, Boston, MA.

Jones, Steven (ed.). 1995. *CyberSociety: Computer-Mediated Communication and Community.* Thousand Oaks, CA: Sage Publications.

Joos, Kristin and Kendal Broad. 2007. "Coming Out of the Family Closet: Stories of Adult Women with LGBTQ Parent(s)." *Journal of Qualitative Sociology* 30(3): 275–295.

Kang, M. 2003. "The Managed Hand: The Commercialization of Bodies and Emotions in Korean Immigrant-Owned Nail Salons." *Gender & Society* 17(6): 820–839.

Katz, Jonathan Ned. 1996. *The Invention of Heterosexuality.* New York, NY: Plume Press.

Kaw, Eugenia. 1993. "Medicalization of Racial Features: Asian American Women and Cosmetic Surgery." *Medical Anthropology Quarterly* 7(1): 74–89.

Kelly, Deirdre M., Shauna Pomerantz, and Dawn H. Currie. 2006. "'No Boundaries?' Girls' Interactive, Online Learning About Femininities." *Youth & Society* 38(1): 3–28.

Kendall, Lori. 2000. "'Oh No! I'm A Nerd!:' Hegemonic Masculinity on an Online Forum." *Gender & Society* 14(2): 256–274.

Kendall, Lori. 2002. *Hanging Out in the Virtual Pub: Masculinities and Relationships Online.* Berkeley, CA: University of California Press.

Kennedy, Pagan. 2008. *The First Man Made Man.* New York, NY: Bloomsbury.

Kessler, Suzanne J. and Wendy McKenna. 1978. *Gender: An Ethnomethodological Approach.* Chicago, IL: University of Chicago Press.

Kimmel, Michael. 2005. *The Gender of Desire: Essays on Male Sexuality.* Albany, NY: SUNY Press.

Kimmel, Michael (ed.). 2007. *The Sexual Self: The Construction of Sexual Scripts.* Nashville, TN: Vanderbilt University Press.

Kleinman, Daniel. 2005. *Science and Technology in Society: From Biotechnology to the Internet.* Malden, MA: Blackwell Publishing.

Kleinman, Daniel. 2008. *Science, Technology, and Democracy.* Albany, NY: SUNY Press.

Kling, Rob. 1996. "Hopes and Horrors: Technological Utopianism and Anti-Utopianism in Narratives of Computerization." Pp. 40–58 in *Computerization and Controversy: Values Conflicts and Social Choices,* edited by Rob Kling. San Diego, CA: Academic Press.

Koch, Jerome R., Alden E. Roberts, Myrna L. Armstrong, and Donna C. Owen. 2005. "College Students, Tattoos, and Sexual Activity." *Psychological Reports* 97: 887–890.

Kollock, Peter and Marc Smith. 1996. "Managing the Virtual Commons: Cooperation and Conflict in Computer Communities." Pp. 109–128 in *Computer-Mediated Communication: Linguistic, Social, and Cross-Cultural Perspectives,* edited by Susan Herring. Amsterdam, Netherlands: John Benjamins.

Kollock, Peter and Marc Smith. 1999. "Communities in Cyberspace." Pp. 3–25 in *Communities in Cyberspace,* edited by Marc Smith and Peter Kollock. New York, NY: Routledge.

Kosut, Mary. 2000. "Tattoo Narratives: The Intersection of the Body, Self-Identity and Society." *Visual Studies* 15(1): 79–100.

Krizek, Claudette, Cleora Roberts, Robin Ragan, Jeffery J. Ferrara, and Beth Lord. 1999. "Gender and Cancer Support Group Participation." *Cancer Practice* 7(2): 86–92.

Kulick, Don. 1998. *Travesti: Sex, Gender, and Culture Among Brazilian Transgendered Prostitutes.* Chicago, IL: University of Chicago Press.

Kwan, Samantha and Mary Nell Trautner. 2009. "Beauty Work: Individual and Institutional Rewards, the Reproduction of Gender, and Questions of Agency." *Sociology Compass* 3(1): 49–71.

Lamb, Warren and Elizabeth Watson. 1979. *Body Code: The Meaning in Movement.* London, England: Routledge.

Langer, Ellen J. 1989. *Mindfulness.* Reading, MA: Addison-Wesley.

Laqueur, Thomas. 1990. *Making Sex: Body and Gender from the Greeks to Freud.* Cambridge, MA: Harvard University Press.

Laumann, Anne E. and Amy J. Derick. 2006. "Tattoos and Body Piercings in the United States: A National Data Set." *Journal of the American Academy of Dermatology* 55(3): 413–21.

Lestoil. 1968. Advertisement. *Life Magazine* 64(14): 81.

Linden Research, Inc. 2009. "1 Billion Hours, 1 Billion Dollars Served." Retrieved October 29, 2009 (http://www.lindenlab.com/pressroom/releases/22_09_09).

Link, Bruce G., Jo C. Phelan, Richard Miech, and Emily L. Westin. 2008. "The Resources that Matter: Fundamental Social Causes of Health Disparities and the Challenge of Intelligence." *Journal of Health and Social Behavior* 49(1): 72–91.

Lonmo, Charlene, and Chuck McNiven. 2007. "Selected Results of the Biotechnology Use and Development Survey 2005." *Statistics Canada, Life Sciences Section*, Retrieved July 30, 2009 (http://www.statcan.gc.ca/pub/88f0006x/88f0006x2007006-eng.pdf).

Lorber, Judith. 1993. "Believing is Seeing: Biology as Ideology." *Gender & Society* 7(4): 568–581.

Lorber, Judith. 1996. *Paradoxes of Gender.* New Haven, CT: Yale University Press.

Loseke, Donileen R. 2001. "Lived Realities and Formula Stories of 'Battered Women.'" Pp. 107–126 in *Institutional Selves*, edited by Jaber Gubrium and James Holstein. New York, NY: Oxford University Press.

Lyon, David. 1995. "The Roots of the Information Society Idea." Pp. 52–73 in *Information Technology and Society: A Reader*, edited by Nick Heap, Ray Thomas, Geoff Einon, Robin Mason, and Hughie Mackay. London, England: Sage Publications.

Mackenzie, Donald and Judy Wajcman (eds.). 1999. *The Social Shaping of Technology*, 2nd edition. Philadelphia, PA: Open University Press.

MacKinnon, Richard C. 1995. "Searching for the Leviathan in Usenet." Pp 112–137 in *CyberSociety: Computer-Mediated Communication and Community*, edited by Steven Jones. Thousand Oaks, CA: Sage Publications.

MacKinnon, Richard C. 1997. "Punishing the Persona: Correctional Strategies for the Virtual Offender." Pp. 206–235 in *Virtual Culture: Identity and Communication in Cybersociety*, edited by Steven Jones. London, England: Sage Publications.

MacKinnon, Richard C. 1998. "The Social Construction of Rape in Virtual Reality." Pp. 147–172 in *Network and Netplay: Virtual Groups on the Internet*, edited by Fay Sudweeks, Margaret L. McLaughlin, and Sheizaf Rafaeli. Cambridge, MA: MIT Press.

Madden, Mary. 2006. "Internet Penetration and Impact." *Pew Internet and American Life Project*, Retrieved August 11, 2008 (http://www.pewinternet.org/PPF/r/182/report_display.asp).

Mansell, Robin and William E. Steinmueller. 2000. *Mobilizing the Information Society: A View from Europe.* Oxford, England: Oxford University Press.

Marx, Karl. 1977. *A Contribution to the Critique of Political Economy.* Moscow, Russia: Progress Publishers.

Mason-Schrock, Douglas. 1996. "Transsexuals' Narrative Construction of the 'True Self.'" *Social Psychology Quarterly* 59(3): 176–192.

"Maxim's 2007 Hot 100." (n.d.) *Maxim.com.* Retrieved April 14, 2008 (http://www.maximonline.com/articles/index.aspx?a_id=+7564&src=RSSArticles).

McGinn, Robert E. 1991. *Science, Technology and Society.* Englewood Cliffs, NJ: Prentice-Hall.

McGlen, Nancy and Karen O'Connor. 1998. *Women, Politics, and American Society.* Englewood Cliffs, NJ: Prentice-Hall.

McKenna, Katelyn Y. A., Amie S. Green, and Pamela K. Smith. 2001. "Demarginalizing the Sexual Self." *The Journal of Sex Research* 38: 302–311.

McKenna, Katelyn Y. A. and John A. Bargh. 1998. "Coming Out in the Age of the Internet: Identity De-Marginalization from Virtual Group Participation." *Journal of Personality and Social Psychology* 75(3): 681–694.

McKenna, Katelyn Y. A. and John A. Bargh. 2000. "Plan 9 from Cyberspace: The Implications of the Internet for Personality and Social Psychology." *Personality and Social Psychology Review* 4(1): 57–75.

McKinley, Nita Mary. 1999. "Women and Objectified Body Consciousness: Mothers' and Daughters' Body Experience in Cultural, Developmental, and Familial Context." *Developmental Psychology* 35: 760–769.

McLuhan, Marshall. 1970. *Culture is Our Business*. New York, NY: McGraw-Hill.

McLuhan, Marshall. 1994. *Understanding Media: The Extensions of Man*. Cambridge, MA: MIT Press.

Mead, George Herbert. 1934. *Mind, Self and Society from the Standpoint of a Social Behaviorist*, edited by Charles W. Morris. Chicago, IL: University of Chicago Press.

Messner, Michael A. 2000. "Barbie Girls vs. Sea Monsters: Children Constructing Gender." *Gender & Society* 14: 765–784.

Meyerowitz, Joanne. 2002. *How Sex Changed: The History of Transsexuality in America*. Cambridge, MA: Harvard University Press.

Meyers, Daniel J. 1994. "Communication Technology and Social Movements: Contributions of Computer Networks to Activism." *Social Science Computer Review* 12(2): 250–260.

Middleton, Catherine A. and Christine Sorensen. 2005. "How Connected are Canadians? Inequalities in Canadian Households' Internet Access." *Canadian Journal of Communication* 30(4): 463–483.

Mitchell, George J. 2007. "Report to the Commissioner of Baseball of an Independent Investigation into the Illegal Use of Steroids and Other Performance Enhancing Substances by Players in Major League Baseball." New York, NY: Office of the Commissioner of Baseball. Retrieved March 8, 2009 (http://files.mlb.com/mitchrpt.pdf).

Moran, Leslie J. and Andrew Sharpe. 2004. "Violence, Identity and Policing: The Case of Violence Against Transgender People." *Criminal Justice* 4(4): 395–417.

More, Sam Dylan. 1998. "The Pregnant Man—An Oxymoron?" *Journal of Gender Studies* 7(3): 319–328.

Morgan, David and Sue Scott. 1993. "Bodies in a Social Landscape." Pp. 1–21 in *Body Matters*, edited by David Morgan and Sue Scott. New York, NY: Routledge.

Morley, David and Kevin Robins. 1995. *Spaces of Identity: Global Media, Electronic Landscapes and Cultural Boundaries*. New York, NY: Routledge.

Moscucci, Ornella. 1990. *The Science of Woman: Gynaecology and Gender in England, 1800–1929*. Cambridge, England: Cambridge University Press.

Muñoz, Vic. 2009. "Gender Sovereignty." Paper presented at *TransRhetorics Conference at Cornell University*, Ithaca, NY. March 6–8.

Murray, Samantha. 2008. *The 'Fat' Female Body*. New York, NY: Palgrave Macmillan.

Nakamura, Lisa. 2002. *Cybertypes: Race, Ethnicity, and Identity on the Internet*. New York, NY: Routledge.

Nakamura, Lisa. 2008. "Neoliberal Space and Race in Virtual Worlds." *The Velvet Light Trap* 62: 72–73.

Namaste, Viviane K. 2006. "Genderbashing: Sexuality, Gender, and the Regulation of Public Space." Pp. 584–600 in *The Transgender Studies Reader*, edited by Susan Stryker and Stephen Whittle. London, England: CRC Press.

O'Brien, Jodi. 1999. "Writing in the Body: Gender (Re)Production in Online Interaction." Pp 76–104 in *Communities in Cyberspace*, edited by Marc A. Smith and Peter Kollock. London, England: Routledge.

O'Brien, Jodi. 1999. *Social Prisms: Reflections on Everyday Myths and Paradoxes*. Thousand Oaks, CA: Pine Forge Press.

O'Brien, Jodi. 2005. *The Production of Reality: Essays and Readings in Social Interaction*, 4th Edition. Newbury Park, CA: Pine Forge Press.

"Objection to DSM-V Committee Members on Gender Identity Disorders." *The Petition Site*. Retrieved September 10, 2008 (http://www.thepetitionsite.com/2/objection-to-dsm-v-committee-members-on-gender-identity-disorders).

Olszewski, Lori. 1993. "Transsexuals Protest at Psychiatry Meeting." *San Francisco Chronicle* May 24, A13.

Orenstein, Peggy. 1995. *Schoolgirls: Young Women, Self-Esteem, and the Confidence Gap.* Garden City, NY: Anchor.

Oudshoorn, Nelly. 1994. *Beyond the Natural Body: An Archaeology of Sex Hormones.* New York, NY: Routledge.

Oudshoorn, Nelly. 2000. "Imagined Men: Representations of Masculinities in Discourses on Male Contraceptive Technology." Pp. 123–145 in *Bodies of Technology: Women's Involvement with Reproductive Medicine*, edited by Ann Rudinow Saetnan, Nelly Oudshoorn, and Marta Kirejczyk. Columbus, OH: Ohio State University Press.

Oudshoorn, Nelly. 2003. *The Male Pill: A Biography of a Technology in the Making.* Durham, NC: Duke University Press.

Pääbo, Svante. 2003. "The Mosaic That is Our Genome." *Nature* 421: 409–412.

Padavic, Irene and Barbara Reskin. 2002. *Women and Men at Work.* Thousand Oaks, CA: Pine Forge Press.

Pardo, Seth T. 2008. "Growing Up Transgender: Research and Theory." *ACT for (Trans) Youth, Part 1.* New York, NY: Cornell University. Retrieved June 8, 2009 (http://www.actforyouth.net/documents/GrowingUpTransPt1_March08.pdf).

Pardo, Seth T. and Karen Schantz. 2008. "Growing Up Transgender: Safety and Resilience." *ACT for (Trans) Youth, Part 2.* New York, NY: Cornell University. Retrieved June 8, 2009 (http://www.actforyouth.net/documents/Trans2_final.pdf).

Park, Katharine. 2006. *Secrets of Women: Gender, Generation, and the Origins of Human Dissection.* New York, NY: Zone Books.

Park, Katharine and Robert Nye. 1991. "Destiny is Anatomy." *The New Republic* February 18: 53–57.

Park, Regina (dir.) 2007. *Never Perfect.* One Drop Pictures.

Pew Internet and American Life Project. 2007. "February–March 2007 Tracking SPSS Dataset." Washington, DC: Pew Research Center, Retrieved August 11, 2008 (http://www.pewInternet.org/PPF/r/64/dataset_display.asp).

Pew Internet and American Life Project. 2009. "Trend Data, March 26–April 19, 2009." Washington, DC: Pew Research Center, Retrieved October 29, 2009 (http://www.pewinternet.org/static_pages/trend_data/whos-online.aspx).

Pew Research Center for People and the Press. 2007. "How Young People View Their Lives, Futures and Politics: A Portrait of 'Generation Next.'" Washington, DC: Pew Research Center, Retrieved July 22, 2009 (http://people-press.org/reports/pdf/300.pdf).

Pfäfflin, Friedemann. 1997. "Sex Reassignment, Harry Benjamin, and Some European Roots." *International Journal of Transgenderism* 1(2). Retrieved March 22, 2009 (http://www.symposion.com/ijt/ijtc0202.htm).

Phelan, Michael and Scott Hunt. 1998. "Prison Gang Members' Tattoos as Identity Work: the Visual Communication of Moral Careers." *Symbolic Interaction* 21(3): 277–298.

Phillips, David J. 1996. "Defending the Boundaries: Identifying and Countering Threats in a Usenet Newsgroup." *The Information Society* 12(1): 39–62.

Pitts, Victoria. 2003. *In the Flesh: The Cultural Politics of Body Modification.* New York, NY: Palgrave Macmillan.

Plummer, Kenneth. 1995. *Telling Sexual Stories: Power, Change and Social Worlds.* London, England: Routledge.

Poster, Mark. 1995. *The Second Media Age.* Cambridge, England: Polity Press.

Postmes, Tom, Russell Spears, and Martin Lea. 1998. "Breaking or Building Social Boundaries?: Side-Effects of Computer-Mediated Communication." *Communication Research* 25(6): 689–715.

Preves, Sharon E. 2003. *Intersex and Identity: The Contested Self.* New Brunswick, NJ: Rutgers University Press

"Professor Assigns Students to 'E-Fast.'" 2007. *Tell Me More.* National Public Radio. July 30. Retrieved August 1, 2008 (http://www.npr.org/templates/story/story.php?storyId=12346287).

Quart, Alissa. 2008. "When Girls Will Be Boys." *New York Times Magazine*, March 16, pp. 32–37.

Reagan, Charles E. 1996. *Paul Ricoeur: His Life and His Work.* Chicago, IL: University of Chicago Press.

Reis, Elizabeth. 2004. "Teaching Transgender History, Identity, and Politics." *Radical History Review* 88: 166–177.

Reskin, Barbara F. and Patricia Roos. 1991. *Job Queues, Gender Queues: Explaining Women's Inroads into Male Occupations.* Philadelphia, PA: Temple University Press.

Rheingold, Howard. 1993a. "A Slice of Life in My Virtual Community." Pp. 57–82 in *Global Networks: Computers and International Communication,* edited by Linda M. Harasim. Cambridge, MA: MIT Press.

Rheingold, Howard. 1993b. *The Virtual Community: Homesteading on the Electronic Frontier.* Reading MA: Addison-Wesley.

Ricoeur, Paul. 1991. *From Text to Action. Essays in Hermeneutics,* translated by Kathleen Blamey and John B. Thompson. Evanston, IL: Northwestern University Press.

Ritzer, George. 1993. *The McDonaldization of Society.* Thousand Oaks, CA: Pine Forge Press.

Rodino, Michelle. 1997. "Breaking Out of Binaries: Reconceptualizing Gender and Its Relationship to Language in Computer-Mediated Communication." *Journal of Computer-Mediated Communication,* 3(3). Retrieved September 10, 2008 (http://jcmc.indiana.edu/vol3/issue3/rodino.html).

Rogers, Thomas. 2008. "What the Pregnant Man Didn't Deliver." *Salon.com.* Retrieved May 23, 2009 (http://www.salon.com/mwt/feature/2008/07/03/pregnant_man/).

Ronai, Carol R. and Carolyn Ellis. 1989. "Turn-on's for Money: Interactional Strategies of a Table Dancer." *Journal of Contemporary Ethnography* 18(3): 271–298.

Rooney, David. 1997. "A Contextualizing, Socio-Technical Definition of Technology: Learning from Ancient Greece and Foucault." *Prometheus* 15(3): 399–407.

Rupp, Leila. 2001. "Toward a Global History of Same-Sex Sexuality." *Journal of the History of Sexuality* 10(2): 287–302.

Sanders, Clinton. 1989. *Customizing the Body: The Art and Culture of Tattooing.* Philadelphia, PA: Temple University Press.

Sandstrom, Kent L. 1998. "Preserving the Vital and Valued Self in the Face of AIDS." *Sociological Inquiry* (68)3: 354–371.

Sandstrom, Kent L., Daniel D. Martin, and Gary Alan Fine. 2006. *Symbols, Selves, and Social Reality: An Interactionist Approach to Social Psychology and Sociology.* Los Angeles, CA: Roxbury Press.

Santoni-Rugiu, Paolo and Philip J. Sykes. 2007. *A History of Plastic Surgery.* New York, NY: Springer.

Schiebinger, Londa. 1987. "Skeletons in the Closet: The First Illustrations of the Female Skeleton in Eighteenth-Century Anatomy." Pp. 42–82 in *The Making of the Modern Body: Sexuality and Society in the Nineteenth Century,* edited by Catherine Gallagher and Thomas Laqueur. Berkeley, CA: University of California Press.

Schlenker, Barry R. 1980. *Impression Management: The Self-Concept, Social Identity, and Interpersonal Relations.* Monterey, CA: Brooks/Cole.

Schrock, Douglas, Daphne Holden, and Lori Reid. 2004. "Creating Emotional Resonance: Interpersonal Emotion Work and Motivational Framing in a Transgender Community." *Social Problems* 51(1): 61–81.

Schwartz, Lori A. and William T. Markham. 1985. "Sex-Role Stereotyping in Children's Toy Advertisements." *Sex Roles* 1: 157–170.

Seale, Clive. 2006. "Gender Accommodation in Online Cancer Support Groups." *Health: An Interdisciplinary Journal for the Social Study of Health, Illness and Medicine* 10(3): 345–360.

Segal, Howard P. 1986. "The Technological Utopians." Pp. 119–136 in *Imagining Tomorrow: History, Technology and The American Future*, edited by Joseph J. Corn. Cambridge, MA: MIT Press.

Shapiro, Eve. 2004. "Transcending Barriers: Transgender Organizing on the Internet." *Journal of Gay and Lesbian Social Services* 16(3/4): 165–179.

Shapiro, Eve. 2007. "Drag Kinging and the Transformation of Gender Identities." *Gender & Society* 21(2): 250–271.

Shields, Rob (ed.). 1996. *Cultures of the Internet: Virtual Spaces, Real Histories, Living Bodies.* London, England: Sage Publications.

Shilling, Chris (ed.). 2007. *Embodying Sociology: Retrospect, Progress and Prospects.* Oxford, England: Blackwell Publishing.

Shilling, Chris. 2007. "Sociology and the Body: Classical Traditions and New Agendas." *Sociological Review* 55(1): 1–69.

Shilling, Chris. 2008. *Changing Bodies: Habit, Crisis and Creativity.* London, England: Sage Publications.

Shostak, Arthur B. 1999. *Cyberunion: Empowering Labor Through Computer Technology.* New York, NY: M.E. Sharpe.

Smith, Marc and Peter Kollock. 1999. *Communities in Cyberspace.* New York, NY: Routledge.

Snow, David A. and Leon Anderson. 1987. "Identity Work Among the Homeless: The Verbal Construction and Avowal of Personal Identities." *American Journal of Sociology* 92(6): 1,336–1,371.

Snyder, Mark, Elizabeth Decker Tank, and Ellen Bercheid. 1977. "Social Perception and Interpersonal Behavior: On the Self-Fulfilling Nature of Social Stereotypes." *Journal of Personality and Social Psychology* 35: 656–666.

Soemmerring, Samuel Thomas von. 1796. *Tabula Sceleti Feminine.* Frankfurt am Main: Traiecti ad Moenum, Apud Varrentrapp et Wenner.

Soukup, Charles. 1999. "The Gendered Interactional Patterns of Computer-Mediated Chatrooms: A Critical Ethnographic Study." *The Information Society* 15(3): 169–176.

Spiegel, Alix. 2008. "Q&A: Therapists on Gender Identity Issues in Kids." National Public Radio. Retrieved August 11, 2008 (http://www.npr.org/templates/story/story.php?storyId=90229789).

Spiegel, Alix. 2008. "Two Families Grapple with Sons' Gender Preferences." *All Things Considered.* National Public Radio, May 28. Retrieved March 22, 2009 (http://www.npr.org/templates/story/story.php?storyId=90247842).

Staav, Yael and Tim Piper. 2006. *Evolution.* Toronto, Canada: Reginald Pike Films. Retrieved February 16, 2009 (http://www.campaignforrealbeauty.com/home_films_evolution_v2.swf).

Stanford, Jacqueline N. and Marita P. McCabe. 2005. "Sociocultural Influences on Adolescent Boys' Body Image and Body Change Strategies." *Body Image* 2(2): 105–113.

Steward, Samuel. 1990. *Bad Boys and Tough Tattoos: A Social History of the Tattoo with Gangs, Sailors, and Street-Corner Punks, 1950–1965*. New York, NY: Haworth Press.

Stolberg, Michael. 2003. "A Woman Down to Her Bones: The Anatomy of Sexual Difference in the Sixteenth and Early Seventeenth Centuries." *Isis* 94: 274–299.

Stone, Allucquère Rosanne. 1991. "Will The Real Body Please Stand Up?: Boundary Stories About Virtual Cultures." Pp. 81–118 in *Cyberspace: First Steps*, edited by Michael Benedikt. Cambridge, MA: MIT Press.

Stone, Allucquère Rosanne. 1995. *The War of Desire and Technology at the Close of the Mechanical Age*. Cambridge, MA: MIT Press.

Stratton, Jim. 2007. "Largo Reaffirms Firing of Transgender Official." *The Orlando Sentinel*, March 24.

Strauss, Stephen. 2004. "Bradshaw + Blahniks = Tippiness Factor." *Globe and Mail*, March 24, R1.

Stryker, Susan. 2006. "(De)Subjugated Knowledge." Pp. 1–15 in *The Transgender Studies Reader* edited by Susan Stryker and Stephen Whittle. New York, NY: Routledge.

Stryker, Susan. 2008. *Transgender History*. Berkeley, CA: Seal Press.

Stryker, Susan and Stephen Whittle (eds.). 2006. *The Transgender Studies Reader*. New York, NY: Routledge.

Sullivan, Nikki. 2005. "Somatechnics, or, the Social Inscription of Bodies and Selves." *Australian Feminist Studies* 20(48): 363–366.

Sullivan, Nikki. 2006. "Somatechnics, or Monstrosity Unbound." *Scan: Journal of Media Arts Culture* 3(3). Retrieved December 4, 2008 (http://www.scan.net.au/scan/journal/display.php?journal_id=83).

Summers, Leigh. 2003. *Bound to Please: A History of the Victorian Corset*. Oxford, England: Berg Publishers.

Swann, William B. Jr. 1987. "Identity Negotiation: Where Two Roads Meet." *Journal of Personality and Social Psychology* 53: 1038–1051.

Sweet, Nova and Richard Tewksbury. 2000. "Entry, Maintenance, and Departure from a Career in the Sex Industry: Strippers' Experiences of Occupational Costs and Rewards." *Humanity and Society* 2(1): 136–161.

Sweetman, Paul. 1999. "Anchoring the (Postmodern) Self? Body Modification, Fashion and Identity." *Body & Society* 5(2/3): 51–76.

"The Tattoo Fad." 1897. *Boston Morning Journal*. December 25, p. 3.

Thompson, J. Kevin. 1999. "Body Image, Bodybuilding, and Cultural Ideals of Muscularity." *Mesomorphosis* 30: 1–6.

Thorne, Barrie. 1993. *Gender Play: Girls and Boys in School*. Buckingham, England: Open University Press.

Throsby, Karen. 2007. "Happy Re-Birthday: Weight Loss Surgery and the 'New Me.'" *Body & Society* 14(1): 117–133.

Tolman, Deborah. 1994. "Doing Desire: Adolescent Girls' Struggles For/With Sexuality." *Gender & Society* 8(3): 324–342.

Tomlinson, Barbara. 1995. "Phallic Fables and Spermatic Romance: Disciplinary Crossing and Textual Ridicule." *Configurations* 3(2): 105–134.

Turbin, Carole. 2003. "Refashioning the Concept of Public/Private: Lessons from Dress Studies." *Journal of Women's History* 15(1): 43–51.

Turkle, Sherry. 1994. "Constructions and Reconstructions of Self in Virtual Reality: Playing in MUD's." *Mind, Culture, and Activity: An International Journal* 1: 158–167.

Turkle, Sherry. 1995. *Life On The Screen: Identity in the Age of the Internet*. New York, NY: Simon and Schuster.

Turner, Bryan S. 1984. *The Body and Society: Explorations in Social Theory.* Oxford, England: Blackwell Publishing.

Turner, Bryan S. 1997. "What is the Sociology of the Body?" *Body & Society* 3(1): 103–107.

Turner, Bryan S. 2007. "Culture, Technologies and Bodies: The Technological Utopia of Living Forever." Pp. 19–36 in *Embodying Sociology: Retrospect, Progress, and Prospects,* edited by Chris Shilling. Oxford, England: Blackwell Publishing.

United Nations Educational Scientific and Cultural Organization. 1985. "Technology Education within the Context of General Education." Working Paper presented at the International Symposium on the Teaching of Technology within the Context of General Education, November 18–22, Paris, France: Retrieved July 3, 2008 (http://unesdoc.unesco.org/images/0006/000664/066416eb.pdf).

United Nations. 1992. "The Convention of Biological Diversity." Retrieved December 4, 2008 (http://www.biodiv.org/convention/convention.shtml).

Vidal-Ortiz, Salvador. 2002. "Queering Sexuality and Doing Gender: Transgender Men's Identification with Gender and Sexuality." Pp. 181–233 in *Gendered Sexualities (Advances in Gender Research, Vol. 6),* edited by Patricia Gagne and Richard Tewksbury. New York, NY: Elsevier Science Press.

Vidal-Ortiz, Salvador. 2008. "Transgender and Transsexual Studies: Sociology's Influence and Future Steps." *Sociology Compass* 2(2): 433–450.

Walker, Danna L. 2007. "The Longest Day: Could a Class of College Students Survive Without Ipods, Cellphones, Computers and TV from One Sunrise to the Next?" *Washington Post Magazine,* August 5, W20.

Waszkiewicz, Elroi. 2006. *Getting by Gatekeepers: Transmen's Dialectical Negotiations within Psychomedical Institutions.* Master's Thesis, Georgia State University, Atlanta, GA. Retrieved March 19, 2009 (http://etd.gsu.edu/theses/available/etd-11182006-151959/).

Weber, Max. 1947. *The Theory of Economic and Social Organization.* New York, NY: Oxford University Press.

Weber, Max. 2005. "Remarks on Technology and Culture." *Theory, Culture & Society* 22(4): 23–38.

Webster, Juliet. 1996. *Shaping Women's Work: Gender, Employment, and Information Technology.* London, England: Longman.

Wesely, Jennifer. 2003. "Exotic Dancing and the Negotiation of Identity: The Multiple Uses of Body Technologies." *Journal of Contemporary Ethnography* 32(6): 643–669.

West, Candace and Sarah Fenstermaker. 1995. "Doing Difference." *Gender & Society* 9: 8–37.

West, Candace and Don H. Zimmerman. 1987. "Doing Gender." *Gender & Society* 1: 125–151.

Wolkowitz, Carol. 2006. *Bodies at Work.* London, England: Sage Publications.

"Woman's Emancipation (Being A Letter Addressed to Mr. Punch, With a Drawing, by A Strong-Minded American Woman)." 1851. *Harper's New Monthly Magazine* 3 (August): 424.

Wood, Elizabeth Anne. 2000. "Working in the Fantasy Factory: The Attention Hypothesis and the Enacting of Masculine Power in Strip Clubs." *Journal of Contemporary Ethnography* 29(1): 5–31.

Xavier, Jessica M., Marilyn Bobbin, Ben Singer, and Earline Budd. 2005. "A Needs Assessment of Transgendered People of Color Living in Washington, DC." Pp. 31–47 in *Transgender Health and HIV Prevention: Needs Assessment Studies from Transgender Communities Across the United States,* edited by Walter Bockting and Eric Avery. New York, NY: Haworth Medical Press.

Yee, Nick and Jeremy Bailenson. 2007. "The Proteus Effect: The Effect of Transformed
    Self-Representation on Behavior." *Human Communication Research*. 33(3): 271–290.
Zammuner, Vanda L. 1987. "Children's Sex-Role Stereotypes: A Cross-Cultural Analysis."
    Pp. 272–293 in *Sex and Gender*, edited by Phillip Shaver and Clyde Hendrick.
    Newbury Park, CA: Sage Publications.
Zipern, Andrew. 2001. "Technology That Aims To Do Good." *New York Times*.
    November 8.

INDEX